ALL BULL recounts the experiences – funny, brutal, frightening, sometimes downright farcical - of twenty-four men who, along with millions of others from all over Britain, were obliged to undergo National Service.

Some of these men are now famous, others are comparatively unknown, but they all retail vividly the time they were forced out of civvies into uniform – and the sometimes devastating effect this brush with the military had on their future life.

B. S. Johnson was born in London in 1933. He worked as a bank clerk and accounts clerk before going to King's College, London at the late age of 23 to read English. His first novel *Travelling People* and a volume of *Poems* won a Gregory Award in 1962. Many other books have followed these, including *Trawl* and *House Mother Normal*, and another volume of poetry. His first film, *You're Human Like the Rest of Them*, won the Grands Prix at the 1968 Short Film Festivals at Tours and Melbourne. He has also done a lot of work in television, consisting mainly of documentaries which he has written and directed. These include *Evacuees, The Unfortunates, On Reflection: Samuel Johnson* and two programmes on architecture. His thirty-minute play, *Not Counting The Savages,* has also been televised.

He is married with two children, and still lives in London.

ALL BULL:
THE NATIONAL
SERVICEMEN

Ω————————————————————

edited by
B. S. JOHNSON

QUARTET BOOKS   LONDON

First published in Great Britain by Quartet Books Limited 1973
27 Goodge Street London W.1.
Reprinted 1973

This was originally published simultaneously with Allison & Busby
Limited

ISBN 0 704 31002 3
Printed in Great Britain by
Hunt Barnard Printing Ltd., Aylesbury, Bucks.

for the kittens
DIANA
so nearly had...

ACKNOWLEDGEMENTS

THE EDITOR has spoken to many people about the subject of this book over the last ten years; to them a general acknowledgement is due. More specifically, he wishes to thank his wife, Nicola Gentle, J. E. Blishen, Gordon Gridley, George Hartwright, Mike Pottle, Iorwerth Davies, John Berger, David Wolton, Ian Yeomans and the Kasmin Gallery.

ALL BULL:
THE NATIONAL SERVICEMEN

INTRODUCTION

It seems there is something of a choice as to who was the last National Serviceman. 23819209 Private Fred Turner, Army Catering Corps, at the time attached to 13/18 Hussars, was discharged on 7th May 1963. Lieutenant Richard Vaughan, Royal Army Pay Corps, left his unit in Germany on 4th May 1963, but because he had to travel back to England he was not officially discharged until 13th May. As to dates, then, Lieut. Vaughan has it; but Pte. Turner had the latest number issued to a National Serviceman, so was certainly the last man from that point of view.

Whichever it was, they were both out by the middle of May 1963, and National Service had officially ended. The perspective of ten years is a good one from which to look back on eighteen years of conscription in peacetime: not sufficient for the distortion caused by real nostalgia, short enough for incidents to be remembered with a reasonable degree of sharpness, yet time for its effects to have begun to be noticed and isolated.

The British had a long history of opposition to conscription, and of being able to manage without it, right into this century. The Army raised to fight the Boer War was wholly made up of Regulars, and it was half-way through the First World War before the stream of volunteers dried up. The introduction of conscription in 1916 was strongly but ineffectively opposed by the trade unions and much of the rest of the country. It was accepted again in 1939, less than six months before the war started, only because it was so evidently near.

But universal conscription in peacetime for an indefinite period? Nothing like that had ever been seen in Britain. The large standing armies kept by countries like France and Germany whether there was a war on or not were thought shameful by the British; no really civilised nation kept a standing army. Indeed, the small Regular Army we did have was generally looked down on, and as a result was rather like a caste apart.

So history was against any attempt to introduce or keep on conscription after the war, yet it came to seem normal, and even natural, for the next eighteen years. That virtually no one at all objected to it, that the TUC backed it through both Labour and Tory governments, must have been largely due to the fact that everyone realised what a narrow escape Britain had had through insufficient preparation for the Second World War, and that the English Channel no longer released us from the need for a standing army. The transition in enemies from the defeated Germans to the exhausted Russians was smoothly made, and Parliament felt it could take three years after the war before bothering to address itself to tidying up the conscription laws which had been in force ever since. The 1948 National Service Acts consolidated wartime legislation, did away with demob suits and gratuities, and fixed a limit to service for the first time. From 1st January 1949 this was to be eighteen months' full-time service followed by four years' part-time in the reserves. In 1950 another National Service Act increased the period of full-time service to two years, but reduced that in the reserves to three and a half years to maintain the total length at five and a half years. The forces considered that it took at least nine months to train a man to be of real use to them, and that any subsequent posting should last from ten to twelve months in order not to disrupt units too often; leave and similar factors made a two-year period the minimum. From the nation's point of view, it would have been convenient if conscripts could have gone in straight from school (which ended for the vast majority at the age of fifteen) to avoid an awkward interregnum. But the forces would not accept them as young as this, and even thought that eighteen was a compromise; they would have preferred them somewhat later and more mature.

Responsibility for registering as soon as he became eighteen lay on the youth himself, though the BBC regularly broadcast information concerning the relevant age-groups which had to report to the Ministry of Labour and National Service. Local posters gave more precise details as to which day to register on and at which office of the Ministry. If the eighteen-year-old missed (or chose to miss) both of these, then he could still be traced through school, National Health or Income Tax records.

Exemption from National Service was granted without qualification to British subjects in government posts abroad, to mental defectives, to the blind, and to clergymen. As long as they stayed in their jobs, indefinite deferment amounting to exemption was also granted to coalminers, oil shale underground workers, merchant seamen and seagoing fishermen, agricultural workers in essential food production, graduate science teachers, and police cadets.

Deferment was readily given if the youth was an apprentice completing indentures, or a student engaged on a course. Proof of exceptional domestic hardship could also result in deferment. The limit was eight years, to the age of twenty-six, which covered the long courses doctors and dentists undertook; later this was extended to twelve years and finally, in 1955, to eighteen years to cover certain men who had been out of the country in their last year before reaching twenty-six.

At the time of registering it was also possible to declare conscientious objections to military service, though this could still be done at later stages before actual call-up. There were very few conscientious objectors indeed. Appendix A contains a breakdown into acceptances or rejections (for all reasons) of those liable for National Service for the sample years 1951-1955.

Within a couple of weeks of registering, the eighteen-year-old would normally receive notice to attend a medical examination. If he missed this without good (in their definition) cause, then he could be given up to two years' imprisonment and a fine of £100. And he still had his time to do after that; like all prison sentences (within the forces, too) they did not count towards service.

The medical was often held in the same Ministry of Labour and National Service building at which registration took place. In my case it was a large hall with cubicles along the sides each the province of a doctor specialising in a different part of the body or its functions. Waiting at the end of the hall to be called to the first cubicle, a large sign opposite us read something like: DO NOT

3

PASS WATER AS YOU WILL BE REQUIRED TO GIVE A SAMPLE. The man next to me could not survive the long wait, and went to find another place to relieve himself. As soon as he came back he and I and a third man were called to begin the rounds. We were handed our flasks, and sent behind a screen to fill them. Two of us could, but the man who had been unable to wait looked as though he had just committed his first treasonable offence. As my first comradely action I offered him some of mine, which he was pleased to accept.

The medical examination was designed to determine into which of four grades the potential recruit fell. The last of these grades was for those unfit for National Service, and something like sixteen per cent of those examined found themselves exempted on medical grounds; a perhaps surprisingly high proportion.

It remained comparatively difficult, however, to fail on medical grounds; anyone who did so was either genuinely incapacitated or a great actor (Andrew Sinclair has told how Peter O'Toole and other drama students used to hold extra-curricular classes in how to fail the medical, aided by too much alcohol and too little food and sleep). A Government Report on National Service in 1956 (see Bibliography for further details) commented that the medical boards of the Ministry were so keen on seeing that malingerers did not escape the net that they were tending to pass an inordinate number of genuinely unfit men who had subsequently to be rejected by the forces. This is confirmed by my own case: I was passed by the initial medical board, but found to have the disqualification (for what reasons I was never told) of a perforated eardrum within three days of entering the Royal Air Force. Reference to my family doctor would have discovered that I had suffered this slight inconvenience from the age of three as a side-effect of scarlet fever.

After his medical, and usually on the same day and in the same building, the youth had a talk with the Military Interviewing Officer. It was the duty of this man, usually a retired senior officer, to help him choose which service, arm or regiment he would like to join, and which occupation he would like to follow in it. It appears that in the majority of cases these MIOs did not have time to explain that they had no power to implement the choice of a regiment or trade which they helped the youth to prefer. In a large number of cases, therefore, a youth went away thinking that his service and job had been settled, only to be disillusioned (and having a reasonable complaint) a few months later when he found himself in and doing something quite different.

Five to six weeks after his medical, the youth would receive his 'call-up papers': an enlistment notice telling him where and when to report, a rail warrant from his home to the station nearest to the reception camp, and leaflets giving information. The date on the enlistment notice would be at least fourteen days ahead, in order for him to be able to give notice at his job and settle such other affairs as he could.

The shock of the first couple of days was intentionally brutal. The new recruits would usually be met at the station, given food reasonably soon after arrival at the camp, and provided with the means to write and say they had arrived safely. But these were virtually the last kindly acts for eight to twelve weeks in a system of basic training designed to suppress individuality, restrict freedom in every possible way, instil instinctive obedience without question of any kind, increase physical fitness, and generally so depress the conscript into a common mould that he would instantly serve the forces' purposes in anything that it asked him to do: to the point of killing fellow human beings, or of offering himself to be killed. The forces had learnt how to train men quickly and intensively in the Second World War; the absolute necessity of training them to this zombie-like state had been taught in the trenches of the First, when an order over the top to almost certain death had to be obeyed instinctively or it would not have been obeyed at all.

There are some eloquent and moving accounts of basic training in this book: how intelligent men were brought to resemble robots by the system, how they were forced to join in, how they are ashamed of it now yet how they actually came to enjoy the drilling, the precision, the uniformity of it. Yet I find it very strange that not one of the twenty-three contributors mentions taking part in that shattering exercise that all of us heard about (and perhaps properly dreaded) before we went in: bayonet practice, being urged by a vicious NCO to compete in making bloodcurdling noises as each plunged his foot or so of cold sharpened steel into the belly of (but no distinction was made) a stuffed sack hanging from a gibbet. Have they all so assimilated it that it was not worth mentioning that they learnt (and presumably still know) how to kill a human being in one of the nastiest ways possible? Are they still therefore conditioned? Was the system that good?

This systematic brutalising of men in basic training had to drive them to the limits, of course; and those limits could only be defined by the number of conscripts who, rather than continue with it, were driven to commit suicide. The Ministry of Defence has been unable or unwilling to give me figures for the number of National Servicemen who committed suicide; indeed, there seems some suggestion that either such figures were never kept or that, if they had been, they would have been inaccurate since many units preferred not to let the matter go as far as the War Office, and covered it up as accidental death, or even as death in action, in order (for one reason) to spare the families some misery or distress. Whatever the rights or wrongs of this, I feel that not too much significance should be placed on the fact that some National Servicemen undoubtedly (too many conscripts have tales of them, even of the rest of the billet being given forty-eight-hour leave passes 'to get over it' as a result) did commit suicide, for I imagine that the proportion would not be larger (and is possibly very much smaller) than that for undergraduates at universities, or new members of any comparable institution.

The 1956 Report referred to previously also revealed that there was no specific training given to the officers and NCOs who were in charge of this very important course of basic training, despite there being parallels in industry and elsewhere for specialisation and direction in this field as in any other; though they were 'very carefully selected', in the words of the Report.

Each recruit had an interview during his basic training with the Personnel Selection Officer attached to the unit, who had also had no specialised training for his job. He had to weigh up each recruit's qualifications and preferences against the needs of the force in which he was to serve, and place the man accordingly. This was the point at which the impression made by the MIO was liable to become distorted, and disappointment and frustration ensue; for the decision of the PSO could not easily be altered at any time afterwards.

During or at the end of this period of basic training suitable conscripts were sent for interview by an Officer Selection Board; others went for specialised further training in a skill or trade, and the unskilled were simply given a posting to a unit at once. Eventually all were posted to units either at home or abroad. The chances of being posted abroad varied from time to time during the eighteen years of National Service: in 1952, during the Korean War, the chances were about one in two; in 1957, they had dropped to about one in three. It was claimed that all National Servicemen serving abroad were volunteers, and, while there is no doubt that many conscripts did volunteer as a way of seeking some benefit from their service, there is equally no doubt (and it is confirmed by one of the contributors) that the time-honoured forces' method of drafting volunteers was also used.

The vast majority of conscripts seem to have kept demob charts; that is, pieces of paper with every day of their service written down to be crossed off as each was done. When the final day came, they handed in their kit (all except for certain items which would be needed during their reserve service) and then they were relatively free.

In less than a year they would become twenty-one, and so entitled to a vote in the affairs of the country they had just spent two years of their lives serving.

How useful and important was National Service to each of the armed forces? In numbers, they were affected disproportionately. Figures for the relative strengths of each service, broken down by years into both Regulars and National Servicemen, will be found in Appendix B, but, very roughly, in a typical year, for every National Serviceman in the Royal Navy there were about twelve in the Royal Air Force and thirty-one in the Army. In assessing the importance of conscription to each, therefore, they should be taken separately.

ROYAL NAVY

The Senior Service, as it was fond of calling itself, was traditionally a force composed mainly of Regulars, men brought up to go to sea by ancestry and geographical accident of birth. Even during the war it used far fewer conscripts than either the Army or the RAF.

But there were also reasons which had nothing to do with tradition. The Army might train cannon-fodder in a few months and fight reasonably efficiently with it, but no destroyer or aircraft-carrier could successfully see action with even half a complement of conscripts that raw; they required not so much training as experience at sea over a far longer period to make an effective contribution to the strength of the Navy.

So, while the Navy's traditional sources of volunteer recruits were adequate, it could afford to pick and choose its National Servicemen to an extent not possible in the other services. In the main it chose two kinds of conscripts: those whose civilian skills were relevant to whatever special needs it had at any particular time, and those who had shown some interest in going to sea (without necessarily wanting to make it their career) by joining the Royal Naval Volunteer Reserve as cadets before reaching eighteen.

But the National Serviceman was certainly useful to the Navy. Whenever there were gaps to be filled in the pattern of Regular recruitment, then the conscript filled them. This could be done without disrupting the scheme of training the Navy had established over many years; the conscript simply fitted in.

Thus, during the whole post-war period, the Navy was able to meet its commitments (the prevention of illegal immigrants into Palestine, support operations off the coast of Malaya, general defence of such of the Commonwealth as could not look after itself, and the landing at Suez) without having to rely very much on National Servicemen. It must also have been a factor that the Navy's pre-war role of defending far-flung outposts and showing the flag had been taken over more and more during the period by the RAF, and the service was inevitably a contracting one.

ARMY

National Service was an enormous success from the point of view of the Army; during the period concerned it was a much more efficient and effective force than it would have been without conscripts.

First, National Service enabled the Army to meet widespread and heavy commitments throughout the period in Germany, Palestine, Malaya, Korea, the Suez Canal Zone, Kenya, and Cyprus; besides providing for the basic defence of Britain.

Secondly, it obtained its manpower very cheaply indeed, especially pre-trained technicians of certain kinds; in 1960 it was calculated that the Regular cost the Army four times as much as his National Service comrade.

Thirdly, it resulted in the building up of very large reserves of men trained (and kept trained) to a reasonable military standard.

The enormous influx of National Servicemen to be trained did, of course, cause the Army great administrative problems; while the Navy could fit the conscript in, the Army had to re-design the whole of its intake procedures. From January 1949 to early 1960, for instance, it accepted 1,132,872 recruits; and trained them. It was no light task, and that the Army could train National Servicemen sufficiently well for its own purposes is indicated by the general agreement both inside and outside the Army that they fought for their country just as effectively as Regulars.

But so they should have done; perhaps even better than Regulars, in fact. In a 1955 Report, *Citizens of Tomorrow* (again, see Bibliography), there is the remark: 'the material coming into the Services is, in the main, very good.' Since they had the pick of the whole of the fit male population of the country at the relevant age, it is difficult to see how the intake could possibly have been better.

National Service also helped the Army with its public relations. Before the war it had tended to be a caste apart, as I have suggested, isolated and somewhat derided. Now, everyone knew someone who had been in the Army, the man-in-the-street had a quite clear idea of what it was like and roughly what it was doing.

The truth is that the Army did very well out of National Service. The quality of the intake was far higher than it could possibly have expected from normal voluntary recruitment, a virtually complete cross-section of the community, and it was able to select for intelligence, ability, skill and every other factor to deploy its manpower accordingly in the most effective manner.

The Army must have regretted the ending of National Service more than any other Service.

ROYAL AIR FORCE

The RAF experience of National Service lies somewhere between that of the two older services.

In its favour, the RAF seemed attractive to a potential conscript because of the undoubted novelty, at that time, the romance and adventure of flying or being associated with flying and aircraft, however false that might be in reality. Furthermore, rumour had it for new conscripts (and apparently in fact) that discipline was less draconian than in the Army and living conditions (because the camps were that less old) were better. Again, life could be more settled and comfortable on a permanent airbase than in (say) tented encampments on the banks of the Sweet Water Canal. Thus the RAF tended to attract the more intelligent and skilled youths who regarded the Army, rightly or wrongly, as the worst of the three options.

So the RAF had much more success in persuading its conscripts to sign on as Regulars; between 1949 and 1960 approximately one-third of the National Service intake signed on, mostly for the three-year engagement that gave them double the pay and far more privilege than the conscript, and made them of more real use to the RAF.

The importance of the National Serviceman to the RAF declined as its equipment became more complicated and sophisticated. As with the Navy, it found it simply could not train a conscript to a sufficiently worthwhile standard of efficiency in two years. It was possible immediately after the war to train National Service pilots and navigators on Vampires and Meteors sufficiently quickly that they could render some valuable service, but the introduction of Hunters, Javelins and V-bombers in the middle fifties meant the end of National Service aircrew well before conscription itself ended. Nevertheless, the RAF continued to use conscripts for unskilled or semi-skilled jobs at the lower levels in order to release Regulars for more specialised trades.

THE RESERVES

Reserve organisations like the Territorial Army, the Royal Naval Volunteer Reserve, and the RAF Volunteer Reserve all originally had a volunteer basis. The element of compulsion introduced by the 1948 Act into service in these organisations virtually killed them; or at best changed their character out of all recognition.

In practice (that is, the Suez call-up of reserves in 1956) it had been found that the reservist had not in fact kept up his training, that he was not as ready for service without further extensive training as had been hoped.

So no one was pleased with the part-time aspect of National Service: not services, nor volunteer organisations, nor conscripts, nor the taxpayer.

The primary object of National Service at the outset, said a Government White Paper in October 1955, was the building up of trained reserves; and it went on to say that this was no longer strategically and internationally necessary. It was therefore intended to reduce the armed forces in strength by about one-eighth.

The end of National Service was in sight, though it was still nearly eight years away. Conscripts would still be needed until enough Regulars could be recruited, but there would be a gradual run-down of those called upon to serve Her Majesty. In order to maintain the principle of universal liability for service, the call-up age would be progressively raised until by March 1958 it was intended to be nineteen. In addition, there would be three instead of four registration dates each year, and from May 1956 those placed in medical Grade III would not be called up.

Somebody had clearly realised that the forces were not quite up to date. This had been a not uncommon condition with the British Army, always notoriously and scrupulously training to fight the last war. At Balaclava we were still using the same pattern of musket as we had fought with at Waterloo, and the waterbottles dated from those in use at Blenheim even earlier; when one of the thirteen generals credited with over seventy years' service happened to want to consult the Drill Book in 1860, he found it had been drawn up in 1788; and then there were all those lovely horses we used to terrorise the German machine-gunners with in the First World War. But it would, of course, be dishonest not to give the British Army credit for ending up on the winning side in most of the wars it had fought, as well.

It was the Suez adventure of October and November 1956 which more than anything else led to the release of the nation's youth from the burden of National Service; even though, for some tiny few of them, this release took the form of violent injury. For the invasion of Egypt proved once and for all that bull, bullet and bayonet were a pathetic arsenal in the league in which Britain was playing. Krushchev's relatively delicate hint that he could have picked up the phone and ordered someone to press a button to deliver a series of nuclear weapons within minutes could have been equalled only in its shocking effect by the Americans' sour note telling us to get the hell out of the place.

Until 1956 there had been very few voices against National Service, but even before the actual Suez invasion there had been some indication that there was not universal acceptance of it though it did not find much of a place in the newspapers. Those Z-reservists who, on receiving their recall papers for the Suez crisis, sent them back with the one word BOLLOCKS scrawled across them were the avant garde in a movement which was soon to grow to establishment proportions.

In the next month, December, there was published a Government Report which concluded that it found it hard to justify 'the employment of National Servicemen in some of the occupations in which we have seen them at work'. It recommended that more civilians be taken on to do those jobs (like clerking, stores, and pay) which could not possibly convince a youth that he was engaged in the vital defence of his Queen, country, home and loved ones. This would clearly, if implemented, have cost the forces a great deal of money. So would another recommendation: 'It is clear to us that if National Service is to continue, many millions of pounds must be spent, and very soon, in providing reasonable quarters'.

If the financial implications of this Report were obvious, even more so were the democratic ones: 'The increasing need to justify the continuance of National Service has not been met', it said, and went on to insist that all conscripts should be made clearly aware:

a) That the future of Great Britain in world affairs must depend in part on the strength of our armed Services.
b) That the necessary strength depends in present circumstances upon a degree of compulsory military service.
c) That the nation owes a great debt of gratitude to those who are thus compelled to interrupt their normal peacetime lives in the service of their country.
d) That only through public recognition of this debt can the National Serviceman feel proud of performing his duty.

Within a few months the Sandys White Paper had resolved the whole thing. It was intended to end the call-up of National Servicemen by 1960 as one result of a thoroughgoing (I had nearly written radical) change in defence strategy. Instead of having our resources spread around the world in garrisons, naval bases and airfields, we were going to have forces with a high degree of mobility stationed in far fewer places but ready to strike at an instant's notice. To look after us at home, there would be a Central Strategic Reserve, equally ready, equally mobile. And the new forces would be all-professional, all-Regular, with men earning notably increased pay and living in what amounted to luxury, by comparison.

As a result, between 1957 and 1963 the morale of the National Serviceman was at its lowest. The Regulars tended to think him hardly worth training as they gained in confidence and professionalism. He was at the same time markedly poorer and more intelligent than the Regular, less able to compete in taking a girl out for the evening yet just about to become (say) one of the country's top mountaineers and make a major contribution to geophysics at university. It was a difficult time for both the forces and the National Serviceman, and (the final indignity) since recruitment lagged behind the expectations of Duncan Sandys, John Profumo had to announce to the House that some nine thousand two hundred of the last men would have to serve an extra six months to fill the gap; but he was able to reassure the Leader of the Opposition, Mr Harold Wilson, that no general return to conscription was envisaged.

And so we come back to Dick Vaughan and Fred Turner, and your choice as to who is favourite for Last Man Out.

One heard a great deal at the time about the benefits of National Service, most bizarrely as though it were a kind of mass alternative to Borstal. The forces took a lot of credit for 'character development' (and how oldfashioned and imprecise that phrase sounds now) which would in fact have happened anyway. But there were benefits, of course. Most men came out physically fitter than when they went in, many benefited by mixing with people from widely varying backgrounds and areas of Britain, a few gained educational qualifications who might not otherwise have done.

But about the other benefits there was considerable doubt. Men were said to come out more mature; but any eighteen-year-old is going to be more mature at twenty. Employers were said to regard a man's success in the forces as a pointer to his future; but surely this can have applied only to a relatively few occupations fairly directly linked to what the man had been doing during his service; there were far more instances either of men being totally misemployed, or of being carefully trained to do the jobs they were already able to do. There was also foreign travel, but under such restrictive conditions that its value could not have been great and the contact with foreign nationals prejudiced by the uniform. Then there was the comradeship; but hardly anyone seems to have kept up with friends he had in the forces. Even the much-advertised value as a social leveller seems to have been true only of the initial eight weeks or so of basic training: for the upper and middle classes tended to become officers, and the working-class lads almost invariably stayed privates, in the strict hierarchy of the forces. Some National Servicemen learnt to exploit the system in which they found themselves, and learnt lessons that were to stand them in good stead for the rest of their lives; but these are in a minority, and would probably have learnt the same lessons in some other system. Certainly they and everyone else also learnt things that were of no conceivable use outside the services.

Yet there were the laughs. Every ex-National Serviceman has his riotously comic stories to tell, and perhaps telling them is the only time he talks about his service. In this book, virtually every contribution has at least one great laugh, a residual benefit not planned or encouraged by the military system.

No, almost all benefits that came out of National Service seem to have been incidental, marginal to the main experience which was tedious, belittling, coarsening, brutalising, unjust and possibly psychologically very harmful. No amount of physical fitness and social levelling could make up for the fact that a youth had his liberty and his right to earn his living severely restricted for two years. National Service seen at its extreme was an indignity and an injustice imposed upon youths at an age when few of them had learnt to think for themselves; and most were not considered mature enough to have a vote. This contempt for common democracy must have had an effect on their later lives.

National Service may well turn out to be a classic case of short-term gains for incalculable long-term losses.

The cost of National Service to the country was cheap in military terms but expensive in other ways, even at the time. Between 1945 and 1960 the total called-up was 2,301,000, and therefore there was a net loss to the labour force each year of something like a quarter of a million workers. A majority of these were youths capable of doing men's jobs; others were being delayed by two years from reaching the point where they could begin to pay back by way of work the investment in their education. The economic price paid was high, and it should not be underestimated; no doubt the fact that the Germans had no conscription from 1945 to 1955 must have played some part in the *Wirtschaftswunder*.

Another cost was occasioned by the three-year gap for most youths between school and National Service; their efficiency, their keenness to learn a job (and the keenness of employers to teach it to them) was inevitably affected for the worse. The expectation of two years of hard discipline and little money meant that they tended to concentrate more recklessness and wildness into those three years, and they took higher-paid but deadend jobs rather than lower-paid ones with prospects.

It is often said that eighteen-year-olds today would not put up with National Service, that they ask questions and demand answers whereas we, in general, did not. It certainly seems to need explaining that, for the generations which came to manhood in the period, National Service was a fact of life present from as early as one could remember. They grew up knowing that their nineteenth and twentieth years did not belong to them, that they were going to be told what to do with them. So much was this true that when I was discharged so peremptorily from the RAF it had a profoundly disturbing effect on my life: the pattern I had expected had been radically disrupted, I now had to decide for myself what to do with those two years, I had to make up my mind about an enormous number of things concerning my immediate future which I had complacently thought would be decided for me. I felt equally balanced between relief at not having to undergo the privations of service life. yet dismay at the prospect of my sudden responsibilities. It was four years before I had created another pattern.

Then there is the untold psychological cost, which may be heaviest of all and still largely to pay, the effect on a substantial section of the nation which is still continuing and may indeed result in unknown changes in the national character over a long period, since there has been (it can bear repeating) nothing like it before.

And almost finally there is the actual financial cost, of course. No government has ever been satisfactorily able to define the objectives which Defence Expenditure was designed to achieve, and consequently it is impossible to tell whether we saw value for money or not. Are we safer now than then? We were certainly safe then, we see in retrospect, and it was much cheaper, too, than it is now.

395 National Servicemen were killed in action.

Some of the contributors to this book are surprised at the bitterness with which they have found themselves writing about their experiences; a few found it the most formative experience of their lives; most condemn it, looking back from at least ten years and sometimes from more than twenty, and are critical of its value both to themselves and to the country. It is difficult to remember that, at the time, one thought oneself well out of it, for whatever reason, if one could avoid it; in retrospect, it still seems better to have missed it. Several of these National Servicemen are clearly somewhat embarrassed, if not ashamed, of what they did or allowed to be done in their names, or what they allowed themselves to be conditioned to become. No one forced you to become an officer, for instance; but the moment you volunteered to become one you ceased to be a pressed man, and became as responsible a part of the system as any career militarist. Perhaps the strongest of those in this book is now revealed to be the conscientious objector. Again, it is difficult to remember how unfashionable, courageous and stubborn such an act was, how pejorative the term *conchie* was, and how few there in fact were. In this case the objection was political, too, and not (as was far more common) religious.

Together with those of this one conscientious objector, this book contains the reflections and experiences of some twenty-three National Servicemen. It has been edited to read as a continuous narrative might be read. I have tried to cut repetitious detail wherever possible so that the broad pattern of a National Service-man's career is roughly followed; that is, those contributors with most to say about basic training tend to come at the beginning, those with more relevant things to say about a particular posting come later, and those who were able to reach some serious conclusions usually come towards the end. Where there is an abbreviation or a piece of service jargon, it is explained only the first time it occurs.

I would not claim the book is representative, since I do not believe it would be possible to choose any twenty-four men who would form an accurate sample. It may be objected that it is over-burdened with officers, but anyone who cares to check up will find that the services, too, were overburdened with officers. And again, there is more than the statistical average of writers in it; but after all this is a book, and writers on the whole tend to write better than most other people. But it does roughly reproduce the 1:12:31 proportions of Naval:RAF:Army National Servicemen, and I think it may contain as much truth about the national experience as we can at this moment, ten years on, discover.

B. S. Johnson
February 1973

JEFF NUTTALL

It was a warm mellow spring, as they go. We used to eat a late breakfast in Poppa Conde's, coffee and fresh rolls. Sometimes we went to lectures at Senate House. Sometimes we hung around Russell Square arguing about whether the great Victorian hotels were good or not. I drew sparrows and went back to my studio in the basement of the hostel in Coram Street and turned them into mad ghosts by fiddling around with the textures and the scale. We used to go to listen to Humphrey Lyttelton and the Crane River Jazz Band at 100 Oxford Street. Cy Laurie's had not opened at that time. It was an urbane life being a student in the early fifties. No protest. No drugs. You could buy all the amphetamines over the counter but we didn't bother. We could not afford to drink much. We read and talked and drank gallons of coffee and tea and then read and talked some more. We were all wretchedly in love.

During the five years of my course I had forgotten a number of things. I had forgotten that there are people around who expect to be obeyed. I had forgotten utilitarian things, cheap gloss paint, cheap disinfectant, cheap linoleum. I had forgotten the structures of rank and fear. So when I walked across Russell Square to the Army Medical Centre that warm mellow spring I walked into a curious archaic dream. It was like meeting an eccentric old man. It was all unreal and quaint and funny. After my half-hearted attempt to plead flat feet and a weak heart we were ushered, one at

17

a time, into the CO's office for an interview. Very few of us were able to take it seriously. So the commanding officer spent his days, seemingly, in a series of enraged confrontations with supercilious students. I was far too naïve at the time to see that this was a fine extension of the class war. I was a callow, introspective, vain, ambitious, obsessive little sod. I walked out of the medical, savoured its musty quality for a day or so, and forgot about it.

It was an odd term. The end of a five-year course. Nobody knowing whether they had passed anything or not. The summer making it all mirage-like. All of us determined not to forget we were artists, whatever the Army or the teaching profession might do to us. My paintings were doing well. I had a show. I used to go, at the invitation of one of my patrons, to the Savile Club. Sitting drinking at the expense of a lot of charming and famous old queers, I was not a little surprised by their disgust at my diffidence about the Army: if I felt so bloody clever about the Army why didn't I plead conscientious objector? Either I believed in it or I didn't. What was I playing at?

I decided, curiously, that I felt that conscientious objection would be precious and false. I felt that the Army was to do with the state of the world and the state of humanity, and although I might feel the greatest contempt for the state of humanity, it was by no means a state from which I wished to escape. If people were suffering something, I could suffer it also. I could take my share of pathetic discomfiture. And sooner or later there was the bomb. One never mentioned it but everybody knew it. So what the hell did anything matter anyway?

The term wound up with a number of parties. They were somewhat libidinous and I disgraced myself. I took the train back home to Hereford in a pale green orgy of remorse, and I got married the following Saturday. We thumbed it to Les Saintes-Maries with a tattered old tent. There, on the beach, amidst midges and oceans of Volpar-Gell, we started our daughter off in life. We got back to Hereford with a few days left. We went up on the Black Mountains and made love in the sun, amongst the ferns, and I carried the image of that time with me for years as a sort of talisman against loneliness or despair. And then I caught the train to Catterick.

It was a long, disjointed, awkward journey. I arrived late and had difficulty finding Mosul Lines. Catterick was as big as a city. I was amazed. And it was still funny, ludicrous, archaic. Was one indeed going to sleep in buildings like public urinals for two years? The orderly corporal who took all the details down was bored and sarcastic. I had to hand in my civvies. It was a suit my mother had bought me. As the quartermaster bundled it up and threw a pair of denims at me I had a quick humiliating wave of self-pity. I made my way to my billet, dragging my mattress and blankets. I met a bunch of ex-students and we spent all the money we had left on NAAFI beer. The next day I had to borrow money for all the polishes and dusters I had to acquire.

They taught us to do silly things. We had to press thick military frieze to a system of razor-sharp creases. We had to polish belt brasses inside and outside. We had to polish the studs on our best boots. We had to polish the lockless seatless shithouses, the concrete floors, the rusty stove. There was a wooden trestle table we all shared: each day the sergeant dug his stick in the earth and dragged it up and down the surface of the table and each day we had to scrape it smooth with razor-blades and scrub it white. Everything was covered in newspaper before we used it. No man entered another man's bed-space. It was my first Army catch-phrase: 'Get out of me bed-space!'

And it was all still funny. Like Alice. Apart from missing my wife and having no money I was lapping it up. Then, about the third day, a little Scottish boy was late on parade.

'Where the fuck d'you think you've been?' shrieked the sergeant, one of those wonderful men whose voices only operated at double-forte.

''Avin' a shit, sarge.'

'When you're in the Army, son, you don't go for a shit when you're on parade. You stand on the fuckin' square and shit yourself.'

The lad's face reddened and his eyes filled.

'Understand?' The sergeant placed his stick against the soldier's nose and prodded. 'Under-fucking-stand?'

The boy raised his arm and brushed the stick away. The sergeant exploded. It was no longer a voice guying itself, larded with all the old sergeant-major witticisms. It was a voice of purposeful violence. The boy was frog-marched off the square and we all stood rigid for fifteen minutes, shaken, waiting for the sergeant's return. He came back alone.

That afternoon we saw the Scottish lad on his hands and knees clipping the mangy grass between the billets with two armed guards standing by. His face was swollen and his head was shaven and the Army wasn't funny, suddenly.

The next day I got a letter from my wife. She had enclosed ten bob. I sat on the edge of my bed and started to cry. The other lads in the billet gawped. They were mostly slum lads from Glasgow, Liverpool and Dublin. Tears were taboo to them.

''E's fuckin' cryin'.'

'Fuck me, ey, come and look 'ere. 'E's fuckin' cryin'.'

They were delighted and amazed. They gathered round chortling. One of them ruined the layout of his bed by collapsing with laughter. And quickly the Army became funny again, a different sort of funny, very very funny. Mad. Violent. Tragic. Hilarious. They saw that my sobs had turned to giggles. Somebody said, 'You're fuckin' puddled, you', and I, I had become a different person. Quite different. For ever.

After that the Army was the theatre of a sort of majestic farce. When Crosby in the next bed to me was sent in disgrace to stand at the edge of the square at full slope, and the sergeant forgot him, and, some five hours later, we had to carry him into the billet, faint with cold and exhaustion, I laughed. When the sergeant persuaded a naïve squaddy that he was to be shot for violation of the rifle range regulations, and stood him against a wall, and had him dictate a last letter to his mum and his girl friend, I laughed. When I tore all the skin off my stomach and arms and half my face trying to get over a wall on the assault course, I laughed. The silliness was extended by the violence and the cruelty, and the moors stretched off to the left and right all round. There was a lot of bright weather with splashes of cold rain and brisk winds that banged the billet door. It was a month of cold shocks, shouting men, muscle, and farce.

We moved on to the old cavalry barracks in Colchester. They were rich and Kiplingesque. Then we moved on to the Royal Army Educational Corps training depot at Beaconsfield. We were all graduates who had either refused commissions or failed them. I refused mine through inverted snobbery. The upper-middle-class charade of the officers' mess repelled me.

I was home to my pregnant wife for Christmas. We had a good Christmas but I was not the man she had married and I think she sensed it then

Then I went to Central Ordnance Depot, Weedon, as Unit Education Sergeant, or 'Schoolie'. And I stayed there the rest of my service.

COD Weedon was built by George IV as an emergency royal residence for the expected French invasion. He calculated the point in the British Isles which is furthest from the sea on all sides and he put the major arms store of his Army there. He put it in beautiful symmetrical redbrick warehouses along a branch of the Grand Union Canal. With its iron bridges and regal proportions the place had the air of some of the best London docks. Canaletto might have designed it. Some way up the hillside he built three four-storey pavilions. The central one was to be his own residence.

When I was at Weedon the central pavilion was the billet for the Royal Pioneer Corps detachment whose job it was to lug cases of FLN rifles around the depot and send them off to Kenya and Cyprus. They had long ago stripped the roof of lead so that rain poured straight through into many of the rooms. They were rough simple lads. They slept in their clothes, many of them, handing in perfectly clean pillowcases and pyjamas for laundering every week. Occasionally one of them would shit on the landing. I got to be very fond of them. They were like big sleepy clumsy smelly dogs. I used to wake them in the morning when I was orderly-sergeant and it was very moving to see such a combination of fresh downy sleepy flesh on their faces and pricks (they all woke with a hand on the gear lever) and the powerful stench from their warm blankets.

The other two pavilions were the officers' and sergeants' mess respectively. I moved into a beautiful room on the top floor of the latter from which I could see most of Northamptonshire. I stuck up a piece of hardboard the first day and started to paint. There was a Georgian marble fireplace. Somebody had painted it battleship grey and picked out the mouldings in bright red. This pleased me immensely.

As I arrived a War Office ruling came through that all ranks above corporal must have their Army Certificate of Education, Second Class (about third-year secondary-school level). Many soldiers were illiterate. Long-serving staff-sergeants came to me with handfuls of money. I started classes in a dusty old Nissen hut at seven thirty in the morning. There they sat, my handful of worried NCOs, battle-scarred and beribboned, chanting the phonetic alphabet. It was a hopeless job. Eventually I did all their papers for them by chalking the answers on the board. Even then some of them failed. One of them died before he took the exam. He was reluctant to die because what little he had would go to his wife and he detested her so much.

Terrible and fabulous things happened at Weedon while I was there. There was a pathetic pioneer called Lewis. He was a high-grade mongol who should never have got into the Army. He had a soft Devon accent. A thick drunken Liverpudlian called Scruggs used to pay Lewis half-a-crown for a gobble every so often. He was enuretic and particularly malodorous. On route marches nobody would go down-wind of Lewis. Sergeant Charley Smart, another Liverpudlian, was the NCO in charge of the Pioneers at Weedon. Whenever there was an inspection he would lock Lewis in the cellar of the pavilion with all his belongings. Eventually, Lewis, lonely and frightened in his dark cellar, tried to hang himself with a piece of string. The string broke. When Charley released Lewis he found the loop hanging round his neck.

'Good job for you you're so fuckin' thick,' he told Lewis. Everybody, including Lewis, laughed about the incident for days.

Charley Smart was adored by his primitive charges. He was a seven-foot slum father to the lot of them, brutal, compassionate, and just.

Periodically he would hit me. We used to do weekend weapon training and I was allocated to Charley Smart's squad. Having the fucking Schoolie in his team was more than Sergeant Smart's dignity could stand. He therefore told me to put my tin hat on. When I had done this he struck me on the head with the flat of his sten-gun. Dazed, I staggered off the square out of his way.

We had a ritual in the sergeants' mess that was supposed to be observed every time anyone was made up to sergeant. A huge pint cocktail was made up of a little bit of everything in the bar. The night Taffy Rivers was made up this concept was expanded to include a dash of every liquid we could find in the entire mess building, from tomato ketchup to Brasso, and on to the unmentionables. Taffy was out for two days in a coma. I suppose we should have sent for a doctor but the motto was 'Don't flap', and, sure enough, in two days Taffy was as right as rain.

Taffy was a curious combination of sexual vanity and complete virginal naïvety. We used to travel back to camp by the same train on Sunday nights. The train from Cardiff to Birmingham would steam into Hereford Station and there would be Taffy, with his specs and his immaculate white stripes and his terrible stutter, calling:

'S-Schoolie. Over b-b-by yer, Schoo-oolie.'

One Sunday night there was a woman sharing Taffy's compartment. She was a pleasant enough spinster in a two-piece tweed costume and brogues, sitting knitting and politely listening to Taffy's incredible saga of prowess. She got out at Worcester with a smile and an unruffled goodbye.

'There you are,' said Taffy, nudging me heavily in the ribs. 'C-c-cock-'appy.'

The company sergeant-major was an awful mess. He was an arrogant little Scot called McKay, with white hair and a purple face. He was a pathetic boozer and bed-wetter. Every Sunday morning he would fork over pounds to his favourite mess waiter who was the only one who had the stomach to clean his room and change his bed. Sometimes he would wander into my room late, pleading for a little sympathy and affection, but it was hard to give. Other times he wandered into the guard room late at night and beat shit out of the prisoners.

There was a branch depot at a place called Barby which was a square mile of black Nissen huts in the middle of a curious plain of waste land grown over with high white grass. Every so often a two-day guard came up and I, as sergeant, had to be guard commander. I used to try and fix it so that my second-in-command was a big cockney corporal in the Pioneers called Spud. Spud and I would pass a hat round the eight patrolmen, then stop the lorry in Daventry to pick up extra grub and a couple of crates of ale. When the duty officer had made his routine check we would call in the picket and enjoy the magnificent fry-up which Spud had been preparing. Then we would open the ale and begin the circus. Everybody had a role to play: mouthy buggers were made ringmaster, fat buggers were made elephants, everybody wanted to be lions and tigers, and there was no shortage of clowns. I was always tightrope walker and Spud was the band. One night the duty officer came back, having forgotten his gloves. I was wearing a vest and pants, grey Army socks, gaiters for garters, my beret, and a webbing belt made into a kind of bra. I had a copy of *Reveille* over my head, under the beret. I was balanced halfway along the edge of an upturned bench and Spud was giving his enthusiastic rendering of 'The Entry of the Gladiators'. There was a full minute's silence. After the silence the major who was on duty asked what the hell I thought I was doing. I told him we were having a circus. I don't think his face actually changed at all for a long time, but various lights passed through his eyes, the lights of betrayed courage, the lights of despairing patriotism, the lights of disbelief, of leonine wrath, of rank terror.

'Well,' he said. 'Well, you'd better get this place cleared up – yes, get this place scrubbed out.'

And then he fled.

I was forever being dragged up before the commanding officer, usually for over-identification, which is Army jargon for not sticking to your rank socially, for being too friendly with the lads. Once I marched off a squad to the left and went in to the mess bar for a pint. Fifteen minutes later the lance-corporal was breathless at the mess-door.

'Sarge, the squad's markin' time up against a brick wall over there. What d'you want 'em to do now?'

I was up on the mat about that as well.

And there was the time I sent Charley Smart off to Nottingham on an education course. That night Charley's wife came down to the mess bar and I made a pass at her. The next day Charley came storming back, drew a sten out of the stores and hunted me up and down the camp. I locked myself in the Unit Library cupboard until his rage had abated.

And there was the night Scouse Jenkins bottled the duty officer and was arrested in the act of masturbation, with his head in a pool of vomit, immediately afterwards.

And there was the milky-faced, ex-LSE NS officer whose communist integrity lasted about six weeks in the officers' mess.

And there was the kid who ran away from the unit stark naked and hid in a cornfield. Two NCOs found him and beat him up, out there in the corn. Then they ran him round the parade-square naked, and the wives came out of the married quarters to laugh at his prick.

The Army changed me immeasurably. I got to know the urban working-class intimately by being forced to live with them. They shattered my middle-class fastidiousness and the intolerance that goes with it. I became capable of extreme callousness.

I acquired a will-power and with it the knowledge that there is very little a determined man cannot do, the belief that there is nothing a determined man cannot do. I learned that energy and ability will stretch much further than idleness and fear normally allow it to.

Most of all, best of all, I learned that life is a desperate, terrible, magnificent joke. You can distinguish ex-National Servicemen by this sense.

I met a British Council official recently who was home on leave and wanted to sample the fruits of the sexual revolution. I introduced him to some girls who might be noted for their lack of sexual inhibition. None of them fancied him. He, however, seemed blind to this and persisted in his advances. Finally one of the girls let him have it just to shut him up. Later he said:

'Things haven't changed, you know. You've still got to fight for it.' A National Serviceman, to the very bone. Mad, ironic, left-wing male chauvinist pigs.

In my room on the top floor of the mess I could watch thunderstorms advancing right across the county. I used to sit in an open window with a crate of beer and my clothes drenched, roaring with delight at every flash of lightning. I painted a lot and my painting registered the changes in myself. All the mystery went out of it, all the subtlety, and a kind of brutal exultant quality came in. My vision since then has oscillated between that brutalism and the subtle mysticism returning.

The other sergeants used to invade my room every so often to stand perplexed and sceptical before 'Schoolie's mad fuckin' pictures'. When I was demobbed they bought me ten quid's worth of paint as a farewell present. It was very difficult making a speech afterwards. There they were, the drunken brutalised old fascists, and there I was, more deeply moved than ever in my life.

I went back a couple of years later and had a drink with them. They told me I was the worst fucking soldier they had ever seen.

WES MAGEE

1960 meant, for me, call-up into the Army. I had no grounds for exemption either through physical disability or involvement in a continuing educational course. As a bank-clerk working in Carlisle I was eminently suitable for conscription and in early March, when the frost still had its claws in place, Army service loomed before me like a dark hill.

The late fifties had been a strangely quiet period. The Teds had put away their drapes and drainpipes and the early hard-rock of Elvis, Little Richard and Bill Haley had faded into a middle-of-the-road pop. Espresso coffee had drugged the youth of the day into a froth-sipping, café-sitting trance, and the dance halls were packed with neatly dressed youths all searching for their living dolls. As a part of this inoffensive mood I raised no objection to being called up, being made to leave home and friends, and told to give up my job. On 3rd March I merely boarded a train at Carlisle station and journeyed south, as ordered, to an infantry training depot at Preston.

Preston. I knew nothing of the town, except that Tom Finney once ran the wing for PNE. And a grammar school 'C'-stream education had done nothing to encourage me to find out, investigate, question. I accepted the notion that what had to be, had to be. That sweet gal, Doris Day, had turned out a similar message – *Que sera, sera* – and made it a best-selling record.

On that train to Preston there were a number of young men all looking slightly tense and keeping very quiet. They were obviously conscripts and were just about as far removed from the image of the soldier as it was possible to get. They sat in isolation, and none were pissed or stretched out along the seats or even chatting up birds. They looked very young. As I stared out at the fleeing countryside with its crusts of snow and frost I saw the roof of my sheltered life blown away by a wind of change. I had a picture of my parents, sister, friends standing in a group, waving, becoming smaller and smaller as the train rushed on, on.

Fulwood Barracks, Preston, turned out to be an ugly place. As the Army lorry swept us past its dirty high walls and through the massive wooden gates the soldier who was with us said, 'That's the last you'll see of civilisation for a few weeks, lads!' He had a pasty complexion, an uneven moustache, and missing teeth. He had a hungry look and was not a pretty sight. The infantry depot looked even worse.

The wooden gates slammed and we had entered, for eight weeks, a prison. Within minutes we were lined up and marched to the quartermaster's store. Kitting out was a pantomime. It was an overworked joke in which the comedians were the bored storemen who wore stripes on their arms. ('I'm a corporal, lad, and don't you forget it!') A huge pile of kit was dumped on each sprog and we stuffed most of it into a drab-green kit bag. If battledress, beret, and boots were not available in the correct sizes then it was a case of anything goes. Finally a poor quality mattress was draped over each head and this little lot had to be carted to a barracks building a hundred yards away. The barracks surrounded the 'square'. They were brick-built and each billet room held a dozen men. Upstairs were store rooms and the corporal's quarters. The buildings had names stencilled over the doorways – Waterloo, Alamein, Gallipoli – and the appearance was Army architecture at its most brutal.

The 'square' was a vast tarmacadam and it was holy ground. No one stepped on to it without permission. A few trees grew around its perimeter. In March they wore a thin, starved look.

I was part of a squad of thirty conscripts and we dumped our kit on to wire-framed beds and looked around the billet, saw the windows nailed down and unopenable (to obstruct thieves), the fire-place blackened by previous squads, the tall metal lockers beside each bed, and the stone floor.

'I'm Bob.'

'I'm Wes.'

'I'm Jack.'

'I'm Phil.'

'I'm Frank.'

'I'm buggered!'

We looked at the joker. He shrugged and scratched his wild mane of hair, and somehow he set the tone for our basic training course. He could not read or write, yet he managed to confront the Army with an awkward face and he would not be put down easily. Even with his hair shorn he succeeded in exuding a raw humour and kept up a running battle with authority.

The squad corporal came round to welcome us. He had two stripes, was once a sergeant but had been stripped for some drinking offence. He looked lean, and as hard as concrete.

'I'm your godfather,' he said bluntly, 'a corporal, that's what these two stripes mean. Got it? A lance-jack like the bloke upstairs has only got one. And I don't mean one ball!'

'Where do we find you if we want you?' someone asked nervously.

'Want me? What d'you think I am, lad, an old shag-bag? I live off camp. The lance-jack'll see to you lot.'

He dandered up the billet, looked closely at each man in turn.

'Those bed sheets,' he said eventually, 'you'll need to keep them clean. They'll have to last you while you're here. So no wanking in your pits!'

He stopped in front of the joker and eyed him carefully.

'I can tell about you, lad,' he said, 'you'll be over the wire, AWOL, I'll put money on it. Bet you now you'll end up in the guard-room.'

With that he left us, switching on the billet radio as he went.

All the depot radios were controlled from the guard-room and they were perpetually tuned in to Radio Luxembourg. For our eight weeks' stay we had nothing but pop, advert, pop, advert, pop. Never a news-cast or a play came within hearing range.

Someone (there's always someone) had wandered about the depot and returned with news about the cookhouse. When a siren blew we moved off there still in our civvies, casual as holiday-makers, and were chased back to the billet by a bulled-up little runt who brandished a black stick and turned out to be the guard commander.

'Get back and get your uniforms on!' he bawled. 'What d'you think this is? Your Daddy's yacht?'

We fled in panic, too good-natured to argue against such an unreasonable attitude. So we missed dinner, but grabbed tea dressed up in prickly khaki shorts and hairy battledresses, our BDs. The meal was lousy. The cooks seemed tired, and they affected a disenchanted manner as they slopped out tinned toms and greasy bangers and diabolically sweet tea. On the way back to our billet we saw the cooks in their rooms, fighting and yelling and hurling bedding. Grievous bodily harm seemed imminent and I found myself wondering how one evaded such violence, defended oneself, or sought out justice if attacked. To fall into such a situation or to become ill seemed fates to be avoided at all cost.

That night a fire was lit in the billet and one sprog began burning the pimples off his leather boots. He used a spoon heated in the fire.

'What's the point of that?' I asked him.

'It's to make the boots smooth. Then you can bull them,' he explained.

We crowded round and he told us how to take a dab of water and a bit of polish on a rag and how you rubbed it round and round on the smooth patch on the boot, until a shine came up. He had got hold of inside information, stolen a march on us, and was already a day ahead of most. I watched him suspiciously as if he were some sort of agent working for 'them'. And what was the point of issuing boots with pimpled leather if you had to burn them smooth? But such a question merely displayed my innocence in dealing with the Army.

When the lance-jack came down he was half-stoned. He had a face remarkable for its number of black-heads and a habit of calling everyone 'tit'. After his visit he himself became universally referred to as Tit. He now looked into someone's locker.

'All that kit's to be laid out proper,' he stated. 'There's a place for everything.'

'Where's the right place?'

'You'll be told, you'll be told.'

We were all thirsty and hungry but no one left the billet that first night. We went to bed late but could not sleep because no one had the gumption to turn the blaring radio off. And it became freezing cold as the fire died, as well.

Somehow I fell into a worried sleep only to be awakened, seemingly after about two minutes, by a piercing stream of vitriolic language. It was still dark and apart from the awful voice there was a metallic thumping. The lights were switched on, and the voice screamed louder.

'It's five o'clock, you black swine! Get your feet on the deck! Come on!'

The voice belonged to a white-faced sergeant, impossibly smart at such an ungodly hour, and he was bashing his swagger stick on the end of a bed. The noise resounded horribly in the harsh light.

'Come on up, you idle gits! Up!'

And he stomped along the row of beds, banging his stick. He stopped before a locker and threw back its metal door.

'What's this, then? Powder! What is this, a Chinese brothel?'

He pulled the locker to the stone floor where it crashed like a dustbin. The contents scattered and skidded away.

'That kit will be stacked pro-per-ly!' the sergeant stormed, his mouth less than an inch away from the poor man's eyes. Lance-jack Tit appeared, all black-heads and bacon grease. He took over as the sergeant left.

'Outside by 0800 hours, the lot of you,' he said, 'full BD and boots!'

We scuttled around like scared rabbits and tried to grab a quick wash and shave in the ablutions block. It was crowded and resonant with crude shouting and singing. There was scum on everything and a stale stench. The water was icy. Outside the early morning frost sparkled in the glow from the naked electric light bulbs.

With knife, fork and spoon clutched in one hand firmly behind our backs we went for breakfast.

'Swing that free arm! Up!' a voice boomed out across the semi-darkness.

For all the world we seemed to have landed in an outpost of Hell where no instructions were clearly given, but where you were just expected to know, to know.

The first days passed in a predictable welter of confusions and misunderstandings and bawling-outs. After a civilian life of fairly low intensity the Army seemed determined to shake me up and keep me jumping. The problem was to get one move ahead of the NCOs rather than one pace behind. It was important to set up an intelligence service so that we would know in advance what was expected of us. We contacted earlier squads and learned much from them. But even so we were worked like coolies. Eventually things began to take shape and a calmer atmosphere prevailed. Our sergeant made daily inspections but even his early morning temper and stick-banging cooled and abated.

Sleep was the only real privacy, but for me even that was

disturbed by the lad in the next bed having nightmares. The poor sod could not march in time and the corporals were making his life a misery.

All contact with the outside world had virtually ceased. Those men who were married grumbled quietly, but all such murmurings were swept aside as the bulling, the blancoing, the polishing really got under way. After a week our kit was sufficiently bulled for us to be allowed on the 'square', the holy of holies. We paraded in a bitter gale, snow flurries whipping through the bordering trees. The regimental sergeant-major came to look us over. He seemed displeased with what he saw.

Here was a figure I had previously observed only in comic films about the Army, and true to type his face was shaved to rawness, his hair cropped painfully far up his neck, and his uniform stiffened with what could have been wooden boards. He carried a stick rigidly under his armpit. He was rumoured to have a daughter who would lay down her arms to senior NCOs, but when he opened his mouth you forgot all about his daughter. His stream of invective and vituperative language showed an almost poetic quality. He could reel off line after line of crudities and make them sound like drawing-room pleasantries, such was the power of their cadences. Then he would stop in mid-flow and for no apparent reason grip some unfortunate and take him apart bit by bit. Psychologically it was all most disturbing, and to add to these mental difficulties I began to lose the feeling in my frozen hands and feet. A muck sweat spread through my body at the very thought of fainting in front of such a man. He would very probably ram his stick up my nostril!

Here we were, doing our duty, only to be turned on and railed against and generally treated like the lowest form of life. But not only us; for now the RSM turned his attention to the squad corporal and made the man double up and down the 'square' for having his beret askew. Then, suddenly, he turned sharply and left us standing in the bitter cold.

'He gobs more than a tart with no teeth!' the corporal said, and as he wiped his face we actually laughed. A bond had been established with the corporal. As a group we had made our first 'friend' in the Army.

Lance-jack Tit remained outside our approval. He came downstairs one night and said that his bog was blocked.

'You, you, and you, up and clear it!'

Docile as sheep we scooped the trough clear with spoons, and this dirty job became a regular punishment for slackers and idlers.

After a few days we told him to get stuffed and he shrugged and went meekly away. He was another first for us; the first superior we had refused. The lesson seemed clear. The Army was a con, just refuse to act and they are powerless to do anything. The joker, swallowing whole this philosophy, went over the wire and was dragged back the next day by scowling military policemen. He ended up in the guard-room sleeping on the floor under naked lights. His head was virtually shaved and he was doubled everywhere around the camp in bare feet. And this was a frost-bound March. Later he was transferred to some obscure unit and we never heard of him again. The lesson now seemed even clearer: *don't push your luck too far!*

But the Army was successfully breaking down our individuality. We were being moulded into a solid unit, and to assist this metamorphosis squad rivalries were encouraged. After football matches and drill competitions the NAAFI was a common ground for argument about which squad was best.

'You're crap, you lot!'

'Oh, come on.'

'Don't give us that, you country bums!'

'Better than being scouse scabs!'

The fights and strugglings were broken up by MPs and the Army smiled blindly on such activities; it was all part of a hardening process which swiftly followed on from the initial softening up and breaking down. We even began to look upon our squad sergeants as father figures.

Although already working from dawn to near midnight, a whole series of new activities were added to our training programmes: PE, weapons instruction, cross-country running, map-reading, assault course, lectures on Army organisation, and some education talks. The education officer – a Major – singled me out at the first of his bizarre talks.

'You, Magee. GCE, haven't you?'

'Yes, sir.'

'Good man, good man.'

After that he never spoke to me again. He was content to ramble through such subjects as American Bases in the Far East, music exams, sea shanties, and how to avoid the pox, all coming from his apparently bottomless pit of useless knowledge.

'We'll be testing you soon,' he told us, darkly, and our tarnished innocence recognised that this could mean anything from digging trenches to exposure to gas.

In fact it heralded an IQ assessment. We were ordered to sit at trestle tables and under the eagle eye of an officer who wore a monocle we sat the examination. I finished the paper and looked around, surprised to see that others were still on page one, or day-dreaming, or picking their noses.

By now, five weeks adrift from home and normality, we watched new squads arrive and settle in. Despite all our moanings against Army life we smirked at the ill-at-ease reactions of the new intakes. By some roundabout way we had come to identify ourselves with our squad, our NCOs, the 'Kings Own Royal Borderers' regimental flashes on our shoulders. We actually looked with pride at our new ID cards and tried hard to break time-records for stripping down and assembling light machine guns. Under pressures I had never experienced (work, fear, lack of privacy) I had taken on a new self-confidence and the Army's attempt to break me down had hardened within me a resolve not to be pushed around. Within the squad morale grew at an alarming rate.

I joined the wood scavengers and under cover of darkness we ripped boards from huts and tore up posts for the nightly fire in the billet. Returning one night laden with planks we found Lance-jack Tit holding court. He sat on a bed and talked about going over the wire.

'You mean out?' someone asked.

'Course.'

'But what about the alsatians and the MPs? How d'you miss them?'

'Simple,' Tit explained, 'if the dog comes at you you stand still and let it come. Just put your hands together and when it jumps push its front legs apart. You'll break its breast bone. Trouble is that some of them dogs are dirty buggers. They go for your balls. Only way then is to kick them hard, real hard, in the kidneys. They'll soon push off.'

As we neared the completion of our basic training, guard duties arrived. Our kit had reached the impeccable stage (it would go downhill for the rest of the two years) and each night seven men had to parade for duty at the guard-room. They were all dressed in best BDs and the guard commander inspected them in detail. The best dressed was declared 'stick man' and released from the night's duty. For this 'honour' we bulled and rubbed and polished all the harder. Belts were covered in unblemished blanco, brasses sparkled, boots shone like mirrors, and battledress trousers had creases that could cut. Despite all the threats and verbal violence and ill-temper that we had lived through we did our level best to be the best. Those callow youths who had come down from Carlisle to Preston were changed utterly. The downcast looks had been replaced by hardbitten ready-for-anything faces that were more than a little ready for the giant piss-up that would mark the end of our basic training.

'Well, lads,' the corporal asked, 'where'll we go? Come on, Magee, you're a bright bugger, what's it to be? Strip-show or booze-up or what?'

Here I was, hardly ever having tasted alcohol and certainly never having seen a naked woman in the flesh, being asked to advise on the fleshpots of Preston.

'How the tit-slinging hell should I know?' I said, aggressive as a trapped rat, 'ask some of these fornicating friggers who live in this one-horse town!'

The corporal nodded his head approvingly. I had passed his language acid test and ever since have been able to make people gape at the virtuosity of my spoken crudities.

But I was not so outspoken on the assault course. Given time I would have enjoyed clambering over brick walls and swinging across water-logged trenches, but the instructors insisted we fill our packs with bricks and turned the whole thing into a race. The last one home was allotted fatigues, as a booby prize. To avoid this extra stint of work we went like maniacs at the first wall. Wrists were sprained, heads were split, and I ended up with a wrenched knee which gave me some sleepless nights. Eventually I turned out on sick-parade complete with the lengthy list of kit that one had to take. The MO took one look at me and said:

'Keep working on it.'

He had been on the beer the previous night and his face was as green as an Irish country lane. I bandaged the knee and 'kept working on it'. On recovery I felt a sense of achievement, a victory against the odds. Yet another victory for Army psychology.

The padre offered the only real rest in our eight-week course. In the depot chapel he held forth on honour and love and duty and comradeship and compassion and the flag. He was almost as dull as the food in the cookhouse, which had become becalmed on a diet of spuds, canned meat and cabbage.

But the question now on everyone's lips was 'Where do we go from here?' I asked an officer from my regiment.

'The Cameroons, laddie, and I suppose you don't even know where that is.'

'Central Africa, sir.'

'Well, don't get too smart, son, they've got some lovely diseases out there and the women are all riddled with the clap. You'll need to keep more than your nose clean!'

The final weapons session took place at the range, but I could not hit the targets (cardboard men) for fear of the SLR rifle smacking me under the eye. Most of us went round with bruised cheeks, and I managed to get a round stuck in the barrel. The sergeant gave me a gripping and snatched the rifle from me.

'Godsake, Magee, can't you find the hole? If it had hair round it you'd have no difficulty!'

The rifle went off suddenly and the sergeant nearly fell backwards in fright.

But that incident could not disguise the fact that the course was over, finished. The passing-out parade was our final fling and the sun shone weakly as we turned and wheeled and slow-marched across the 'square' before a smattering of mums, dads, and girl-friends. The Cameroons lay ahead, but right now we were due for a week's leave, release! The faces of the eight-week soldiers were ruddy and worldly-wise. Innocence had been swept away. My hands told me this. They had been lily-white and used to counting pound notes, but now they were horny and ingrained with dirt. Like the others I had become soiled.

My prospect of a week back at home was rudely shattered the following morning. We were all packed and ready for the off when the squad corporal came down to see me.

'Magee. You're to report to the Intelligence Corps depot at Maresfield, Sussex.'

'What's that?'

'Six months training course, old son. Serves you right for being so bleeding clever. It was the IQ test that did it.'

He laughed, and clapped me on the shoulder. It was a gesture of friendship, but all the same by my barrack room locker I could have sat down and wept. The nightmare seemed ready to start all over again. *Your life is not your own* was a warning given to us by an NS man on our first day in this place. The truth of his message was indeed hard to take.

I clambered aboard a lorry with all my kit and was soon speeding south on a train bound for London, while my pals in the squad were heading north for Cumberland, and home.

EDWARD LUCIE-SMITH

It is easy to remember events; less easy, perhaps, to envision oneself as one looked more than twenty years ago. We get so used to inhabiting our bodies that we forget the slow process of change. At eighteen, with my public-schooldays just coming to an end, I was, I think, less different from my present self than many of my contemporaries. Short, loose-jointed, rather clumsy, bespectacled, flat-footed, verging on plumpness and afflicted with colds and sinus (I had spent my childhood in Jamaica), I was never a success on the playing field, or, indeed, at anything which required violent physical exertion. Fortunately, mine was a tolerant school: if you were bad at games, it was possible to get out of them.

What I dreaded was the prospect of National Service, to the point where it had become a kind of phobia. On the other hand, I had more or less convinced myself that my various physical deficiencies were sure to get me exemption from it; which was just as well, as I already had both a place and a scholarship waiting for me at an Oxford college.

In due course, the summons came for my medical examination. At breakfast time one winter morning I left Canterbury, where I was at school, for Chatham, where the medical was to take place. The local train puttered along through the frozen neatness of the Kentish orchards. It was all familiar and reassuring. Familiarity and reassurance stopped abruptly at the doors of the medical board building, which stank of disinfectant and perhaps slightly of urine, and which was full of long corridors painted shiny green and cream. A miserable bunch of us was shepherded from one cubicle to another. Perfunctory tests were made. Nervously, I asked one of the doctors, a stooped, grey-haired man with a cigarette dangling from his lower lip, if he wanted me to change position.

'No, I want you to speak when you're spoken to,' he snarled.

By mid-morning I had been passed fit for service.

Later, matters arranged themselves, or, at least, were subject to a few adjustments. My Oxford college had been assured many times that I was certain to fail my medical. Now that I had so inconsiderately passed it, everyone agreed, even the military authorities, that it would be best if I got my degree first. In that way, I would become eligible for a commission – a soft option, many people told me.

When the last day of my last term came, I went home. The summons had not yet arrived, and I hung about for several weeks until it did. I was to report to RAF Cardington in Bedfordshire. From there, since I had already passed a selection board, I would go straight to an Officer Cadet Training Unit.

At Cardington, I had my first stroke of luck. In charge of my hut was a Jamaican corporal. Even though I was white, I was nevertheless the first Jamaican he had encountered among all the recruits entrusted to him. As a tribute to this fact, he insisted on sewing on for me all the numerous name tags and badges with which we had been issued. Meanwhile my companions (all of them destined for the RAF ground officers' OCTU like myself) struggled with unfamiliar needles and thread. They also struggled with newly issued black boots, passing round tips gleaned from elder brothers, or from school-friends who had already served their time. Spoons were heated over matches, and the hut soon had a fine stink of warm boot-polish. Boots, indeed, immediately became one of the main topics of conversation amongst the members of our squad. Only I was debarred from offering an opinion. In a determined effort to avoid having to look after these fetish objects (I knew they would get me into trouble), I had already persuaded the camp doctor that boots were something I was medically unfit to wear. This exemption was to single me out for the rest of my service career.

The other main topic of conversation at Cardington was how to get leave. Newly inducted conscripts were told that everything off camp was also off limits. Weekend passes were quite out of the question. As potential officers, we took this as an affront to our as yet untested sense of responsibility. Particularly affronted was the man who had the bed next to mine. Splendidly blond, typically public school in accent and bearing, he gave, within twenty-four hours of our arrival, every sign of being an accomplished skyver in the true service tradition. His bed-space never got swept; his kit was never ready for inspection. It fell to me, and to his other next-door neighbour, to remedy his deficiencies in these respects: the team-spirit of the hut already demanded it. Yet Stephenson (as I shall call him) never attracted blame for this because he obviously felt no guilt. His lazy charm conquered all. It even conquered the commanding officer at Cardington, who was persuaded to issue Stephenson with the only weekend pass that any member of our squad received. So far as we could discover, it was also the only pass issued to any of the new intake of conscripts. When the weekend came, the rest of us mooned aimlessly about, looking for something to do.

The RAF, wiser in these matters than we had taken it to be, came up with at least one answer to the problem. A disused hangar had been converted into a vast dance hall; bus-loads of local factory and shop-girls were shipped in every Saturday night to serve as dancing partners. It must have been strange for them, arriving week after week to find a complete change of partners. But much practice apparently made perfect: I soon discovered that all the girls were formidably good performers, with a fierce intolerance of those, such as myself, who were not as skilled as they were. After a few sweating, embarrassed turns round the vast floor, which was bathed in a dim red light, I lost my courage and slipped away to the barrack hut and a paperback.

The day soon came when we were to be shipped out of this limbo. We crammed our kit into our kit-bags, and were in turn crammed on to a train for London. A change of stations; a long, dismal wait, and we found ourselves on another train for Liverpool, en route to the RAF OCTU at Jurby, on the northernmost tip of the Isle of Man. The journey was broken by a night's stay in a squalid barracks at Birkenhead – it was our first glimpse of the soft underbelly of service life, with its peeling paint, dirty beds, stinking toilets and shortage of cutlery. Most of us had not as yet washed and polished our mess-tins. Dinner tasted slightly of sewing-machine oil.

Next morning we boarded the ferry for Douglas, then took the toy train which linked the two ends of the island. Any hopes we may have entertained were immediately dashed by the sight of Jurby itself. The camp was bleak, fit for its function as a kind of purgatory. Its low huts were built of asbestos, and they were arranged in regular lines under an enormous sky. As we arrived, the sun was just setting, and the whole of this sky was filled with tones of mother-of-pearl, salmon-pink and silver. The characterless low buildings and concrete paths dwindled to insignificance beneath this display.

Tension filled our lives at OCTU. We knew we were always under observation; always on trial. Every action, however trivial, counted for something in the dossier that was being built up. In addition, we were always tired. The course involved a tremendous amount of physical exertion.

Everything at Jurby was organised by 'courses'. Within the camp at any one time there were always three of these, at various stages of their training. The courses, in turn, were divided according to the huts which their members happened to inhabit. In theory, course-loyalty took second place only to hut loyalty. You hung together, or were liable to be hanged separately.

It soon became obvious, however, that our course would not be a good one: at least as the authorities defined it. Few of the ingredients of group loyalty were present. We fell into three different and opposing categories. First, there were the senior NCOs qualifying for commissions at the end of their service careers. They would never get beyond Flight Lieutenant, but it meant a better pension. The members of this category were old sweats to a man; wise in the ways of the service, hard-drinking, cunning and (in their own estimation) tough. But, whatever else it had taught them, the service had not encouraged them to think for themselves. Then there were the cadets who had signed up for short-service commissions, three years instead of two. Most were on the rebound from something, either a failed examination or a failed love-affair. Nevertheless, in comparison with the members of the third category, ourselves, the National Service cadets, the short-service men enjoyed a privileged position, not only in their own eyes, but in those of the authorities. Their skills were those which the RAF thought it needed; most of them were accountants. And they had committed themselves for long enough for these skills to be of some use. In return, they were not only paid better than the National Servicemen, but (as it later appeared) there was heavy pressure on the camp commandant to pass them as fit for command. We alone could expect no mercy.

The OCTU had a deliberately exhausting routine. What free moments we had were passed either in studying air force regulations, or in cleaning our kit. We robbed ourselves of sleep in order to maintain the standard of smartness required of us. There was no official lights-out, and the lights burned very late in our huts. This lack of sleep and lack of regulation soon caused tension in the barrack-room which I inhabited. One of our number, a National Serviceman like myself, was a man whom I shall call Mooney. He was plump, pale, slow, disorganised and obsessional. The lights blazed until well past midnight as he sat cross-legged on his bed, clumsily blancoing and reblancoing his webbing, or polishing and repolishing his boots. Reveille was at five in the morning, and tempers rapidly grew frayed.

As it happened, I alone had some reason to be grateful to Mooney. He was to some extent my companion in misfortune. He and I were undoubtedly the two least military-looking cadets in the camp. RAF battledress did not become either of us: we looked like two sacks of potatoes, tied in the middle. On the barrack-square, when ordered to slope arms, we tended to wrap our rifles round our necks, as if they were lengths of limp spaghetti. We marched, so the two of us were told, like a couple of pregnant ducks.

Mooney always had particular trouble with his uniform. Any pair of trousers he put on immediately fell out of crease. His battledress jacket looked as if he kept it wadded up in a ball at the bottom of his locker. My sartorial difficulty was perhaps less serious, since it led to ridicule rather than black marks. The first time the drill-sergeant addressed me, it was on the subject of my beret.

'Change it at stores!' he yelled. 'The one you've got on looks like a pimple on a pumpkin.'

I duly changed it for a larger size, but however much I twisted this, wadded it or folded it, it continued to look absurd.

I also, as it turned out, had a slight advantage over Mooney in two other ways. The more obvious of these became apparent when we were detailed, as every cadet was in turn, to drill a squad of fellow-cadets. Mooney was unable to raise his voice. I, on the other hand, had a loud voice and used it without inhibition. As they marched, wheeled, changed step, came to a halt, stood at attention, stood at ease, all to my word of command, the warrant officers and the short-service commissions eyed me with a mixture of resentment and respect.

The other advantage appeared when we were turned loose on the camp assault-course. Of all the rumoured horrors of service life, this was the one which had frightened me the most in prospect. As on other occasions in my life, I soon discovered that if one cannot be spectacularly competent, it is sometimes best to be spectacularly incompetent. I frightened myself silly on the nets we were asked to climb, the narrow planks we were expected to traverse. But I frightened the officer in charge of us still more. He was in bad odour for the number of broken limbs that his methods produced. He did not want to add me to his score. His nerve cracked slightly before mine did. Unobtrusively, he began shepherding me away from the more dangerous corners of his domain. Poor Mooney, pleased to excel me in this, trundled round after the others, always out of breath and a moment or two behind.

Neither he nor I could avoid attracting the unfavourable attention of those responsible for training us. This tended to make us pariahs among our fellow cadets. No one wanted to be associated with potential failure. This was made plain to me when the time came for our first night exercise. We were arbitarily split up into small parties of four or five. My party included two of the younger NCOs, who told me bluntly I would be in all senses a burden upon their progress, and must do exactly as I was told. Our set task was to cross a long stretch of moor and bog high up in the centre of the island, with the help of flashlight, pocket compass, and map. A bus dropped us at regular intervals along one road, and we were instructed to rendezvous at a pub on another road which ran parallel to the first, but some miles distant. As we got off the vehicle, my arms were grabbed by my two burly companions.

'Come on,' they said. 'We're going to do it this way.'

Thus linked, we set off across country at a brisk gallop, ignoring easier gradients and possible detours. Once we encountered a small stream. My companions jumped; I stumbled, and fell about six feet down the steps of a small waterfall which had been hidden by the darkness and the bracken. Drenched but uninjured, I scrambled out, and our headlong progress was resumed. As it happened, this dunking in mountain water made little difference, as the ragged clouds which had from time to time hidden the moon now thickened, and a downpour started. Everyone was soon as wet as I was. It did not seem to matter. I shook off the hands which still clutched me under the elbows, and began to run, more easily and freely than I would have thought possible. We found a small cart-track which we had already marked on the map as leading almost directly to the point of rendezvous. It sloped downhill, and we pelted along it, jumping from tussock to tussock on the middle ridge. The moon reappeared, and shone in the water which brimmed in the ruts on either side.

At the pub, we were the second party to arrive. Seeing me, our predecessors greeted us with something like incredulity. It took the edge off their success when one of the course duds turned up hot on their heels. Our speed did us little practical good, however. The camp transportation arrangements had broken down, and we spent hours shivering by the roadside, even after the last stragglers had arrived, waiting to be picked up.

Warned by this experience, I resolved to tackle our next exercise, 'escape and evasion', in a more practical spirit. We were to be dropped individually at various points some distance from camp. Our task was to make our way back into the camp itself without being spotted and captured. I already knew, from camp gossip, that few cadets succeeded in this. The pursuers knew the chosen stretch of countryside well; we knew it, of course, not at all. Basically, there were two choices. The first, and most logical if one meant to succeed, was to stay off the roads, to skulk from farmyard to farmyard and hilltop to hilltop, until at last one got near enough to the objective to make a dash for it. The obvious points of danger were any roads which one might have to cross, and the flat, bare land which surrounded the camp itself. On the other hand, there was another choice, preferable if one thought success to be not only improbable but unnecessary. This was to make what progress one could on the road itself, thus pursuing one's pursuers.

Equipped with a packed lunch and a paperback, I waited tranquilly for some hours in a small wood, until I thought the first captures would already have been made; a distant droning of motor-engines told me that activity was taking place somewhere in the neighbourhood. I then walked down to the nearest road, and began to plod in the direction of Jurby. For an hour or so, nobody appeared; I began to wonder if insolence might not carry me through, at the price of a long and tedious walk. But suddenly, blessedly, there was a shout. I made the ritual attempt to escape, but was soon seized, and was bundled into a bus, already occupied, I was happy to note, by seven or eight other cadets. We motored through the Manx lanes and more and more captives were shoved through the door. Once again, I pulled out my paperback. As it happened, nobody succeeded in getting through, though two cadets were caught only as they approached the camp perimeter.

I had not made myself fatally conspicuous.

One day, in the middle of the course, I was summoned to the camp commandant's office, handed a rail warrant, and told to report to a medical board in London. My hearing, so it seemed, must immediately be retested. Something in the medical record was causing concern.

I rattled down from Jurby in the toy train, and boarded the ferry. The weather was threatening, and I had provided myself with sea-sickness tablets from the camp dispensary. Two were to be taken an hour before sailing, so I swallowed them immediately. Almost at once an announcement was made over the ship's tannoy: due to adverse weather conditions, departure would be delayed. Similar announcements were made at intervals for the next twelve hours. Gradually I consumed my whole supply of tablets, becoming aware, as I did so, of a strange buzzing in my head.

I recall very little of the voyage or the train journey, and equally little of the medical examination, for which I arrived in the nick of time. Glancing at myself in a mirror in the hall of the building, I noticed that my pupils were much dilated. The buzzing was still with me, like a distant hive. I explained the circumstances to the ear-nose-and-throat specialist, who grimaced, and scribbled something almost at random on his pad. I was still, in his opinion, fit for service.

In the afternoon, before catching the return train to Liverpool, I was free to visit Richard Buckle's Diaghilev Exhibition, then on at Forbes House near Hyde Park Corner. My head buzzing louder than ever I wandered through the successive rooms within which Buckle had created the first of the 'multi-media environments', though the term itself had not yet been invented. Wafts of *Mitsuko* (Diaghilev's favourite scent) and the strains of Stravinsky ballet music crept up on the visitor at every turn. The exhibition was hot, luxurious, secretive, magical, claustrophobic and almost deserted. I could hardly believe that Jurby and Forbes House existed on the same planet.

Back on the Isle of Man, I found that, though my medical status had been settled, my future as an officer was still very much in question. The climax of the course, an ordeal much whispered about, was a week's camp on the shores of the Irish sea, at a spot yet bleaker than the one occupied by Jurby itself. This camp would be entirely officered and run by the cadets; our instructors would be there as observers only. I had been selected as camp commandant for one of the six days (posts changed in rotation

43

every day) and as chief warrant officer for another day later in the week. To be thus singled out was no compliment, as honours of this kind were usually given to those most likely to founder beneath them.

My mood, therefore, was not particularly cheerful as we marched towards the appointed spot. Our rifles were carried slung on the shoulder, a simple knack I had never mastered. Every few hundred yards the sling dropped jarringly, and I was forced to hitch it up again. The camp-site, when we reached it, was as unprepossessing as we had been promised: a stretch of sand dunes, covered with scrubby grass and a few thorn-bushes, and pocked with innumerable rabbit holes. The rabbits themselves were absent, for this was the period when myxomatosis raged. Occasionally one found a pathetic heap of bones at the entrance to one of the burrows.

We fell out of ranks, and began to set up camp. The results were predictably chaotic. We knew very little about tents, tarpaulins, field-kitchens and the rest. As I watched the panicky, bad-tempered efforts of my companions I began to revise, not so much my estimate of them, as their estimate of me. My turn as commanding officer began at dawn the next morning, and I promised myself that things would go rather differently.

They were indeed different. I shouted, I raged, I bullied, I ran up and down. By the end of the day we were organised. I had knocked down one image of myself and created another.

The days passed; I found to my surprise that my spirits had risen and continued to rise. Everyone else's seemed to sink in about the same measure. The inhabitants of the camp became increasingly dishevelled, bad-tempered and exhausted. Nevertheless what seemed to come back to me, at this incongruous moment, was the pleasure of childhood picnics, open-air eating and sleeping, barbecues and bonfires. The weather was warm for late autumn; sky and sea alike were mantled in a gentle haze. At night, there were more exercises, conducted with hilarious incompetence by cadets and instructors alike.

The fifth day came, and it was my turn to be chief NCO. Mooney was to be commanding officer. We were packing up, ready for next morning's departure. Already conscious that I myself had escaped the axe, I was determined to rescue Mooney if I could. My plan was simple. The instructors lived in a wooden tower, once a coastal signalling station, at one end of the camp, which straggled away northward under the lee of a dune. There was plenty to be done. I would therefore organise matters near the tower and cookhouse; Mooney would busy himself in the distance where minor errors and muddles would, with any luck, remain undetected. I had reckoned without Mooney himself. Every five minutes or so he would come drifting up to me, like the matchstick in a bucket which inevitably seeks out the other matchstick floating there. I was aware that these constant consultations (and the reasons for them) were being noted. But even when I managed to drag Mooney out of earshot of official eavesdroppers, my warnings had no effect.

It was a sad little band that shambled back towards Jurby, and our comfortable central-heated huts. In many cases the facade of military toughness had been badly fissured. I tended to get some of the blame for this; perhaps I now wore a slight air of self-satisfaction. But in any case there was no need to keep up the pretence of mutual liking. The course was at an end; the results were posted. An unusually high number had either failed, or were to be 're-coursed'. The camp commandant was overheard shouting down the telephone line to London, arguing with some personage at the Air Ministry, who was issuing instructions that the short-service accountants must be saved at all costs.

As one of those who had passed, my next posting, with the rest of the education officers, was to the RAF Education School near Grantham in Lincolnshire – a kind of holiday after our ordeals at Jurby, so everyone assured us.

The Education School, when we reached it, was a guest-unit at a station largely concerned with other things. With our stripes newly on our epaulettes, we were quickly made aware that we counted not merely as second-rate but as fourth-rate citizens. This applied particularly to our position in the mess, a gaunt red-brick building with freezing cold bedrooms, inadequately warmed by coal fires for which there was never enough coal (we were now in the depths of an East Anglian winter). Unable to use our rooms during the day, we also found that a great many other parts of the building were barred to us at most times, including the only comfortable bar and the television room. In a draughty ante-room, specially assigned to us, another television set blared, making it impossible either to read or to talk. It was not a cheap mess, and fixed charges made heavy inroads into the slaary of a National Service pilot officer. We felt that our miserable pay was being used to subsidise the comforts of others, and the atmosphere was soon one of discontent.

The commandant of the school reacted to our complaints with governessy prissiness. It was clear that his main anxiety was to avoid offending the officers from other branches of the service who shared the mess with us. He soon singled me out as a threat to the precarious harmony he maintained with the rest of the station, and nagged me with especial persistence. My classroom experiences were also discouraging. The airmen and airwomen whom we were set to teach had served as guinea-pigs to so many young educationists that they eyed us with hostile cynicism.

Luckily, the course lasted only a month. At the end of that time our real service careers were to begin. I found that I had been assigned to Upavon, the headquarters of RAF Transport Command, to serve as junior education officer in the small unit which did the necessary housekeeping and donkey-work.

It was not, at first sight, a plum job. Upavon went back to the days of the Royal Flying Corps. It lay in the middle of Salisbury Plain, and it was thirteen miles from the nearest railway station, from which, in any case, as the timetable showed, the trains ran very infrequently. When I arrived, it was to find a mess almost as large as the one I had just left at Grantham. It was filled with a frightening swarm of high-ranking officers, almost nothing lower than a wing commander. But the atmosphere was very different.

My first duty was to report officially to my new commanding officer. He was a thin man of medium height, with a red face, a toothbrush moustache and startlingly blue eyes. He glared at me, and I quaked. His opening remarks gave me to understand that he did not think much of the education service or education officers. He then read me my confidential reports, a little ceremony which took place on the occasion of every new posting. That from Jurby was flattering; indeed, quite startlingly so. That from Grantham was quite the opposite. My new CO finished his reading, looked up at me, and, for the first time, smiled.

'Well, we know which of those two to believe, don't we?' he said.

It was clear that, from his point of view, the two opposing opinions did not cancel one another out; they were both commendations.

The next thing was to meet my new colleague, the head of the station education section. Peter was a north-countryman, holder

46

of a short-service commission, and only a few years older than I. I liked him at once. Though by nature very easy-going, he was also a congenital enthusiast, ready to be pleased by almost everything life had to offer. He had a light, rapid voice, always in full spate, with characteristic short north-country vowels. I found his accent and manner of speaking infectious, to the point where, after only a few weeks, we were often mistaken for one another on the telephone.

My duties turned out to be rather curious. At that epoch, RAF education officers undertook two different kinds of professional activity. The first was general education. All airmen and airwomen were required to attend classes at the education section for a given number of hours a week. This provision was linked to the acts which enforced conscription itself; it served as a kind of sop to those who felt that military service should be used in order to raise the general quality of life. The educational 'opportunity' was extended not merely to conscripts, but to young regulars and to members of the WRAF.

Even if one had taken it seriously (which, it must be confessed, Peter and I did not) it would have been hard to make the system of general education work. Since the RAF did not accept illiterates, we did not find ourselves with the burden of remedial teaching which seemed to fill up the time of educational sergeants in the Army. Our job was merely to 'extend horizons'. But how? Our pupils, for the most part, were reluctant. They felt that they had finished with the classroom when they left school, and thanked God for it. The other section-commanders on the station were disinclined to release their airmen and airwomen into our charge at times which always turned out to be inconvenient. We could never count on regular attendance. Every period in the classroom had therefore to be a separate disquisition on some topic that the audience might with luck find interesting, but most probably would not.

In despair, we fell back on poetry-readings and music appreciation classes. The latter, in particular, were moderately popular with both teacher and taught, because no effort had to be made on either side. On one occasion I played a whole side of the Tchaikovsky Violin Concerto at 78 instead of 33 r.p.m. A wild screeching filled the room, but nobody commented.

The only kind of general educational activity which had much hope of making an impression on our pupils was the 'educational visit', but these, since each of them swallowed up a whole afternoon, were harder to organise. We would take a three-ton truck and set out for some local point of interest: a pork-pie factory at Calne, or the railway works at Swindon, or even Stonehenge. The pork-pie factory was chiefly notable for the neatness and speed with which the women who worked there removed the shells from the hard-boiled eggs which were put at the centre of mass-produced scotch eggs and veal-and-ham pies. They did it one-handed, crushing the shell and stripping it off with a single rolling motion of palm and fingers. The railway works were splendidly old-fashioned, a series of tableaux from the early days of the Industrial Revolution. Stonehenge was Stonehenge. It impressed even our young airwomen, the toughest nuts of all in the classroom.

The rest of our teaching work pursued different and more strictly limited aims. We prepared people for promotion examinations within the RAF, or we tried to tutor them for examinations outside, sometimes up to university entrance level. The service examinations were very simple, tests of competence in writing English and in simple arithmetic. To a middle-class product of a scholarship-mill, such as myself, these classes were (and I do not think I exaggerate at all) the revelation of another England. I was shattered to discover how poorly most of those who came to me had been taught during their years in the clutches of the state education system. True, they now had quite specific reasons, such as they had not possessed before, for wanting to acquire basic skills with words and figures. But it was also a little frightening, as well as depressing, to discover what inhibitions they had about the learning process, and how much they tended to under-value their own intelligence. Few of my pupils were genuinely stupid, though most of them wrote an English so poor as to be almost unintelligible.

Within a few months, however, I had managed to devise a rough-and-ready, but also effective and rapid, way of teaching all but the most inhibited to express themselves. A topic was chosen; a random list of words and ideas associated with it was put together, using a process of free association; the contents of these lists were then categorised. By the time this was done, the pupil discovered that his essay, in outline form at least, already lay before him on the paper. When he could no longer protest that he could 'think of nothing to say, sir', it was easier to instil the knack of constructing coherent sentences and paragraphs. Using this method, it was often possible to achieve a dramatic improvement within the space of two or three sessions. Those I taught were openly grateful to me, as well as being astonished to find that matters went so easily. I was equally grateful to them, and equally astonished. I discovered that I was, if only intermittently, getting more satisfaction from RAF life than I had from my time at university.

The pupils we had to prepare for outside examinations, mostly School and Higher Certificate, were a more difficult problem, and sometimes stretched our joint resources uncomfortably. I grappled with a classical Latin I had largely forgotten, and with mathematical methods which I had never learned.

Only occasionally did one meet with a difficulty which proved to be insoluble. The strangest of these concerned a strapping young corporal, newly married, who was anxious to celebrate his marital status by getting promotion. In every respect but one he was well qualified. At his service duties he was excellent, by all accounts, and certainly his English showed perhaps the most dramatic improvement that I encountered among any of my pupils. But Corporal Smith had no head for figures. The mere sight of them on the page seemed to throw him into a kind of catatonic state; you would see his big shoulders stiffen while his eyes became fixed and glazed. The twice-times multiplication table was an unhappy guessing-game, the three-times table most visibly a nightmare. Try as I would, even to the point of suggesting that he jot seven threes down on the margin of his paper and add them up to find the answer to three times seven, I could discover no means of getting numbers to perform the most elementary of their evolutions for Corporal Smith. Frustrated in his hopes of promotion, he became less of a paragon. The last time I saw him, he was in the station guard-room, locked up for taking a bicycle without permission. We sat on the edge of his mattress together, and went through the multiplication tables, once again, with the familiar lack of success.

In speaking so much of our teaching, I ought not to leave the impression that the Education Section at Upavon was overburdened with work. Peter and I spent many pleasantly idle afternoons, chatting, drinking cups of coffee, glancing at the new books which had come in for the station library (also our responsibility) or simply gazing out of the window.

If this lotus-eating mode of existence became boring, then there was an officially-approved means of escape. Though Upavon was a headquarters station, and therefore, by definition, a seat of bureaucracy, it did have attached to it a small aerodrome. This was used by the aircraft of the communications flight, and also by the trainers (Chipmunks mostly) in which the officers of the flying branch kept up their necessary quota of flying-hours. Ground officers were encouraged to take to the air as much as possible, and if work seemed dull, it was quite all right to make one's escape into the sky, hitching a lift from whoever might happen to be going up. These joy-rides could be intensely exhilarating, with the whole of Wiltshire spread out beneath one, and the slender needle of Salisbury Cathedral spire rising in the distance, but they were seldom sedate. The younger pilots took pleasure in trying to frighten the groundhogs out of their wits. The splendidly manoeuvrable little Chipmunks were thrown about the sky in loops, turns and mock dog-fights until one's stomach seemed to be left lingering several miles behind.

The one serious worry I might have had about these flights, though it never prevented me from asking for another ride, was the physical condition of some of those who piloted me. There were a small number of junior officers at Upavon who formed no part, either of Headquarters staff, or of the service-station complement. They were with us on attachment. What this meant, most usually, was that they had been severely injured in crashes during training, and had been sent to us to await the verdict of the doctors, who would say whether or not they were physically fit to remain in the service. A wall-eye, a limp, hands with badly distorted or missing fingers: these were the marks that singled them out. Most had a rather desperate gaiety, a commitment to high jinks and high spirits, which served as a cover for what must have been their real feelings. Understandably, it was the pilots in this group who were keenest to make use of the training facilities of the place, and who were the wildest in the aerobatics they performed. Every flight was a proof, even if no one who mattered was there to witness it, that flying skills were still theirs in full measure. Yet one or two of them were also at pains to point out to me, as I climbed, perhaps rather pale, from the cockpit behind them, that these lively but, in terms of actual speed, very slow light aircraft were a very different proposition from the jets which fully-active pilots flew. In military jets, notoriously, no slightest mistake or fumble was forgiven by the mechanism itself.

Brief forays in training aircraft over a small patch of south-west England were not the only flights I made. A month or two after I arrived at Upavon, I discovered from Peter that the station had a very important 'perk' reserved for its two education officers. In fact Upavon had an out-station, administratively united to it but physically separate. This, in itself, was not unusual. But this particular out-station happened to be situated in the South of France.

Transport Command maintained a small staging-post at the huge French military airbase at Istres, which lay behind the Etang de Berre, a marshy lagoon which itself lay slightly inland from Martigues. The unit there was much too small to have its own education officer, and therefore, to keep things within the framework of the regulations, one or other of us from Upavon had to spend a few days there at regular intervals. If nothing much got done on these trips, apart from a little careers guidance or educational counselling, no matter: the proprieties had been observed.

Peter was much less interested in 'abroad' than I was. He had already visited Istres, and, besides this, he was in love – an endemic condition with him, as I had rapidly discovered. Thus it was that, about six months after my conscription into the RAF, I found myself flying southwards towards the sun. Our communications flight was still equipped with Ansons, small twin-engined aircraft which went back, in design at least, to the middle thirties. We would make a leisurely journey to Istres, at extremely moderate height and speed. Because of prevailing weather conditions (being unpressurised, the Anson could not climb above a storm which lay in its path) we had in any case decided to fly a semi-circular route. We lunched in the Channel Islands, dined in Biarritz, then next morning flew along the line of the Pyrenees to our destination.

Istres itself was a small, old-fashioned provincial town, with dusty squares and winding alleys. A statue of some pre-First World War radical politician adorned the main *place;* it may even have been Jean Jaurès. The inhabitants sat on wooden chairs outside the doors of their houses, watching the world go by.

If the town was small, the airbase was enormous; it was said to have the longest runways in Europe. Because of this, and because of its comparative isolation, the French had chosen to make it their main experimental centre. All sorts of strange products of French engineering ingenuity, as weird yet as logical as certain French cars, lay scattered about on the aprons, or were visible within the gaping doors of the enormous hangers. Conspicuous among them were the pick-a-back aircraft which had been the first to achieve manned supersonic flight: a small jet plane mounted on the back of a lumbering propellor-driven aircraft.

In the bustling mess, which served far better food than we ever tasted at home amid a roar of talk and a clatter of thick white plates, the small group of English officers seemed very isolated.

The French, it was said, regretted having given us a foothold on this top-secret base. A more likely reason was that, of all the officers who belonged to the English unit, only the CO spoke adequate French. We visitors were greeted slightly less than cordially by our fellow-countrymen. The squadron leader in charge made slightly edged jokes about people from Command Headquarters who came to France simply in order to get drunk and get in the way. Had I had any illusions on the subject, it would soon have been made plain to me that any formal attempts at 'education' on my part would be unwelcome. The unit was understaffed and working overtime. I could make myself available for consultation, that was all. Anxious not to be left hanging about, I asked if I could make myself useful in some other way, since my French was sufficient for most purposes. This suggestion was greeted with relief. Perhaps I would like to make a start straightaway, by taking one of the corporals over to the French doctor.

The corporal turned out to be an outstandingly handsome man of about my own age. His spectacular good looks were highlighted by the fact that his hair was already completely grey. He complained of stomach pains, fever and a slightly loose bowel. Together we went to the surgery, and I explained his symptoms. The doctor listened carefully then, with a vivid pantomime to reinforce what he was saying to me, he asked me to tell the patient to remove his trousers and underpants. Obediently, but clearly somewhat puzzled (as was I) the corporal did so. Immediately, the doctor produced one of those huge rectal thermometers favoured by the French medical profession. When my companion realised what was to be done to him, a deep blush appeared on his handsome face. A moment later, the same blush could be seen appearing below the tails of his shirt. To make matters worse, the doctor then announced that he intended to prescribe suppositories, which would soon deal with the symptoms complained of. Another and even deeper blush could not disguise the mulishness of the corporal's expression. The suppositories, it was clear, would be thrown away the instant he got back to his own quarters.

That evening, we visitors began to discuss what we should do with our free time. A visit to the local brothel was jokingly canvassed, but it was decided to settle for dinner and a bit of quiet drinking instead. We ate strongly-flavoured Provençal food at a little restaurant in the main *place,* just beside the gesticulating statue I have already mentioned. It was at this juncture that the women materialised. Nobody seemed to know quite who had invited them to join us, but at any rate it was clear that they were known to the officers of the Istres unit, two or three of whom were dining with us. It seemed to me that the residents greeted the ladies with a certain reserve. After dinner, at any rate, they rapidly excused themselves. We were left with our new friends, three of them to five of us. It was now suggested that we move on to 'a sort of nightclub'. This turned out to be a house which was almost, but not quite, like a private residence, done up in dusty velvets, filled with awkward lumps of oak furniture, but nevertheless with the echoing tiled floors of the region. Nobody else was there. The owner/proprietor hovered, offering drinks at high prices. What could we have? 'Oh, almost anything.' Mindful of the unit commander's tirade against drunkenness, I opted for Fernet-Branca. If it cured hangovers, as it was supposed to, then surely it would prevent them too?

As the member of our group with the most French, I was pressed into service as interpreter. Compliments were paid. The drinks came. Glances were exchanged. A game of poker-dice was proposed. The man who lost would pay for whatever drinks were then outstanding. The woman who lost – well, perhaps a kiss would be enough? Early in the proceedings I won, and leaned rather self-consciously towards the most attractive of the ladies. She was pale, with a full face, and a slight double chin. Her lips were cherry-red and glossy, in the fashion of the time. She seized me firmly, and an extremely active tongue was thrust into my mouth. The older men watched me sardonically.

Later, at a lull in the game, I asked her if she had always lived in Istres. There was a moment's hesitation.

'No,' she said. 'My husband works here for the government, but at present he has business in Paris.'

I had by this time swallowed quite a number of little glasses of Fernet-Branca, and was beginning to feel queasy. I took another sip of the bitter drink, and a cold sweat suddenly began to trickle from forehead and upper lip. My services as interpreter were, in any case, no longer needed. It was time to slip away.

I came down to coffee and croissants the next morning with my feeling of queasiness greatly intensified. Only one of my travelling companions was awaiting me at the table in the garden where *petit déjeuner* was set out. He, I recollected, was the one who had announced his engagement the week before. He took in my appearance with a broad grin. Neither of us made any reference to the events of the previous evening.

I spent the rest of the morning doing my best to hide my condition. As long as I was on my feet, and hard at work, nothing would be said. When lunch-time was near, it was announced that a vehicle would be taking off-duty members of the unit to a nearby beach, in order to bathe. Would we like to go along? Only I was free to accept. It seemed as good a way as any of removing myself from the scrutiny of the CO. All morning, his eyes had been fixed on me speculatively.

Aboard the bus I found the handsome corporal, now apparently fully recovered. I was the only officer present, and an educationist and a National Serviceman to boot. It was tacitly assumed that rank could be forgotten. Conversation flowed idly along.

'I hear that Wing Co. you brought with you was around with old Madeleine last night,' the corporal remarked suddenly.

I realised that he was referring to the best-looking of the women we had met the night before. She had finished up by attaching herself to the senior officer in our party.

'Well, Red here,' jerking his elbow towards another corporal lounging in the seat across the aisle from us, 'he used to fuck her regularly a while back. Lasted about six months. Said she was a bit oi a handful, even for him.'

Apparently the impression I made at Istres, despite the Fernet-Branca, was not too disastrous. It was indicated that I should not be unwelcome if I came again, and in fact I paid several more visits to the unit.

The most memorable of these was the journey on which our Anson burst a tyre when landing at the French military airport at Dijon. The accident had marvellous consequences. For three days we ate and drank while we waited for a replacement wheel to be flown out to us. Generous at any rate in this, the government made ample allowances to officers temporarily on service abroad. One night, after a magnificent meal and a splendid bottle of wine, both of them courtesy of the British taxpayer, I wandered out into the streets of the town. Almost at once I came upon a theatre, its architecture based on that of the Roman temple at Nîmes. A performance was just about to begin, as people were pouring through the doors under its portico. The play advertised on the posters was Sartre's *Kean,* and the leading role was to be taken by Pierre Brasseur. On impulse, I went to the box-office and asked for a ticket. A single *strapontin* was left. For the next three hours I sat or, rather, nodded through Sartre's romantic play. Its rhetoric mingled with the fumes of the wine I had drunk, until I did not know if the drama was being enacted inside or outside my head; in the theatre of the brain, or in this real and physical theatre, which was very like those that Kean himself must have acted in. It was perhaps the most unexpected bonus of my time as a conscript.

Service life in England had now settled into a routine. As the months went by, the work of the education section tended more and more to fall into my hands. Peter had a long bout of ill-health, and, in addition to this, he was now in love more seriously than ever before. His 'little bunny', as he always referred to her, filled his thoughts to the exclusion of everything else. When he was not out with her, or on the phone to her, he was talking about her, hands clasped behind his head, legs propped on the desk. His clerk and I got on with things as best we could, while the amorous monologue washed over us.

Some jobs were admittedly a trifle tedious. We were perpetually engaged in stock-taking of one kind or another: checking the contents of the library, or those of some station store. The library inventory had been fudged so often by successive education officers that there was no alternative but to fudge it again. One store, for some reason long unopened and therefore uninspected, turned out to contain thousands of little cardboard boxes, each containing either a crystal or a valve for a different mark of service radio. There were scores, perhaps hundreds, of different types. Many must have been long obsolete. All had to be checked against an enormous list. After three dusty, sweaty days, during which my actual totals diverged ever more widely from what should have been on the shelves in theory, I decided to call a halt. This inventory must be fudged, too.

It was all too easy to fall victim to the prevailing *laisser aller*. As my release date drew near, I became more and more reluctant to look for a civilian job. The RAF was now the devil I knew; it provided me with a sheltered, easy, perfectly regular existence. I could even say, with a show of truth, that it enabled me to do some good in the world.

I was on camp one summer weekend, it being my turn to serve as station duty-officer. In the morning, a group of local farmers, armed with shot-guns, had come to the great oak tree which stood beside the mess. Many rooks nested there; the air was always filled with their cawing. Methodically, our visitors shot them out of the tree. The glossy black bodies flopped like wet rags to the grass, tipping some of the blades with drops of blood. Unreasonably disturbed by this incident, I had gone to bed in the afternoon.

Suddenly, after sleeping for a couple of hours, I sat up, rubbed the glue from my eyes, took my portable typewriter out of its case and began to write the first of a score of letters to prospective employers.

Once out of uniform, I soon lost touch with everyone I had known in the RAF. I wrote a few letters to Peter, now a civilian and working in adult education, and I got a few in return. I met one of the members of the Upavon mess in the street and completely failed to recognise him. As soon as I established myself in London I had become heavily involved with a group of poets who met at a weekly discussion group. It was its members who now supplied the social background to my life. It turned out that I was almost the only one of them who had been a conscript. The others had been exempted for health reasons, or were even, as holders of foreign passports, ineligible for conscription. National Service, the so-called 'universal experience' of my generation, was not something we shared, and for this reason we never discussed it. In addition, the fact that I had held a commission made the subject taboo. Arnold Wesker's play *Chips with Everything* supplied the image which most people subscribed to. It was difficult for me to protest that my air force had not been in the least like that. Would it not seem as if I had betrayed certain principles we now held in common? Memory hung in the wardrobe with my increasingly dusty uniforms. It was some years before the moths got them, and then I threw them away.

PATRICK SNAITH

Do not keep or copy official documents ran the minatory mini-poster on the wall of the orderly-room clerks' office, as I recall it. Or was it DON'T KEEP OR COPY OFFICIAL DOCUMENTS? Yes, perhaps the latter: total recall is difficult fifteen and sixteen years on.

At that time the 1st Battalion of the Royal Norfolk Regiment were in Cyprus turning a deep red-brown colour, potting at Eoka and always failing to catch or notch the hero Grivas. Judging by their returning bravado and soldiers' tales they generally lived it up, wenched it up and boozed it up much more than the contemptible white-skins who lingered out their days of conscription in the Depot at Norwich. Of course, a few in Cyprus got themselves killed (very often in road accidents, as it happened) and there were also some unlucky ones who were severely maimed or disabled. But special cases aside, the general pattern was of intakes arriving at Britannia Barracks and then being shorn, trained and sent to the Nicosia tannery, where in the time-honoured phrase they 'had a job to do'. One or two got sentences of a hundred days or more for sleeping on guard duty or, as a more inventive variant, weeing into a fire bucket while on guard duty. But most apparently conformed to what the Army wanted and said it wanted, give or take the odd trigger-happy adventure on patrol.

But at the Depot (where I was) what great things happened there? What of the arts of peace and leisure, the offspring of evasion and the harvest of tedium? Even inactive service has its special properties. Take dress, for instance: of such high import in our peaceful theatre that it was periodically submitted to most critical attention, *videlicet:*

143. BOARD OF SURVEY

A Board of Survey will assemble in the QM stores at a time convenient to the President and the QM for the purpose of examining and condemning clothing etc, in accordance with Clothing Regulations 1953, Pamphlet 1, para 116.

The board will comprise:
President: Capt. K. B. Root
Member: RSM D. S. Barnwell DCM
Member: CSM M. T. P. Finn

Four months later (as I further recall) a more extreme interpretation appeared to have been invoked: the Board was to assemble 'for the purpose of examining and sentencing clothing, etc . . .' Meanwhile, a new fashion in cap badges was imposed (note 'imposed', not 'encouraged'):

208. DRESS – CAP BADGES

The large-size cap badge is now obsolete. No further issues will be made and soldiers are forbidden to wear the large ones after being issued with the small type. No soldier will proceed on draft wearing the large badge.

Great was the excitement when the QM colour-sergeant was placed on a charge for flogging the deposed fashion to draftees; he got off with a reprimand but, unlike the cap badges, at least escaped reduction. All power to the newer, smaller, staybright Britannia! Britons ever shall be fashion's slaves!

But for the skilful there were independent trends to be set:

185. SKILL AT ARMS BADGES

The u/m of Trg Coy qualified as marksmen with the LMG on 6 Jun 57.

Ptes Knight, Langley, Patrick, Love, Jones, Bell, Lailey and Coleman.

With immediate effect the Skill at Arms Badge will be worn 6½ inches from the bottom of the left sleeve of the battledress.

What else of our way of life? The keeping of pets was permitted, but controlled:

125. ANIMALS – CONTROL OF DOGS AND CATS IN MILITARY CAMPS

In accordance with ACI 635/54 no dog over six months of age may be kept in barracks unless:

(a) it is properly licensed under the Dog Licence Act, 1867 and
(b) the name and address of the owner is inscribed on the dog's collar or on a plate or badge attached thereto,
(c) the owner has the permission of the OC Depot to retain it in camp.

All dogs which do not conform to the condition above, and all surplus cats which are not disposed of by their owners, when so ordered, will be handed over for disposal to the civil police, or to the nearest Inspector of the Royal Society for the Prevention of Cruelty to Animals.

Yet by contrast guinea pigs were warmly welcomed in the name of military science:

145. VOLUNTEERS FOR PHYSIOLOGICAL TESTS
Volunteers are required for physiological tests to be held at the Chemical Defence Experimental Establishment, PORTON, Wilts, during the period 13 Jul– 19 Jul 57.

Names of volunteers are required by 29 May 57. Further details may be obtained from the orderly room.

As to manners, attentive obeisance was paid to royalty, when royalty chose to come for imbursement:

210. THE ROYAL SHOW
During the period of the Royal Show, 2-5 Jul 57, the Regiment will be in the public eye. All ranks are reminded that they must at all times be exceptionally smart and well turned out.

SALUTING During this period Her Majesty The Queen will be in Norwich and at the Showground. The procedure for saluting Royalty if passing on foot or in a car is to halt, turn and face the royal personage and salute. Be alert at all times for a car flying the Royal Standard, or for individuals of the Royal Family walking about the showground.

HOLIDAY On the occasion of the visit of Her Majesty The Queen to Norwich on 3 Jul 57 the Commanding Officer has granted a whole day's holiday to enable all ranks to watch the arrival of Her Majesty at the City Hall and to attend the Royal Show.

Any man who is performing an essential duty, i.e. cooks, mess waiters, duty officers, etc. will be given a day off on Thursday in lieu.

Heads of departments will arrange for a skeleton staff only on Wednesday, 3 Jul 57.

Literature, too, was not neglected:

265. READING OF THE ARMY ACT
The attention of OsC HQ and Trg Coy is directed to QRs, 1955, para 662. Sections 24 to 73 of the Army Act, 1955, will be explained to all ranks on parade on a date and at a time convenient to the above-mentioned OsC.

A certificate to the effect that this has been carried out will be rendered to the Adjutant by 1200 hrs on Tuesday, 13 Aug 57.

Neither were creature comforts neglected:

312. BEDSTEADS – NEW PATTERN
This Depot has received Bedsteads, fixed type, to replace the old pattern folding type. All Companies and Departments in possession of the old pattern will exchange them for the new pattern at the Brick Gymnasium at 1400 hrs on Monday, 9 Sep 57.

But at the beginning and end of the day (though for us the chips were never down) there was both a time for turning out and a time for standing still:

375. BUGLE CALLS
The following action will be carried out when bugle calls as under are sounded:

Reveille: All Guards will turn out. Those armed with rifles will carry same.

Retreat: Everybody will stand still and to attention until the call has been completed, no matter what part of the barrack area he may be in. The time for sounding of Retreat will vary. Revised times will be published in Part One Orders.

The hallmark of my Army career was mismanagement; though perhaps I cannot claim credit for all the confusion I found myself in. But other people certainly did find Answers that were to them satisfactory: some orthodox, some odd.

One Sunday night while I was travelling on a train back to Norwich I got into conversation with a chap of my own age whom I assumed at first to be in the RAF. But he told me that he had got out of doing his service.

'How so?' I enquired. 'You look fit enough. Were you an objector?'

'No,' he replied, 'but just before my medical I broke my leg playing rugger. Now instead of getting a doctor's certificate and sending it to them – as I could easily have done – you know what I did? I hobbled along on my crutches with my leg in plaster. Now it was obvious I couldn't go in but, you know, because I *went* there, they . . . well, they cocked things up somehow in my case. Somehow, going there so surprised them that the result was they forgot all about me after that. I'm all right now and I haven't had to go in.'

There are still occasions when I envy that man, particularly when I find myself dreaming that I still have three months, or whatever, to do – O, Khaki Lord, will these residual days, duties and orders never pass?

As I said, mismanagement was my hallmark and I have continued to mismanage my life as competently since then, with the sure touch of the practised hand. My commitments to the work-ethic, the career-ethic and the monogamy-ethic appear to give fluctuating readings. It cannot be the machine's fault, for that only has its job to do. Furthermore, those twin impostors Orthodoxy and Unorthodoxy do not help much either with their conflicting advice.

Certainly he who resolves in the Army that he will go his own way stubbornly and not take advice and not be buggered about can truly have a field day for the rest of his life in the world outside. So I say the Army was for me a turning-point, setting me firmly on the path along which lumberingly I have travelled ever since. But resentment of the Army's decisions is a great spur to making one's own (however rashly or myopically) thereafter.

I had applied for a university place in London and hence also for deferment during my last year at school. I duly got a place and also my deferment. Then at the end of the school year my father pressed his enthusiasm for my trying to get in at Oxford and so I had interviews there and decided to cancel my deferment, in the hope of passing college entrance exams while in the Army. So now I was in the position of having to hasten my entry into the Army in order to be out in time for the beginning of term two years later.

This sudden volte-face in my arrangements afforded neither time nor incentive to reflect on the morality of what I was about to commit myself to. Nor were there any stirrings in the media of those days: pondering the morality of fighting was not at all in fashion only ten years after Hitler's War, conscription was phlegmatically accepted, and the word 'conchie' had not become obsolescent yet. If I thought anything at the outset, it was that I would just have to do it and that the sooner it was over and done with the better. A mistake! For if there is any one lesson I learned and would wish to pass on for next time (yes, young men, beware a next time!), it is that as a duty to oneself, one should – one must – think such an issue through before one ever dons a uniform. For one thing, the choices will never be so clear-cut again as they are before your service starts, the dilemma never so objective. It is quite immaterial whether basic training screws your balls off or conversely steads you in good stand: or whether what follows that results in boredom, self-improvement, heroism, death, injury, disillusion or lifelong conscience-pangs. The only fact to be considered is that in allowing yourself to be called up you are surrendering your personal morality and integrity to the decrees of others. And you must ask yourself: *Can I in all conscience allow myself to be used by others to commit acts of violence for their purposes – which may well not be my purposes?* Remember that volunteering as a Regular in a 'right-*v*-wrong' Hitler War is not the same as putting yourself at the State's general disposal in peacetime, for any (usually dirty) work or 'jobs' that it wants men to do. And to crown it all (and to mock our timidity all these years on) we did not even have the vote! Tolerance may be a virtue, but what virtue was it to tolerate barbarism? Perhaps the prime example of the barbarism of that Britain was one Albert Pierrepoint, a publican by trade who exulted as the hangman of England and was well rewarded for his abominable pains. It might have been an idea to petition Eden and the top brass to persuade them to put conscripts to carrying out all the executions of the day. What a chance lost!

I did not think. I came in, was more broken by basic training than made a man of by it, and thereafter settled into a sullen policy of minimal contribution for the remainder of my service. I resolved to myself that I would accept no rank other than the honest one of private. I even had some misgivings about taking an extra three shillings and sixpence a week for having passed a trade test. As a Royal Army Pay Corps company pay clerk, I worked under an RAPC sergeant in the Depot Pay Office, next to the orderly-room clerks' office. I got to the office first, cleared out the ashes and lit the fire before the sergeant came. Our work was routine, but at least warm. I lived in the 'T' Room (that is, the top of the 'T') of a large T-shaped barrack-room which could hold as many as thirty-eight permanent staff and holdees. This was so poorly heated by its coke stove that there were some nights in my first winter there on which everybody went to bed to keep warm at nine o'clock when the better-heated NAAFI closed for the evening. The assortment of clerks, MT drivers, batmen and attached REME and RASC blokes were easy to get on with, indeed were amusing company.

The one jarring personality when I first arrived was one Bob Willett who had just been taken on as signwriter/handyman (and occasional bugler at funeral services). He impressed as the most egotistical, crudest, loudest lout imaginable, always reacting to any provocation, however small, always raucous and intrusive. He would bellow for silence whenever he felt a fart coming and then, his audience watching, put his foot up on his bedside chair to assist its birth ('Boy, the state o' my date – honest, it's like burnin' rubber!'). He would take the piss out of all around him at every opportunity and it was noticeable that whenever he borrowed money from someone (which was often), he would always make some joke at their expense in the very act of taking money, as if to indicate that he would allow no curbing of his licence even where he accepted favours. Yet, as often happens, initial antipathy soon gave way to amusement and even a kind of affection for the man. He was so honest, for one thing, about himself and his virginity (summed up in his familiar Norfolk 'I dairunt'), and his curiosity about others and their doings was boundless, making him a catalyst of communication.

When I came in from an evening's squash or table tennis at the Norwich CEYMS (Church of England Young Men's Society) and he would ask: 'Get your thick end in, PeeGee?'

I would say, 'No, did you, Bob?'

Then he (who probably really had been trying to) would shake his head sadly and say, 'No, you know me.'

On occasions, when everybody, or nearly everybody, had gone to bed, Dave Lane, a Londoner, would come in and go straight over to Bob's bed, proffering his fingers to Bob's semi-somnolent nose.

'Fish and chips!' Bob would retort.

'Fish and chips, bollocks!' Dave would reply. 'That's the real thing and you don't bloody recognise it, mate, because you've never bloody had it!'

'Fish and chips,' Bob would go on muttering, turning over on to his other side dismissively.

Again things would be quiet until Keith Clift came in, having taken his girl out. He infuriated Bob by not having his slash on the way in but always going out for it after changing into his Army-issue pyjamas. But after rebuking Keith for keeping the light on and for making a noise, Bob would happily engage him in conversation about football (Keith was a part-time pro with Yarmouth Town, then managed by 'Sailor' Brown) both of them apparently quite oblivious to the increasing annoyance brewing around them.

When lights were out again and all still, Bob's voice might still intrude, growling, 'Someone's having a wank – who is it?'

'Shut up, Bob!' the world would retort, shaking its drowsy head.

So then he would pack it in, rounding things off satisfactorily (in his own mind) by bidding 'Goodnight, Keith,' 'Goodnight, PeeGeesus,' and so on to all his friends (which were many) in turn. It seemed that the final arrival at silence was our major psychological achievement each day.

Bob's warmth and chirpiness made him the life and soul of the place. But then a sad thing happened. One midday I came into the barrack-room and there was Bob, not in his usual denims but in his best BD and packing up his kit. He was chatting away to his Yarmouth mate, Dave, who was a regimental policeman at the Depot. Because Bob was as voluble and apparently as relaxed as ever, I did not realise at first that he was in fact already under arrest and that Dave was his official escort. The matter of it was that he had unofficially driven an Army truck (without a licence, without permission) and had had some minor argument with a brick wall in it; nothing much but enough to result in his exposure. For this offence he received over a week inside: and was so different, so embittered and so savage when he rejoined us that it was at times difficult to believe he was the same person. Gone were his high spirits and accomplished piss-taking: now he sulked and rued and had nothing to give out.

At times he still debated with himself aloud but now in a more sombre vein: 'Oh, well, I did wrong, I know that, and I had to pay – I got no argument with that. No, I've got no complaints – I asked for it, didn't I? I only got what was comin' to me. But that's it – that's *it!* I just want the day to come when I leave this bloody issue now. Sign on! They can kiss my Royal Norfolk rectum! Rectum! Fuckin' near ruined 'em! Sign on? I wouldn't even join a Christmas club in this bloody Army!'

While I thought: if one really warm and decent man can be so twisted up by a week's just sentence, then what of the effect of a hundred unjust days inside on the fire-bucket man from Cyprus? Detention may have a use as a deterrent in the Services, or outside, but once it is applied it plainly does no good to a man, only a great deal of harm. Signing on as a career-assassin for the State involves not only the odd killing of one's own species but also living with and condoning a system of justice of the most vengeful and naïvely barbaric kind.

Fortunately Bob's joy and zest gradually returned. Having had a short spell teaching in a Sec. Mod. of those days, I recognised that Bob was one of those who could have benefited from a better education than his Sec. Mod. had given him. He was so meticulous in his signwriting, talented even, and he told everyone, quite

64

unashamed in his simple, direct way, how moved he had been by a funeral service he had bugled at for a private killed in Cyprus. He was his own man, sincere, confident, basically irrepressible, not knowing so much but yet knowing where he stood and able to articulate his problems, his views and his doubts with clarity and gusto and humour. He was fully what he was and thus had a kind of maturity for which I, with all my inner doubts, envied him

Towards the end of his time he said: 'You know what, PeeGee, when I get home after all this, you know what I'll do? Now I don't go to Church much but that's just what I'll do. I'll go down on my knees and give thanks to God Almighty that I've done my two years and that I've come through it still alive. There y'are.'

I was surprised after all this time to discover that he was in fact a believer, of a sort. I had long been a doubting sceptic and had assumed he was, too. How different we were: and how positive he was, even on such a difficult question. I knew Bob at the Depot only in this, the barrack room situation. I went my own way outside, not attracted either to boozing in 'The Castle' (where Bob exchanged repartee with the RSM) nor to patronising the cock-shows, as Bob and the others called them, at the New Theatre.

A close neighbour of mine, both in the barrack-room and at work, was Nick and he again was different from us both. He had failed his War Office Selection Board Examination and become an orderly-room clerk, responsible for turning out Part One orders three times a week. How he had failed WOSB we could not understand: he was much wiser, more intelligent and fitter than most of the well-spoken erks who did make the grade. But he bore his disappointment with good humour and eventually took two tapes while essentially remaining one of us. I recall that when Bob recited a parody version of 'The Burial of Sir John Moore after Corunna', not knowing that it was a parody (and part of the Norfolks' history), Nick excited his curiosity greatly by responding with part of the original:

> Not a drum was heard, not a funeral note,
> As his corse to the rampart we hurried . . .

The version Bob had picked up and which remained in his repertoire ran:

> Not a sound was heard but the sofa shook
> And the lady looked slightly flurried,
> As between her white legs my position I took
> And Sir Thomas I silently buried.

No useless french letter enveloped his head,
Not in silk nor in satin I wound him;
But he went forward all naked instead
With nought but his foreskin around him.

Short, swift and sharp were the strokes he took
With never a thought of retiring:
And then as sure as the sound of a gun
Sir Thomas was silently firing.

At last when I sadly drew him out,
His head all red and gory,
Who would have thought that he'd once stood –
(*Narrator flexes elbow*) Erect! In all his glory.

We also found that by singing 'flurr-ay-ed' and 'berr-ay-ed' that the words fitted the tune of 'The Wraggle Taggle Gypsies' satisfactorily.

Yes, there were tiny compensations for the donation of those two dragging years. Bob's collection of alternative versions of pop-songs of the day included Davy Crockett ('the women loved his hairy mystery'), 'Love is a many-splendoured thing' ('Love is a big round hairy thing . . .') and

> Walk flange in flange with me,
> You are my destiny . . .

while only

> Walk to the station,
> Jump on the train,
> March at the double
> Down lovers' lane . . .

prevailed, unaltered and unparodied.

But back to Nick, the begetter of Part Ones. It was quite by accident one day that he hit on a pastime that was to occupy himself and myself here and there for the rest of our alleged service. He had to produce Part One orders at the dictate of the CO or the adjutant, though of course much of the material was fed to him by the orderly-room colour-sergeant. At Christmas time, he found he had to include Christmas greetings from the CIGS, the GOC in C Eastern Command, and the CO of the Depot. Unwilling to let the slide stop at that point, he took one copy of the completed orders and was moved to add (as I roughly recall):

> The Editor would also like to take this opportunity of wishing all
> his readers a merry Christmas.

A modest enough beginning, but enough to set us on our way.
After that, Nick's method became more sophisticated: he would
type the given orders, add his or my illicit ones on to the stencil,
and then print the three or four copies that we needed. After that
he would expunge the illicit orders with correcting fluid and print
the twenty or so official copies. Sometimes as he would be typing
the illicit orders the adjutant might pass by, but never stop long
enough to read what was being typed nor to suspect that anything
so flagrantly subversive was afoot.

Of what (you may well ask) did these our sly postscripts speak?
An early one spoke in rebuke of the Army's known cruelty
towards dogs and cats:

> NOTE
> The Editor wishes to make it clear that in regard to Order No 125
> he deplores the callous attitude of the authorities towards Non-
> conformist domestic animals and that he refuses to be implicated in
> their unwarranted persecution.

They also spoke of pay parades,

> 147. PAY PARADE
> Pay parade for holdees and permanent staff will be at 1100 hrs,
> Thursday, 23 May 57. Dress: Money order . . .

of the assistant editor's welfare on one occasion:

> The Editor joins with the CO, the Adjutant, the Orderly Room Staff
> and the Pay Sergeant in sending kind regards to Pte Snaith P.G.,
> hoping that he is enjoying his leave and trusting that he will return
> to his labours as a giant refreshed in due course . . .

of honouring Royalty outside the Norwich City Hall,

> NOTE
> While being not unmindful of the distinction of the honour accorded
> to him in his selection for the Guard of Honour for Her Majesty, the
> Editor would, nevertheless, in future appreciate rather fewer of these
> marks of favour from those in authority . . .

and at the Showground:

> 1. THE ROYAL SHOW
> The Commanding Officer would like to point out to L cpl Rodgers
> and Ptes Snaith and Willett that the reason for the day's holiday this

week is to enable personnel to attend the Royal Show and not, respectively, to play cricket, to attend Wimbledon or to 'get heads down'.

The Editor would like to know how much it is worth to the above-named for him to refrain from putting the bubble in for them with the Adjutant . . .

While Bob's departure on leave too was commemorated:

3. SALE OF SURPLUS STOCK
The following is a catalogue of the sale of Surplus WD stores and equipment to be held at HQ Coy stores at 1500 hrs on Thursday, 18 Jul 57, by kind permission of OC HQ Coy.

Prospective purchasers unable to be present may place their bids previous to the sale with the Auctioneers, Messrs Snaith & Nixon, The Orderly Room, Britannia Barracks, Norwich. Tel: 32

Lot no	Description
1	Sticks, mahl, signwriter for the use of, one.
2	Sticks, breach, rifleman for the use of, one.
3	Socks, green, fluorescent, pairs, one. Guaranteed to reflect the rays of the sun with more than Oriental splendour.
4	Collection, badges, regimental; a veritable cornucopia.
5	Boxes, corn plasters, large, one.
6	Tins, Oxo, large, one. A not inappropriate receptacle for toilet requisites.
7	Trousers, denim, one pair. Slightly disintegrating at the apex of the bifurcation.
8	Bugles, brass, one. 'Dribbles better than Stanley Matthews as well as emitting a stormy blast of penetrating magnitude and intrinsic delicacy of tone.' (Boosey & Hawkes.)

and so was his demob (coming at the time of an inconclusive skirmish with a French *au pair* in Norwich):

268. POSTING TO ERE
23164221 Pte Willett GR is posted to Mrs Willett's domestic and culinary establishment, 11 Lofthouse Road, Gorleston, GT YARMOUTH, Norfolk, for extra-regimental employment as Breadwinner/GD man. Available for fatigues. Transfer will take place on successful completion of Course No 7 (L'amour) of 'Etente Cordiale' at the British Army School of Anglo/French Relations, La Gala, NORWICH.

A special illicit order aimed at enticing Bob to sign on was not successful:

1. SIGNING ON
All National Servicemen leaving the Army are encouraged to sign on for a Regular engagement.

Failing this, they are cordially invited to avail themselves of the opportunity of joining the Britannia Barracks Christmas Club. (Our motto: 'Pay what we say – have what you're given'.)

But in addition to exhortations, firm instructions were also included:

234. During the narration of military reminiscences the following precautions will be observed:
(a) Helmets, steel, will be worn.
(b) Slit trenches will be made available for use when the exceptionally hazardous nature of the story warrants it.
(c) Pendant electric lights will be swung when the speaker embarks upon paeans of self-praise.

New intakes every six weeks were always a matter of interest at the Depot. Bob always declared that he would be getting up early to go to the cookhouse 'to hear the plates go down'; but then on the morrow when anybody suggested it was time he got up to wash (for he made shaving an evening matter), he would stay in bed and retort:

'No, fuckit, I'll go dirty!'

And so he would. Our Editor, however, believed in extending a hearty welcome to newcomers,

NOTE
The Editor joins with the CO, the RSM, OC Trg Coy and the Unit Barber in welcoming the NS Intake of the 29 Aug 57. He hastens to assure them that the first 23 months are the worst and that thereafter they will, in the words of Pte Wordsworth (Cumberland Light Infantry) 'see blessings spread around them like a sea'.

And he was always willing to help people find their way around:

359. EAST ANGLIAN BRIGADE SENIORITY ROLL
A copy of the above roll is held in the Orderly Room. WOs and Senior NCOs wishing to look through the roll may do so in the Orderly Room.
360. GOVERNMENT PROPERTY ROLLS
Rolls of Government Property are held in the annexes to all wash-rooms. Any OR, Regular or otherwise, who wishes to look through the rolls may do so at any time out of working hours.

Finally Nick's own demob approached, and he wrote feelingly of the wrench that was to come:

314. EDITORSHIP
The Editor wishes to state that offers have been made to him by the proprietors, Major Cox and Capn. Boon, to renew his contract, but that he, finding himself in a position similar to that of Mr Malcolm Muggeridge, Editor of 'Punch', wherein his journalistic independence would stand in jeopardy, being too long in the service of one master, has decided to relinquish the Editorship shortly after returning from his forthcoming annual vacation.

But modest fiction competes ill with fact. There was nothing so ludicrous as the capitulation of a whole generation to a State-decreed immorality. How can a man take a State rifle and let himself be pointed in any willed or whimmed direction and then fire when told to fire? Mind, the generation that stuffed Hitler is to be admired, and I respect the sacrifices that were made then. And conversely I applaud present-day youth standing up defiantly for civil rights and representation (and in its own way stuffing the recalcitrant LBJ). But our bewildered lot on the mezzanine floor, what were we at? We were neither one thing nor the other, neither flesh nor fowl, uncertain as we were whether to run with the baby or hunt with the bathwater. We sulked but we would not rebel: or most of us would not. Yet we did not even have the vote, a factor which should have made the position of the successive governments involved quite indefensible. But they got away with it with ease.

Of course, it could all happen again, chaps, you know, were a coalition to gain power again for any reason. Then what would happen? Would the State win? Perhaps not. My vision is of the first great call-up day arriving. Instead of the expected thousands turning up with their call-up papers, there are in fact teeming millions of people all brandishing impeccable (that is, well-forged) papers, all demanding to be documented, kitted out, fed, watered, shorn and trained; a whole host of young men, middle-aged men, women, children, Spanish tourist students knowing little English, old age pensioners, foreign *au pair* girls, pretty girls, plain girls, all sorts and kinds of people taking part in the grand Saturation Excuse-me; and saying not, 'No! Damn you!' but, 'Yes, yes, here we are, you beauts, we've all come as invited! Please cope with us till kingdom come!' And according to plan, at Service depots all over the country, a whole generation will sit itself down on barrack squares, all singing and happy together in the sunshine (yes, the sun must shine that day) while in Whitehall some cloddish Heath or Wilson-like figure will be so consterned as to wearily give up the flock for lost and start penning his peevish resignation-letter.

Ah, happy day! Either that, or again the bent crook of State pens its wee lambs in the copes and folds of its amorality.

JOHN LAWSON

Up till then that was the longest train journey I'd ever made, Dundee to Cardington, in Bedfordshire. I felt excitement but it was tempered with apprehension at leaving the environment I'd lived in eighteen years of my life, apprehension because you don't really know what you're going into. You're going far away, you know you're going hundreds of miles away, it's not just a run up the path.

The first thing that happened to me is we've gathered in a room, I can remember it, we're seated in this room, this is before we're issued with any uniform at all, the sergeant comes into the room and he begins to talk. He tells us the good points about signing on to become a Regular and then he says, 'Anyone like to sign on, stand up and come forward,' so the people who want to sign on stand up and they go forward, they're separated from the rest, the rest stay National Servicemen. There are some Regulars from various parts of the country who haven't actually signed on because they don't sign on till they reach the Induction Centre. They're even given the option of being given their train fare to go home again, they may have just fancied the journey or they may of a sudden feel homesick – this happens to Regulars, not National Servicemen.

The first day I think would be taken up with familiarisation, taking in the new surroundings. We had a medical, quite a strict medical it was, and I was graded A-1 if I remember right; I felt proud at that particular time, yes, I still feel proud of it.

The quality of the accommodation was good, it was about what you'd expect: you had clean sheets and blankets. The food at the initial stages I don't think was all that hot, through basic training the food wasn't too clever; it was only when you went to a permanent station that the food improved. Of course, I'm sure they filled the tea up with bromide, it tasted vile. I'm not really sure what bromide is, but I think it was to stop the lads masturbating because you were away from women for eight weeks. Later, when I was a cook, we never added any chemical of any kind to the tea, bromide in the tea was a lot of hearsay during basic training, though I must admit I never did feel like a bit of the other during those eight weeks, no time.

As soon as they issue your uniforms they take all your civilian clothes and you send them home. All you're left with are your two uniforms, a battledress and a best blue, and then you're ostracised from the outside world from that point on. Basic training's about eight weeks and it wasn't frequent, you being allowed out of camp, and when you did go you had to wear your uniform, your best blue which at that time was somewhat inhibiting because in certain parts of the country the teddy boys would pick on a uniform just for the sake of a fight.

We were given medical lectures, and shown films by a senior technician (a senior technician is a man with three stripes but they're inverted, the chevrons are inverted, which means he's probably fairly high up in the medical business, he's a technician rather than being a medical orderly; he certainly knows his business, he probably holds certificates). The films were in Technicolor, Incredible In Their Stark Reality, sores as big as a saucer, tips of pricks rotting off, and I think that anyone that's seen these films should certainly never contract the diseases. Well, he would tell us about various diseases, and also that there were contraceptives available, and if and when you were allowed out at the weekend you could go to the medical section and ask them for contraceptives. And we were told never to go in with VD and say we got it on a lavatory seat. This was something he was quite strict about. Now whether this is still the general opinion in the medical world I don't know but this was something that he said. Another thing we were told was that if we did contract VD we would have to accept the treatment that the RAF dished out to us; we couldn't ask for any sort of specialised treatment. If they wanted to use the umbrella on you they'd use it. I've never actually experienced this but I've heard people talk about it. It's a sort of needle shaped like

72

an umbrella, and it's usually used for gonorrhoea (syphilis is a far more serious disease and has to be treated by specialists). It comes from a fairly round shape at the bottom to an apex, to a point like a needle; this is inserted right up the middle of the penis and when it's at the top they flick the switch, like an umbrella, and then it's dragged out, and it is agony. I've never had this but they say it's agony. Without an anaesthetic. Anyone that did have that happen to them would certainly remember it, they'd never forget it.

Apart from that, the RAF, or any service for that matter, teaches you to be very hygienic. In this particular camp the water was incredibly hard; I'd been used to very soft water in Scotland because it goes through a different filtering process, but in this particular camp the water wasn't chlorinated with a chlorous gas, it was purified with lime and every time you washed, no matter how clean you were, you got a half-inch of scum on the basin, on top of the water. Almost undrinkable, incredibly bad.

As I see it now today, they had a way of letting you know at once that you were now in the Royal Air Force and you were going to do as you were told. It was a good thing in a way because it steeled you for the discipline that was to follow during your basic training, like learning how to march and how to handle different weaponry; it was a good thing because the discipline there was very severe. I say it was severe, it was really a crash course in growing up. Once you went to the basic training camp the two stripes were all you had to see, nothing else. Two stripes was a corporal, and all the instructors were, if not officers, at least the rank of a corporal, so every time you spoke to one you had to stand at attention, and discipline was, as I say, quite severe.

There was one particular time during part of the Ground Defence training when we had to go into what they called a gas chamber, situated in a playing field. I think it had a window in it, I'm not too sure about that, but certainly the doors and walls were all asbestos-lined so that none of the gas escaped. Normally six or seven men went in at once, and there'd be a small stove in the middle, and the chap would break a couple of pellets in it. You went in with a respirator on first, and then you'd take the respirator off and then the tears would come, it was probably tear gas, and you'd feel a bit sick as well. I don't know if it was CS gas but it was certainly tear gas. When it was my turn to go in, the chap told me to put the respirator on.

I put it on and I told them, 'It's very hard to breathe with this respirator on,' so I took it off again and tried to tell them that it wasn't working. Well, he said it was but I couldn't breathe, that's how I knew it wasn't working, I couldn't breathe, so I took it off again and said, 'There's something wrong, I don't think it's working properly.' He's ordered me to put it back on again and I've refused, so ultimately I've refused to go in the gas chamber, so he's told me to fall out and stand aside so when we marched back to the class (we were going back to a theoretical class on ground defence, this was part of the practical side, we were going back to the theory) he's taking me into the flight-sergeant, the flight-sergeant in his turn is taking me in to the warrant officer and the warrant officer in his turn was taking me in to the squadron-leader who's probably the senior ground defence officer on that particular camp. Well, he's bollocked me rigid for not doing it and then he's asked me where I come from. I said 'Dundee.' He said, 'You're a disgrace to Scotland.' And to the warrant officer he says: 'Mr So and so,' (he always called the warrant officer 'Mister'; we called him 'Sir', but a man of senior rank to him would call him 'Mister'); he asked this Mr So and so to take me back down to the gas chamber and put me in, and this time when they took me back down and put me in they put me in with no respirator on, no respirator; shut the door, broke the pellets, and when I come out, my denims – you always wore denims – the denims were soaked with the tears running down your face, just like water, it's incredible, there must be glands that this particular gas affects. But I never refused to go in again. That was my first taste of bureacracy, with that corporal. He wouldn't believe me, he wouldn't believe it wasn't working, and apart from that he wouldn't test it himself. Once he'd said, 'It is working,' he wouldn't go back on that, and of course there were so many respirators it's a fair bet there'd be a faulty one, when you've got sixty men, all with a respirator each, yet he wouldn't have it that it was faulty. As far as he was concerned, I suppose it was his opinion that the RAF don't make faulty gear, but it was me that had to suffer for it anyway.

There was a shortage of instructors at this particular time, so what normally happened was that the drill instructor would march us down to the gym and we'd spend probably an hour in there but he wouldn't have time to wait for us, so he'd go on to another job and it would be left to one of us to march the flight back. At that time I fancied doing this little job; nobody really liked it but I fancied it because it gave me a sense of power, so one day I decided that I would hang back a bit, so I hung back, and sure enough I was picked up. The sergeant said to me, 'You, march the flight back.' So you're in denims and, underneath the denims, in gym shorts, gym vest, and you wear your combat boots all the time and carry your plimsolls under your arm. The flight assembles outside the gym in the roadway and the sergeant brings them to attention and then he gives the order, 'Forward march!' and we march away. Now it was left to you to get the flight of sixty or seventy men in a column of threes back to the billet, and outside the billet bring them to a halt – it gives you quite a little feeling of power. So this day I got picked for the job and we'd come along from the gym, turned right, and we're marching up this road, and you had to march outside the column of men on the right-hand side at the very rear of the flight. If any officer passes, you give them the eyes-right and all they do is turn their head to the right, give an eyes-right to the officer and you salute, you're the only one that salutes. Well, this day I was feeling quite powerful as it happens, and I'm marching them up this road and I was so engrossed in this new form of power over my fellow men that – when you get to the top of this road you must turn left, it's the only way the road goes – I'm thinking, 'I'll give them a left-turn at the top and they'll wheel round', but when they got to the top of the road I was so carried away with my new-found power that I gave them right-turn instead of left-turn, and the bastards kept marching to the right when they knew well they fucking shouldn't, they should have been marching to the left. They marched straight across the garden and everything – you can picture what happened. I had to pull them to a halt and sort of about-turn and they all marched back down again, the embarrassment you felt was incredible, the embarrassment and the jokes about it afterwards.

When I was doing my basic training I reported sick once, reported sick with sunburn, believe it or not. I got sunburn and I went on sick parade and just before the march down to the sick quarters the chap who was marching us down came up to me and said, 'What are you sick with?' I said, 'Well, I've got sunburn,' and he says to me I shouldn't go sick with that; I said, 'Why is that?' He said, 'Well, you'll get charged;' I said, 'What do you mean charged?' He said, 'Well, you'll get put on a charge.' I said, 'Why?' He said, 'Well, you're damaging the Queen's property,' and this I found out was, believe it or not, true, my body – incredible. The bloke says to me, 'You've damaged the Queen's property and it was self-inflicted wounds; if you wanted to go and lie in the sun you should take precautions. You can go sick if you like but it's more than likely you'll be charged.' So I didn't report sick, I stuck with the sunburn.

Certainly one of the most impressionable things that stays on your mind during basic training is the weapon training, especially when you've never seen any before. First of all they teach you how to march without a rifle and then they give you a rifle and they explain how deadly they are, you know, they're not toys, not to be toyed with; they're chained and padlocked up at the end of the billet anyway and when you do drill with a rifle you see that the psychology of the RAF was very good. First of all, the discipline in the first place was fair so it gave you an idea of what was to come, and then they'd let you handle the rifle, but empty. Later you'd be sent off to a sort of miniaturised rifle range. This one at the camp was twenty-five yards long but the targets were ten times smaller than they would normally be, so actually you were firing at, say, 250 yards, and when I first fired a rifle it was a frightening experience just to hear the explosion. It kicks back if you don't do what you're told, though there were always dodges like putting your beret into the shoulder of your uniform or carrying yellow dusters with you and putting a couple of dusters in, but people still had the odd black eye. It was best to do exactly what you were told; the men teaching you were professional soldiers, they were trying to make you a professional, they were telling you the best. But you still got the odd cowboy merchant, the chap who's watched too many westerns and he lies his eye along the rifle by the barrel, but when it kicks back he finishes up with a right black eye because the rifle, as it kicks up, it comes back as well, it kicks back and up at the same time; well, when it kicks back if your eye's too near the saddle you'll get that and it really whacks you in the eye and you finished up with a right black eye.

Something that gave you a real feeling of power was having a machine gun or a bren gun at your disposal. Of course, you were firing it under very strict supervision. The weapon training was very strict, but you got the odd fool who picked up the bren gun when it stuck and turned around and pointed it at somebody. At that time you thought he's just stupid, or he's not thinking, he'd get a right terrible bollocking. One particular chap – we were firing in a line of about six of us and a bren gun holds, I think, about twenty or thirty rounds of ammunition in the magazine depending on the Mark, there's Mk I, Mk II and so on. Before you even go near the range we'd been taught about these weapons in classes, we'd handled them, taken them to pieces, put them together again; we were told what they could do and could not do, and one of the things you never do when a bren gun sticks is pick it up and turn it round, like this particular chap picks it up and turns round to the sergeant and says, 'The gun is stuck.' Ah, incredible. You see, it could be anything, it could be a round of ammunition with a very slight burr on it that hasn't fallen into the chamber and it could fall at any minute, and of course as soon as it falls if you have it on 'Automatic fire' and you've pulled the trigger back and nothing's happened and the trigger is still back, so – it could just blow the man to smithereens, because they make holes in you like dustbin lids. They go in the size they are but they come out a bloody sight bigger at the other side . . . There were no accidents to my knowledge, anyway.

It was a good basic training apart from a few little incidents, and it certainly taught me one thing: it taught me always to be smartly dressed, not only when the occasion arises but always to keep yourself in a decent manner; always have your hair cut short, you won't see me with long hair. It taught me to look after my body because, as we know, it's the only one we've got. It's amazing how many people neglect little things and little things turn to big things. Basic training taught me, apart from the whole of my service, to respect other human beings. Just because a bloke's got two stripes and he's a bit nasty, it doesn't mean he's always nasty; more than likely he's doing it for my good, he's got a job to do and he would probably just as soon not do it. Drill instructors and education officers get people out of civilian life without the slightest concept of what a military force is about and they have to try and turn them into professional soldiers or airmen; they have a really hard job.

When basic training is finished you have a passout parade and usually a passout party and then you have I think seven days' leave after that, and then you report to your Trade Training Station. I went to RAF Halton in Buckinghamshire. I had chosen to be a cook – well, it was either cook or storeman. I'm not particularly fond of food, no, but at that time I knew exactly what a storeman's life must be like, having worked in a factory; very mundane, very boring, so I chose to be a cook. Also I thought I'll give the RAF some aggravation: if they can make a cook out of me then I'm not surprised they won the Battle of Britain. Before I went there I couldn't boil water without burning it, but they did a very good job.

Different trades take a different amount of time to train for: to train an aerodrome fireman or a cook took basically about the same length of time, twelve weeks, but an aeroplane mechanic or fitter would take a lot longer, plus as you progressed through trade tests it became more technical. Halton stuck in my mind a lot because we had to scrub floors on our hands and knees, a very good psychological point I would say for the RAF. The floor is the very basis of cleanliness: they teach you cleanliness before they teach you how to cook. First of all you get theoretical lectures on cooking as well as practical demonstrations which you take part in. What strikes me now is however they made cooks out of us. In my particular instance they brought me from nothing to a qualified cook, at the end of twelve weeks, who could cook several basic dishes – it seems incredible to me. They teach you always to clean your working space after you, clean your utensils, your knives, things like that. Then they'd start on the basic things like how to make a white sauce, a *béchamel*. They don't just throw you into it and expect you to transform from a nothing into an Escoffier, they do it gradually, they tell you what sauces go with certain dishes and how to make them. You may have interim practical and theoretical tests, and during these weeks they keep telling you that when your final test does come up you'll be expected to make a soup, a meat dish and a sweet and you'll also take a theoretical test. Now out of a hundred marks for each of those tests the pass-mark in the RAF is sixty; if you don't get above sixty you've failed and you're relegated to the job of catering assistant, which means you'll be washing up tins and pots for the rest of your service, so people really knuckle down. I used to be a great table tennis fan at that time; I played a lot but at the same time I used to study a lot, particularly when you've got, say, a mate of yours to study with, you ask one another questions like students. You know, that's exactly what you are, a student, and you think, well, I don't fancy washing tins all the rest of me time, so you start studying and as it happens I was lucky enough to pass. For my test I did: tomato soup, a meat dish – I think it was a pie – and then I think I cooked an apple pie for sweet, something like that. Everything is mixed by hand, pastry, everything, there are no machines. When you go to do your service, when you go to, say, a big station where there are hundreds of men to feed, then you have machinery but at this particular time it's all done by hand. Mixing pastry, say, sweet short pastry for a sweet or, say, for a flan or something, you mix by hand the sugar and the margarine, then you add the egg, then the flour, to get the right consistency.

I was very pleased about passing out, about being a cook. The instructors were chefs really; not cooks, we were the cooks, they were the chefs. These instructors could walk into any hotel in London, however high class it was, and get a job there, because they really know the fancy gear, but when you pass out they tell you your marks and then they tell you which station you're going to, and there's another little bit of excitement, sitting there waiting, sitting as a class, just like a class at school, it's mixed, they have men and women, like airmen and WRAFs as well, and they tell you where you're going; and me and Paul, me and my mate, we finished up going to the same camp; and then they designate you to either the airmen's mess or the sergeants' mess or the officers' mess, depending on your ability.

Actually I did put in for abroad. You're given three choices of posting: I certainly put a posting abroad down but while I was doing my basic training I got a right bout of homesickness. I'd never experienced it before, never having been away from home, and I don't think I've experienced it since, but at that time I really wanted to get out.

Well, my first posting was to RAF Stanbridge, in Signals Command, near Leighton Buzzard. Once you go to a permanent posting, the menus are set, laid down by the catering officer, probably. He puts you down for either the airmen's mess, or the sergeants' mess, or the officers' mess, as he sees fit. Once I saw a mess waiter, this was in the officers' mess, and there was this WRAF officer the waiter didn't like, she'd annoyed him for some reason, and just before he went through the doors from the kitchen, I've seen him, he had a poached egg on toast for her, he undid his trousers and pulled out a single public hair and slid it between the egg and the toast.

There were so many things that happened . . .

Being a cook, I went into the mess one night, and this WRAF came in, so I pulled her into the pantry. Now, there was a window in the pantry, and the window was mesh, very fine mesh, to keep out insects and so on, and I had this WRAF up against the bench in the pantry and I looked up and there was this squadron-leader looking in at the window, watching me, incredible as it may seem. And my mate told me, from outside he said, 'Here watch it, Ballet's outside.' That was his name, Squadron-Leader Ballett, to my mind a very, very repulsive man, I hated him, I detested him, not so much for that incident but for another thing that happened to me . . .

Oh, I could write a book about it all, all the things that happened . . .

But you couldn't go back. It was an experience, an unforgettable experience that remains with you all the days of your life, when people come out they very seldom go back in again, very very seldom. You could go round this pub, and ask a man if he'd done his service, and then ask him what his number was, and he'd rattle it off for you just like that, as quick as that. People have so many good times and so many bad times during their service that it makes it unforgettable, for the simple reason that you're so young when you do it . . .

ALAN BURNS

PETER BURNS

My brother Peter is today general secretary of War on Want. He has worked as an organiser for Oxfam and for Amnesty International. Twenty-one years ago he served in the British army of occupation in Cyprus and in Egypt. I tell his story rather than my own for two reasons: my novel *Buster* covered the ground so effectively (for me) that I am now unable to disentangle fact from fiction; and Peter's story is better than mine.

ALAN BURNS

Starting as a rifleman in the Rifle Brigade, I was indoctrinated with the glories of the Regiment. We were the light infantry, the élite. We only marched in double-quick time. Our drill was unique. We did not slope arms, we did not carry the rifle on the shoulder when marching, we carried it in the right hand with finger through the trigger, on the alert, ready for instant action. We did not wear brass buttons to glint in the sun, but black buttons for camouflage in battle. The nice thing about the Army is that whatever you are in, the Artillery or the Pioneers, they manage to find something in its role or tradition to make you specially proud of it. But the Rifle

Brigade really was something special: I felt superior to the mob.

I thought I was doing quite well. I had done some boxing at school so I entered the regimental championship. I got to the final, and lost. They gave me a medal, which Dad still keeps in the safe. Then I tried for the officers' selection board and failed. I was very, very upset. I could not understand why I had failed. It seemed ridiculous, though they pat you on the back and say you will pass next time. The question is, what do you do in the eight weeks before you are allowed to take the test again? They sent me to Germany, seconded to the Kings Royal Rifle Corps, our sister regiment.

They were stationed at Minden, near Hanover, in ex-Nazi barracks. The panzers had been there. It was Germanic, superbly equipped, absolutely metallic, cold, with an enormous, endless barracks square. It was the worst six weeks of my life, because the sergeant was mad. He was a mad sadist, utterly brutal, and I hated him. I could have shot him in the back. He just made you march and drill, and drill and drill and drill, until you could not drill any longer, until you dropped your rifle like I did. You get to the stage where you can't hold the rifle, not because it's heavy but because your fingers can't hold it. I collapsed on the square. When you fell down they marched over you. It's the equivalent of fainting but you don't black out, you just can't go on, you can't march any more, and why should you? It is totally pointless. I went to the medical officer saying I couldn't go on and was told to piss off. I couldn't understand the point of it. I complained to the very charming, urbane platoon commander, Sir Somebody Cunningham, Bart. I told him I was due to be an officer, that this was not what I was sent there for, but he mumbled something meaningless about the Army. There was no recourse, no redress from this sergeant who simply terrorised thirty men. I was only passing through so I never knew the beginning or the end of it. There was no sign of rebellion among the men, no sense of we are going to get this guy. But if they could not have killed him they should have got him into a mental hospital. That was six weeks out of my life.

When eventually I did become an officer, I passed out near the bottom of the list. Perhaps I was too young. Although I was good at drill and at boxing, and was a marksman, I was not very assertive. I had had a sheltered upbringing, I lacked aggression and self-confidence and it showed. I did not dominate the scene, and that is what they were looking for, the people who lead. I might be selected as officer material from among working-class men because my middle-class background helped. But among these upper-class gents I found it difficult to lead the leaders.

When you are commissioned you put in for the regiment of your choice largely on the basis of where they are serving at the time. My first choice was the Oxfordshire and Buckinghamshire Light Infantry because they were in Cyprus. By some fluke (it must have been a fluke or an administrative error because almost every officer in the regiment was very pukka, very aristocratic) I was accepted. So, after a short embarkation leave, and going out with Dad in my new uniform, I 'joined the regiment'.

I had never really travelled before, and here I was, an officer, travelling First through the Mediterranean to Cyprus. I had this lovely cruise on a beautiful ship. I remember stopping at Tangiers, a marvellous white city.

At Nicosia there is a jeep waiting for you: 'Mr Burns, sir? Let me take your baggage.' And you are whisked off to meet the Adjutant: 'Good morning, Burns, glad to have you with us.' A bit of documentation and you are shown to your quarters, just like in a hotel when the porter shows you to your room. You are assigned a servant, you go to lunch and you are introduced to everybody, you sit and have lunch, then go for a swim in the Med, and suddenly you find it's all fantastic, an exciting and glorious time. This was it, this was what it was all for.

It was a plush life. The troops had taken over a holiday camp called Golden Sands and we led a golden life. I have never had a higher standard of living. I was paid about £30 a month, with all found, no clothes or food to buy. Only drink, and I was very young. My favourite drink in Cyprus was a double-Coca-Cola in a silver tankard, that is honestly what I used to drink. I was a boy, I never amassed great mess bills or anything like that.

We started at eight in the morning with a real officer's breakfast – kidneys, liver, eggs and bacon from silver platters. Then a morning of routine training, perhaps a bit of rifle drill, or a current affairs lecture, telling the troops bits of my School Certificate geography. Lunch marked the end of the working day. You're free. We used to go into Famagusta, swim, sunbathe, ride a motorbike up into the Trudos Mountains in the heart of Cyprus, or to Mount Olympus, or Kyrenia. When the troops got bored I would borrow a truck and take them somewhere like Salamis for the day. It was a beautiful life.

Although we lazed around there was no sense of sloppiness.

Regimental pride was the deciding factor. I had learnt something about regimental traditions in the Rifle Brigade, but this was the Ox and Bucks, the 43rd Light Infantry! In the officers' mess everything was different, with a special name, a peculiar style. We did not have Sam Brownes like everyone else, we had regimental Belts, with two leather straps that did not cross but went straight down. Our caps had an odd black button at the back. We did not carry an ordinary swagger stick but a regimental cane, black with a silver top embossed with a hunting horn, the regimental crest. The last two notes of the Last Post were not sounded because in eighteen hundred and something a bugler had been shot dead at that point. Officers' Guest Nights were the high point of all this nonsense, with the gentry coming in from Famagusta, the regimental band playing *Annie Get Your Gun,* and fairy lights, and caviare flown in from Port Said.

The idyll was briefly interrupted by the Mossadeq oil crisis, when the Iranians tried to take over their own oil. The paratroopers arrived in a bloody great aircraft carrier, and though they were five times tougher than us, our job was to train them up. We had two terrible weeks of manoeuvres at the height of summer, a hundred in the shade. We fought fake battles all over Cyprus, which is very hilly, one hill leading to the next. What saved me were those beautiful water melons which grew close to the ground beneath huge leaves. They were lovely and cold, however hot the weather was. Of course they belonged to Cypriot farmers, and you pinched their stuff, charged over their land, and they never complained.

The basic law of manoeuvres was: first find the gin wagon. The troops each carried a flask of water, and you would lecture them: 'Take care how you use that water, it's got to last you all day, these are war conditions.' Then we would go over to the officers' gin wagon and have a gin and tonic. And the troops knew it, it was part of the game. The majors and colonels would sit down to a full meal, with little tables and chairs, and soldiers acting as waiters.

One or two of the younger subalterns turned a bit nasty 'in the field', because they were weak and felt they had to dominate. I never charged a man on battle-training or on parade. I would tell him to get his rifle cleaned, but never report him for it. They liked me the less for it. They said, Here's a weak bugger.

There was this liberal streak in me always trying to get out, often in a slightly patronising way. One guy in my platoon was a known thief. I made him my batman. I thought I would take care of him, get his confidence, and he would not steal again. He was superb, the best batman you could wish. Then three officers lost all their money and that was the end of him.

The only time I was involved in a court-martial was also the nearest I got to action. Our job was to guard the port of Famagusta. As duty officer I went down in a jeep to check the guards. One night I found the two guards paralytic drunk, with rifles loaded and bayonets fixed. I was too naïve to be scared; I just said: 'Look here, you can't behave like this. Get into the jeep.' I took their rifles off them, drove to the guard room and put them in the cells. When I told the court martial what had happened the presiding officer thought I'd been terribly brave: 'Conscious as you must have been of the danger to yourself, you disarmed these two men.' I had relied on my public school training, a natural assumption that the buggers would do what they were told.

It's this background that enables a young second lieutenant to remain, at least nominally, in command, but nine times out of ten it is the sergeant who runs the show. My sergeant was a leathery bugger who had done twenty-seven years. He knew it all. He treated me okay so long as I did not pretend I was boss. It was a conspiracy of pretence. He would pretend to the men that I was boss (and they would pretend to believe him) so long as I did not pretend to him. I accepted the position. It was the drill. Most officers were not fit to be officers. The NCOs should have been the officers, they had come through it and they knew it, they had fought in the WAR, you see, that was the difference. Most of these sergeants had been in the war, so they weren't mucking about.

What gave me a rather warped view of my brother officers was the fact that I was one of only two National Service officers in the battalion. The rest, Regulars, obviously found us a bit strange. They were gentlemen all, very friendly, very pleasant people, but they would *peer* at you. Apart from subtle class differences, you were only a visitor, passing through, they were there for good. They never said so directly, that was not their way. One joined in and was treated like everybody else but there was this understanding that you were different.

It was because I was a National Service officer that I was shunted out of this cushy post. A subaltern had to be seconded to the Pioneer Corps. Somebody had to go. It had to be an NS man. So I was sent for six rotten months, guarding munition dumps along the Suez Canal. Of course, in terms of prestige, and after all that light infantry stuff, the Pioneer Corps was the absolute end.

They were Mauritian troops, all of them black. And in those days that was partly why I had no relations with or understanding of them. They spoke a kind of French that had nothing in common with the language I had learnt at school. They were self-sufficient. I knew none by name, except the sergeant, a very tubby man with a long Indian name which I have forgotten now. As ever, he ran the show.

The ammunition dumps were strung along the Canal. I was first based near Port Said, then at Ismailia, half-way down the Canal. These enormous dumps of arms were just stuck in the desert, great tarpaulins covering miles of crates. We were never allowed inside, the sentries marched round and round the perimeter. As duty officer I would check the guards four times each day and night, and all the time I was there I never found a thing wrong. I would go round in a bren gun carrier driven by an Army driver. It was pretty eerie out in the desert at two in the morning, and I wrote poems about the moon.

We were at the centre of British power in the Middle East, this is where its strength lay, defending the Canal. But we still averaged only about four hours' work each day. My main relaxation was playing tennis at Port Fuad, the residential area of Port Said. I joined the Tennis Club to meet the girls there. It was well regulated: you could never take a girl out, these were Suez Canal Company girls, their fathers were officials of the Canal. They were Maltese, Gibraltarians, Lebanese, all sorts, and very aristocratic. Once I went to a girl's house and sat in the dining-room, on a chair at the edge. I was introduced to her mother who said, 'Hello,' and shortly afterwards, 'Goodbye.' There were two girls who were friendly, but they were totally non-sexual relationships, because you didn't do that kind of thing. But I enjoyed the tennis, they were superb courts, always in the sunshine, and after the game you would sit on the balcony and have Turkish coffee till six, and then back to the camp for a shower, change for dinner, and then it got really boring. You would read or play solo, while the troops played Bingo.

My essential state was one of unawareness, sexual, political, social unawareness. I did not see through the dreary, decadent life around me, I was ignorant of the imperial set-up I was part of, and I had no comprehension of the real condition of the native Egyptians. I was so young, so immature, that I did not know what day it was. Yet I was responsible for the lives of thirty men.

But apart from being responsible I had no function. I was just there.

What neatly summarised my situation was that I was transport officer but I could not drive. So I learnt. A corporal taught me in a three-ton truck. This is how I learnt to double-declutch. Then he showed me how to ride a motorbike and that was fantastic, that was my excitement, rocketing down the Canal road, a straight road through to Suez. I remember the smell of a BSA to this day.

I also remember the smell of the curry. I not only learnt to drive, I learnt to eat real curry. Even the officers lived on curry. I say even the officers, but it was really only the dregs of officers who ended up there.

This was 1950-51, when Farouk was still King and tanks were always surrounding the palace. There was a continuous national crisis which I never understood. There was simply a big fat fool called Farouk who had venereal disease and lots of women. He was a joke. All Egyptians were jokes, their Army was a joke, the whole nation was a joke. There was never any attempt to explain the situation to the officers, never mind the troops. I never met one Egyptian, not as a man, not even as a servant. One's only contact outside the Army was with fellow-Europeans at the Club. The native people were filthy and degraded. I once tried to take a photograph of what seemed to me a typical wog. He raised a stick to me and I was amazed that he was capable of that much protest. It was as if an ape in the zoo had complained about the invasion of his privacy.

On leave I did all the officer-tourist things. I went to Cairo for the weekend and stayed at Shepherds'. I went to a belly dance in a place like a strip club: there was nothing to it, nothing erotic, nothing doing, there was never anything doing. Port Said was always a filthy port just before you arrived: 'If you'd been here six months ago, my God, we had these clubs where women were doing it with donkeys,' but it was always some time, some place else. But Port Said was even then known as a dangerous place. One did not go into town in uniform. The British were not liked. When I went to collect the cash for payday I went in a truck with an armed guard, and into the bank with an armed guard.

In the Pioneers there was no kind of caste system, as in a posh regiment. There was an officers' mess, but everyone mucked in. My distinctive light-infantry uniform and my Ox and Bucks shoulder flashes marked me out a bit. I was in two minds whether to keep them, but it was just as well I did. From time to time there was a big official party, and one was given by the C-in-C, Middle East. I attended, and the General called me over:

'What's the 43rd doing out here?'

So I said, 'Well, sir, I'm stuck here, actually.'

And I told him how it had happened.

He said, 'You want to get back to the regiment? We'll soon get you back.' He spoke to one of his aides and in a month I was back in Cyprus, much to the horror of the 43rd, who thought I was where I belonged, according to my caste.

So I spent a pleasant few months before demob, in Cyprus. Waiting for the plane home I remember strutting: I really mean strutting. I was a bloody peacock. I had my cane and I felt good and fit and tanned, though I left the cane on the plane and never found it again. And my uniform was later sold to a rag and bone man, which really upset me. That beautiful regimental belt; when I bought it it was probably a hundred years old ...

That two years matured me physically, and I do not just mean my body. The way you bear yourself involves more than the body. I mean a kind of manhood. In the old phrase, I went in a boy and came out a man. But not a very nice man; I was a much nicer person before.

Intellectually it was totally stultifying, absolutely no progress in those two years. In university, you would be asking questions; in the Army all questions were suppressed.

I was in Cyprus a few years before it erupted, and all I knew was that Cyprus was beautiful. There was a Turkish quarter and a Cypriot quarter; I recognised no friction between the two, nor any hostility towards me from either quarter. In Egypt my alienation was total. The Egyptians were not even European. The Cypriots were certainly inferior, but they did not all wear filthy sandals. Egypt was a South African situation, and mine was a typical white-settler mentality. I could have been trained into some kind of Gauleiter. With a political illiterate it is not enough for his heart to be in the right place. I lacked any kind of intellectual understanding of what was happening and where I fitted in. It is appalling to think what happened to me and millions of others. I am ashamed of what I was conditioned to become. I do not want to exaggerate my role, but I was part of a British Army of Occupation. My presence helped maintain it. I never shot anybody. There was no active internal security being carried out then. But that was merely because we were so powerful that there could be no active opposition: though a couple of years later we were chased out ignominiously by the peasants we affected to despise.

I left the Army in 1951 and by 1956 I was in Trafalgar Square listening to Bevan speaking about Suez.

My sense of shame is over my lack of consciousness more than anything. I do not feel the guilt I would feel today as Lieut. Peter Burns in Ulster, for instance, physically terrorising the population. I was not doing that, I was simply 'there'. But if I had been faced with armed revolt, I wonder how I would have reacted? If I had disobeyed orders I would have been almost the only man to have done so. The British Army is notable for its docility in accepting its imperial role. Henri Martin refused to serve with the French in Indo-China, and many Americans have done the same in Vietnam. But obedience is the rule in Northern Ireland. I had certain liberal sentiments but I had no coherent ideology. I had no intellectual basis on which to build an alternative view. So on the one hand there was this very firm imperial ideology based on class interest and two hundred or more years of history. On the other, just a series of vague sentiments, little more than natural good wishes. In such a situation the sentiment collapses quickly, especially when all your mates and the weight of discipline and incipient physical terror are added to the score. So it is a hundred to one that faced with a war situation I would have tamely obeyed orders no matter what they had been, and conceivably have been guilty of all sorts of atrocities.

BILL HOLDSWORTH

My real intention had been to become a conscientious objector. My father called me yellow. I found this difficult to understand: his youth had been ruined as a result of having been gassed four times at Ypres, and he had survived the horrors of Passchendaele and the retreat from Mons. On his return he was deprived of his pension, and later was one of the millions thrown out of work. My childhood memories of my father are composed largely of dole queues, the odd bit of wallpaper hanging, and betting slips. He had no full-time work until the time came to take the countless panes of glass out of the roof of St Pancras Station. It was a strenuous job for a man who coughed his inside up every moment of the day. The mustard gas was slowly killing him, destroying his personality, his humour, his very being. I was twenty when he died. Yet he called me yellow. I just could not understand him.

In the summer of 1950 as a member of the Labour League of Youth I wrote and directed a pageant based on the fifty years' history of the Labour Movement at the International Socialist Youth Camp in Stockholm. Britain had a Socialist government. The war with fascism had been won. It was time for reconstruction. My apprentice and student friends talked of the ideals of international brotherhood. We believed in one world. Reactionaries like John Foster Dulles and General MacArthur were pressing for a nuclear bomb in Korea. In a place called Vietnam the French had finally lost their eastern empire. The tragedy of Stalinist oppression in Hungary was slowly beginning to unfold. But in Stockholm in that summer of 1950 the words on everyone's lips were 'peace and reconstruction'. On my return to England I was to leave for Yugoslavia where I was to join a youth brigade and help in the building of a railway to Belgrade. Journeying through Holland *en route* to Sweden I met up with members of the Pola Zion, a Socialist Youth Movement in Israel, and heard for the first time about the principles of the kibbutzim. My mind was made up. A year in Yugoslavia, and then on to join the young country of Israel, where they welcomed Gentiles as well as Jews to create a new Jerusalem.

I never made it. My call-up papers were on top of the pile of letters on my return. My decision to ignore them led to the first major disagreement with my mother. She felt I was letting my father down. I could never convince her. She said the police would get me at the boat. I wish I had not believed her. Instead of getting a ticket out, I travelled instead to Honiton in Devon, and there, on the railway station, I lined up with dozens of other conscripts while our names were called.

But nobody called out 'Holdsworth'. Was it true? Had they missed me? My later experiences would have led me to whip into the Gents, or walk away as if I did not belong. But I had been well brought up. Like a good boy, I said,

'Corporal, my name's not mentioned.'

He looked down his list.

'What's your name then?'

'Holdsworth,' I replied.

'No, it's not here, but we shall soon put that right. How do you spell it?'

Looking back to the start of my National Service, much of what I felt then may seem naïve in the light of today's values. I was convinced that if there was to be National Service of any sort, then it should be as an International Youth Force, trained to handle emergency situations in any part of the world, as a back-up to a United Nations Peacekeeping Force. And although I had been deferred until I was twenty as a result of serving an apprenticeship as an engineer, I was still green when I went in compared with the youth of today. My socialist ideas were polite and respectable, too, compared with present-day revolutionaries. We sang our songs of revolution with short hair: an intake of youths with long flowing tresses tied with ribbons would have given the barber at

Honiton Basic Training Camp of the Royal Electrical and Mechanical Engineers a pink fit.

As it was, I felt sick and miserable standing in the long queue of 'nig-nogs' (I never did discover the origin of this term for raw recruits: and today it has acquired racial overtones, of course) having our hair shorn off. The more we had, the more was taken off. A moronic corporal and sergeant stood over us shouting,

'Use the razor on that man! Look, his neck is dirty! D'you know what we do to dirty men, sonny? We scrub them with hard bristle brushes.'

The bull-necked Scots sergeant and his acolyte, a Liverpudlian corporal, were of a particular breed. In civilian life they were always in trouble with authority; in the Army they were given authority, position, a mission in life: to bully. When they called you 'sonny' you learnt to watch out. It was a prelude to references to your mother, and the circumstances of your birth. I came to hate these people; and hate for the same kind of people still remains with me. The Army taught me how to fight against authority. Only when you have lived within an authoritarian system can you learn how to fight it.

In retrospect, I think I was foolish not to take the advice of a mate of mine from Kentish Town. Jack's life had really been rough. He had known what it was like to be in Borstal, he was a tough guy in the real sense of the word, and a real mate. It was Jack who gave me my basic training not the Army. The Army showed me how to kill, to use a bayonet, to scrub wooden floors with bricks, to slam my boots down hard on the parade ground and to loosen the rifle magazine so as to make a loud noise when presenting arms. It was Jack who taught me how to use the Army, to accept the orders I did not like by re-interpreting them to suit myself. It was a new life-style, a survival kit.

'Billy boy, be smart, you're educated, you know about things,' he said. 'It's a system, see? and all systems have flaws. Find them out, and then take advantage. Pretend you're religious, take classes. You're clever, Billy boy, become an officer. Don't let them use you, you use them.'

I partly took Jack's advice, but I did not become an officer. Three times I was approached. Each time I turned the offer down. To become an officer would be to become a traitor to the very ideals I had fought for. Having rolled marbles under police horses at Ridley Road in '47, and supported strikes of kitchen porters by lying down in front of oil tankers, the idea of crossing to the other side was unthinkable. In reality I was naïve. Jack was right: by becoming an officer I would have been able to influence greater changes within the Army system than by remaining in the ranks. I also deprived myself of a training that might become useful to some in future years if we are faced with the rise of fascism within our own nation, and have to fight again to retain our essential freedoms.

The main difference between the Regular and the National Serviceman was the latter's attitude of non-permanence. We knew that on a certain date we would be finished with it all. While National Service was to many of us a bore, the very fact that we knew it would not last brought subtle changes to the forces that those in command are probably glad are over. National Servicemen wrote frequently to their Members of Parliament, for instance, without too much fear of victimisation. The Regular Army soldier, having joined as a career, or for whatever reason, now felt that his education was ended, apart from moving up the ladder of command. We talked in draft numbers:

'When are you out, Charlie?'

'51-10.'

'Oh, mine's 50-19, get some in!'

Get some in . . . a reference to having a longer time to stay than someone else. Like prison life, National Service life was surrounded with strange words and phrases, which lost their meaning once conscription was ended.

A film called *Virgin Soldiers* caught the mood of waiting for the time to pass, and also the hope that if posted overseas it would be to a place where life was easy and you could have your first 'bunk-up' with a girl. I bought my first packet of contraceptives because I was issued with a pair of trousers that contained a special long, thin horizontal pocket close to the fly buttons. An old soldier told me it was called a 'Johnny pocket'. The packet stayed intact for months, acting like a badge of office. On my first dispirited and unsuccessful attempt to use the sheaths I left them all hanging on a tree bough. I have hardly achieved a successful experience with french letters since.

Remembering Jack's advice to attend courses, when I was posted to Bordon in Hampshire I studied to become a Vehicle Mechanic and also did German and Economics. All these were activities which helped me to get off fatigues, and inevitably brought me into contact with the Education Corps, an Army group comprised mainly of teachers and ex-university students. I doubt whether there was any planned campaign by left-wing organisations to infiltrate the Army, but after the Lending Library incident the hot line from Bordon Vehicle Training Depot, REME, to MI5 must have been busy.

Amongst the Victorian Barrack Blocks, 1914 spider huts, and 'married pads' that were disposed each side of the London to Portsmouth Road there was a new collection of timber sheds that housed the Education Centre and Library. Compared with the corrugated tin cinema and NAAFI hut it was only sparsely inhabited. Whilst I was browsing among other Michael Caines with steel-rimmed glasses and studious intent, looking for a respite from Micky Spillane and Hank Jansen, I found under the title of *English Wild Flowers* a copy of *Das Kapital* by Karl Marx. Other books under strange titles came to light: works by Lenin, Attlee, William Morris, Sinclair Lewis and Trotsky, Jack London's *Iron Heel*. A job lot, bought off a barrow in Seaton Street market, perhaps. I read everything, and became a regular visitor.

By nature, and my training as a draughtsman, I am neat. As a soldier I was neat. My books were stacked in an upright row on the top shelf of my locker, crowned by a blanco'd helmet and cartridge belt, and the soap-filled creases of my best BD hung beneath in the specified regimental pattern.

'Stand by your beds!'

A duty sergeant, resplendent, a broad red band across his chest, stood framed in the barrack-room doorway. Spot inspection. Standing to attention by our beds, eyes to the central walkway, the duty officer, colour-sergeant and barrack-room corporal walked slowly down the file one after the other. The officer had the impatient, disdainful look of a bored pekinese dog. Suddenly he stopped in front of me.

'Can I have this soldier's door open,' he said languidly.

'Soldier, open your cabinet door,' snapped the sergeant.

'Yes, sir,' I said. I opened my door, and returned to attention. No trouble, I said to myself. Everything was neat as a pin.

'Hmm, yes, yes, hmm . . .' The officer stopped talking through his teeth. He stopped talking. He was breathing. Hard. Blimey, my books, he was reading the titles.

'Sergeant!' he screamed. 'Report this man to the CO!'

'Sir.'

Whilst the officer turned and walked over to the corporal, the sergeant glared at the offending books.

'You're for the high jump, sonny. Name. Report at seventeen hundred hours. Best BD.'

After the inspection, my barrack-room pals crowded round and looked at the books for the first time.

'Blimey, mate, what's wrong with him?'

''Ere, this is all commie stuff. You're for the high jump.'

I felt I would be.

I was having a bath later and had forgotten the time when I heard my unit officer shouting my name. 'Holdsworth! Where are you, man?'

'In the bath, sir.'

'In the bath! Bloody well get out and dress, the Old Man is waiting.'

I was clean and smart and one minute late when I arrived to find a welcoming committee. Along with the commanding officer was a REME colonel and a major dressed in Canadian green and belonging to some queer infantry outfit.

'Stand at ease, soldier.' The colonel was speaking, 'What's your name?'

'22419105 Craftsman Holdsworth, sir.'

'Well, Holdsworth, are you a Communist?'

'No, sir.'

The colonel looked disbelieving. 'These books you have brought into the camp . . .'

'I didn't bring the books in, sir. I have them on loan from the camp library, along with Churchill's *The Gathering Storm* and *The Role of the Individual in History* which are in my pack.'

'Camp library! Are you making fun of me, man?'

The commanding officer, the REME colonel, and the quiet major just sat. I opened the books to prove my point and was dismissed.

Before I left for another unit some weeks later I took a quiet walk around the library. In a corner I found one of the books, and I imagined the others were probably still around. The one I found was *Das Kapital*, the this time bound under the title *50 different recipes for French cooking*.

Arnold Wesker, in his play *Chips with Everything,* portrayed a scene where a man from the monied classes and with a public school education showed a bunch of working-class lads how to stage a raid on a coal store. Wesker based the incident on an experience of mine which he heard during our early days together at the very start of the Centre 42 idea.

It may have been good naturalist theatre, but it was not true to life. To know how to steal coal with finesse is not peculiarly one of the benefits of a public school education. It is part of the natural survival kit which any serviceman acquires for himself. The trick was always to be one step in front. The winter spent at Bordon was particularly cold, and insufficient coal was available for the barrack-room stoves. Each night a raiding party was sent to pinch coal from the stockade.

The greatest success was the night I accompanied Geletly. Born in Palestine of a Scots father and Italian mother, Geletly had lived in ten countries and had the Army organised for his benefit seemingly without effort. Armed with a large tin tub, we skirted the parade ground and crept up to the compound. A dog patrol guarded the gates and the high wire fence. It seemed impossible as we waited and quietly froze into the ground. The sentries changed every two hours, returning to a guard hut from which a warm anthracite fug escaped every time the door was open. We were about to give up when a guard left the hut with a bucket and shovel and stepped round to the rear of the hut. There was a scraping and shovelling noise and he returned with a bucket of coal. Geletly and I looked at each other, and crept to where he had been. There, stacked in a brick compound, was all the coal we could want. Each piece was handled like gold until our tin bath was filled. So far so good. Having got there, how would we stagger back? We were about to leave, when the night was filled with alarm bells, the shouts of the guard sergeant and the clatter of boots. Bugger it, a fire drill! The parade ground was soon filled. We strained to hear the roll call:

'Jackson . . . staff. Holyrood, staff. Holdsworth . . . Holdsworth . . . staff.'

Our mates had not let us down. Someone took off Geletly's high-pitched response. We breathed again. Drill over, another fifteen minutes and the square was still again. It was Geletly who came up trumps.

'Let's become a guard party with a prisoner.'

'Who's the prisoner?' I said.

'The coal,' he answered.

We stood up with the full bath of coal between us. Geletly gave the orders:

'Prisoner, shun. By the left, quick march. Left, right, left, right . . .'

His voice echoed across the square as we tried to appear erect, keep in step and yet hold the heavy load low enough so the bath was not silhouetted against the sky. We got safely back to the barrack room, both pleased and flushed with success. It was the best haul that we gained that winter, but the only response from our mates was a chorus of:

'Bloody hell, what took you so long? The stove's out.'

Without conscription, I would never have joined the Army; although when I passed the junior technical scholarship during the war my first choice was to have been a navigation officer in the Navy. But then I was only thirteen years of age. As a twenty-year-old with a strong political background my attitudes were decidedly different. Although I lived in a tough working-class neighbourhood in North London, it was only when I met youngsters from other parts of Britain that I realised how insular I was. Being suddenly uprooted and thrown together was a little like being a wartime evacuee again, when I had previously learnt to stand on my own legs. In the forces your education widened dramatically. During my time in National Service British troops were fighting in Malaya and Korea. To get a comfortable overseas posting one thought of a cushy number in Germany. My turn came when the British presence in Egypt was starting to wane. At the embarkation camp we paraded at night to depart. Jack had caught up with me. We thought that by shifting from one group to the other we might find ourselves with a mob for Germany. We were not the only ones up to the dodge; the whole square was moving and shuffling. We nearly died of fright when one character said we were bound for Korea. But the SS *Atlantis* finally docked at Ismailia and I found myself doing a sand dance and being told that if I fell into the Sweet Water Canal I would get one hundred hyperdermic needles shoved into my arse.

In England a new recruit was called a nig-nog, but in Egypt all new arrivals were called 'pinkies.' We had left Liverpool on New Year's Day, and arrived to shouts of 'Get some in' from dusty brown veterans of two months.

Tel-el-Kebir occupied twenty-eight square miles of desert centred on a water hole Australian troops had found in the desert campaigns of the second world war. Around it a vast storehouse and repair depot for British land forces in Egypt had grown. Neguib had deposed King Farouk, about whose balls we sang a

97

delightful ditty in the NAAFI whilst swilling an Egyptian brew that tasted like diluted Bluebell polish. Neguib had told all Arabs to stop working for the British, so into the vacuum came thousands of expert personnel: engineers, mechanics, and electricians, the majority of them conscripts. So many of them that the old water hole and battlefield of young Churchill's Omdurman campaign was jammed inside the perimeter wire and minefield. But whereas the Regular soldier would accept without special comment the pitiful state and terrifying poverty of the ordinary Egyptian, the National Serviceman generally would not. Although we mounted guards to look after the mountains of radios, refrigerators, furniture and so on that had been paid for by the British taxpayer, we tried to avoid confrontation with the Egyptian raiding parties that came in at night: they were welcome to as much as they could lay their hands on. And many of us were convinced that the strip of water known as Suez should belong to the Egyptians, or at least be controlled by an international authority. Later, in 1956, I was to demonstrate with thousands of others in Trafalgar Square against Eden's Suez adventure.

A subtle change takes place when the British Army goes overseas. The bullshit goes. Not all of a sudden, and not without a fight. It took the battle of the regimental flag-pole to settle the matter in our case.

Amidst all the paraphernalia of military occupation was Sergeant-Major Fortune's regimental flag and flag-pole. He had it painted white. Three coats. All thirty feet of it. The flag pole was erected on a new parade ground, which was stamped, rolled and its sand brushed like rays from the sun. Fatigue parties were sent into the desert for special lumps of rock and these were painted red, yellow, and black, the REME colours. All was ready. Sergeant-Major Fortune surveyed his symbol of power, his symbol of spit and polish.

'You might think it's going to be different now you're away from England,' he said. 'Well, it's not.'

He was berating the whole vast crowd of us on the parade ground, and complaining of the slipshod ways we were getting into.

'You're living like pigs!' he shouted.

He did not appear to be stirred when a voice shouted back:

'We're eating like pigs.'

That night, Fortune's 'prick' was still standing when I passed on my way back from a smashed-up NAAFI, the result of a fight between the Airborne and the Sutherland Highlanders. The next morning pandemonium broke out. Immediately after breakfast the whole Tel-el-Kebir force of occupation was paraded around the square. What had happened?

'Chopped down.'

'You can't mean it.'

But sure enough, the flag-pole, all thirty feet of it, lay on the ground, neatly chopped.

'Christ, we're in for it now,' said someone into my ear.

Sergeant-Major Fortune was red-faced normally: that day he was vermilion to the tips of his toes. Hours we paraded, with odd fall-outs for a drink, then back again. We stood to attention whilst Fortune and his aides, flanked by military police, marched up and down the ranks stopping suddenly to stare into the face of a soldier.

'Where were you last night? Come on, own up it was you.'

No reply. He promised, cajoled, threatened. Nobody replied. At last he had the parade dismissed. I don't think that man was ever the same again. I never saw him, because I was posted to a small unit of some thirty-four men. After that I discovered that the ordinary soldier can win, and until I left Egypt to be demobbed National Servicemen were considered as equals by all the Regular Army mob, and especially one particular bloke in the REME. Frankie Howerd found a very receptive audience when he came to entertain us; he may have wondered why a little song called 'Keeping Pace with Fortune' brought even more applause than his own performance. He never asked why.

My job at Vehicle Command Workshops was to inspect all the incoming vehicles for performance and repair. I controlled the spare part replacements for vehicles as far away as the Red Sea. The major who commanded us had been in Egypt since the war. He was jovial, not given to harsh discipline, and when I edited *Pivot* (a camp magazine typed out with one finger on a French typewriter, and duplicated on a hand roller by Tent 7's co-editor Gordon Culley) Major Easter would write a little homily on why us boys should be looking after this particular bit of desert for Queen and country. One day he asked to see me.

'Holdsworth, you're in charge of vehicle maintenance.'

'Yes, sir.'

'Good, I want you to find me a twelve-horsepower engine in good nick, the staff-sergeant will tell you the rest.'

The old Major seemed highly pleased with himself; almost boyish, I thought.

The only way to find an engine that was in good nick was to remove one from a fairly new vehicle and then log the vehicle as being in for repair. It was a good team that the major had collected, Tents 7 and 8, consisting of 'Sticks' Linley, a Geordie whom I found still drumming in Jersey five years ago, Gabby Hayes and an eccentric Welshman, Hyde, who was so unconcerned that even the news that his girl friend had given birth and was wearing a ring did nothing to change his slow demeanour. So these three, Culley, and Harpic, as I was called, presented ourselves to the staff sergeant; our engine, covered with oil, brown paper and crated up, was aboard a Dennis truck.

'Where are we off to, Staff?'

'Lake Timsah, lads, Lake Timsah.'

No questions asked. We were off. Away from the sand and flies to the cool of the lake.

We sang all the way as we drove along the side of the Sweet Water Canal, passing the families who existed solely by selling a few bottles of Coca Cola a day. It was remarking on the abject poverty of the fellelah that gave our magazine *Pivot* a political twist which was later to prove an embarrassment to the Army authorities, but on this particular day the excitement was the chance to get out away from the desert cage, to see a woman whatever age or nationality, and to find out for what reason the major wanted the twelve hp engine.

We soon found out.

The boat was of reasonable size and was moored along a small jetty.

'Right, lads, let's get to work,' said the sergeant.

'Work, bloody hell, thought we were on a picnic, should have known,' said Sticks.

The old engine was removed with much swearing, and then as the sun rose up to its zenith we all sweated and swore again putting in the new one. It was Hyde who gave us hope, by suggesting that we were going to have a boat trip for all the concert parties, tramp suppers and the like that Tent 7 had organised. Could be, I thought. At last we had finished, and went on a little test run. After a swim we rested to drink beer and eat our rations.

'The major's here.'

We all stumbled up, a little sleepy, and rough-looking from our labours.

'It's all right, men, at ease, at ease.' He was dressed in civvies, white trousers, blue shirt, yachting cap.

'Well, Holdsworth, does my engine work?'

'Yes, sir, first class.'

'Good. Good.' He turned and walked away. Then he was back carrying a wicker basket, and alongside him walked the most delectable woman we had seen for a year. Greek, or Armenian, it didn't matter. Small. Slim, with fabulous eyes, mouth, skin, legs, breasts, bottom. Our eyes just took her in.

'Well, chaps, this is Minnie.'

He then introduced each one of us, even the staff-sergeant whose tongue must have become inflated. Each one of us stood and shook her hand, speechless. She stepped into the boat, her trim figure (which was to occupy our wanking dreams for weeks) disappearing down into the little wheelhouse. The major, who was round and comfortable, stepped aboard, turned and said:

'Cast off, men, see you in a week or so.'

He started the engine, the boat pulled away. We stood together a forlorn group for some time until the boat was a small dot on the lake. It was Hyde who broke the silence.

'I wonder what he will do for a week?'

We all jumped on him.

Illustrated on the cover of *Pivot* magazine was a pyramid, turned upside down. As National Servicemen in Egypt my friends and I were on the threshold of changes from an old sphere of influence to that of a new one: Russia. The little duplicated magazine echoed the thoughts of young soldiers concerned as to why they carried arms. I bought two books in Tel-el-Kebir: one was a paperback edition of a diary of Bevan's, *In Place of Fear*, the other was Bertrand Russell's *New Hopes for a Changing World*. These writings, along with Camus's *Rebel*, became my platform. The beliefs that flourished prior to and during my National Service days have since remained central to my philosophy.

A Regular Army officer once said to me, 'Holdsworth, you're a ruddy Bolshevik.'

I wanted to point out that politically I had more in common with the Mensheviks, but I did not bother to explain. I do not think he would have understood. There was always a reason for rebelling.

An article published in *Socialist Advance* written while I was still stationed in the Canal Zone was nearer the truth than I could ever have imagined in the light of Middle-East history over the past twenty years. Some awkward questions were asked at the time by a new commanding officer who had replaced our jovial major. But I was past caring. My number (50-19) came up and I was soon on my way to England, home, and demob. In my pocket was my discharge book in which were written the words:

Craftsman Holdsworth has the CORRECT attitude to his superiors.

I wonder what Old Yorky, my father, had had written in his discharge book?

IAN CARR

My National Service, which took place in the period 1956-58, came immediately after I had spent four years at university, and these two experiences could be seen as part of the same process of getting to grips with the business of being alive. Four years of intense thought and philosophical speculation were followed by two years of action in which principles and conclusions might be tested out in a supposedly more real situation.

I studied at King's College, Newcastle-on-Tyne, and after four years had obtained an honours degree in English Literature and a Diploma in Education. Although naturally athletic and practical, I had deliberately cultivated a neglect of the body, hoping that in this way I would refine and streamline the workings of my sensibility and soul. At the time I was obsessed with pursuing the poetic and imaginative life, and probably thought, with obscure logic, that imagination would draw strength like a parasitic fungus from my decaying body. I deliberately avoided all exercise, over-smoked (having seen an early photograph of W. H. Auden rakishly lighting a cigarette), ate as little as possible, and kept very late hours. I also grew my hair very long and wore carefully cultivated rags.

The rub was that my fastidious programme of physical dissolution had not resulted in any masterpieces. My entire output to date had been a few stricken verses about a horrific universe seen through the eyes of a drunken, ill-informed, underfed undergraduate. After four years I had grown sick of this life-style, and I began to look for another road to wisdom.

So it was with a sense of relief and excitement that I reported myself at Strensall, Yorkshire, for basic training in September 1956. Here was the purgative I needed: the drastic revision of the external image, the close-cropped hair, the obsession with surface polish, rough living, physical toughness. Inside I might still be soggy with introspection, but it was necessary to develop a hard external crust. Life was now reduced to physical action and functional intelligence. Apart from the relief of this, though, the period was not a particularly pleasant one and only a few pictures linger in the memory with any clarity: breath puffing white on the air as we drew rifles from the weapon store first thing in the morning; polishing boots and buttons under naked light-bulbs while over the barrack-room loudspeakers Radio Luxembourg blared out the continuous pop music of the day ('Green Door', 'Swinging Shepherd Blues' and so on); lectures on military subjects in stuffy smoke-filled rooms delivered by a lieutenant who projected on to the screen pictures alternately of weapons and nude women, to keep us awake. The official pictures are just a blur in my memory, but I can still see one or two of the women vividly.

It was also during this period that I had my first encounter with that unhappy breed of man, the Army padre. The one who attempted to minister to us seemed to be painfully aware of the philosophical contradictions he represented, and he spent most of the time tying himself in mental knots trying to justify the social role he had chosen. Occasionally he would make a huge effort and attempt to elevate his private and subjective torment to the level of objective or universal truth and would say in a very loud firm voice: 'I AM WHAT I HAVE OVERCOME: YOU ARE WHAT YOU HAVE OVERCOME!' But he failed to maintain this splendour of utterance for more than a few minutes, and inevitably subsided into a muttered soliloquy about good and evil. We would have respected him a lot more if he'd either left himself out of it altogether, or simply said:

'Look, I've got a wife and three kids and this job is a pretty good screw.' But of course that would have cost him his job.

After six weeks of basic training, we were asked if we would like to be officers and I put my name down to go to the War Office Selection Board. There were probably many reasons for this decision, but the most important ones were that I like to feel that I have some control over my own destiny, and saw greater opportunities for freedom as an officer. Additionally, since my teens I had been obsessed with the First World War (I still am) and for years had been seeing myself as a sepia photograph in uniform and puttees. This was my chance to get nearer to the dream.

During the period of the Suez crisis in 1956 I went down to Aldershot (or somewhere south of London) and underwent the various tests to see if I was worthy of the Queen's Commission. I acted what I thought was the part, and when asked by a white-haired colonel why I was looking forward to military service, replied quite truthfully, but in a bright, ringing voice:

'Well, actually, from a quite crude sense of adventure, sir!' On the final afternoon (the whole WOSB thing covered about three days) I was lined up with the ones who had passed, and re-turned to Strensall to join the Leader Platoon.

After another week or so we were given some leave and told to report afterwards to Eaton Hall, Chester, for four months' officer training. As I left Strensall the padre shook my hand, and said:

'Goodbye, Carr . . . Hardly the happy extrovert . . . but good luck!'

I had a rough time at Eaton Hall, and my very first experience within its stately precincts was extremely unpropitious. We were ushered into a building where a cavalry captain with thin, bandy legs and a long, hawk-like face in which sunken eyes glowed fanatically, directed our gaze to a printed notice which hung from the ceiling. As we looked at it he read it out, his voice rising to a falsetto screech on the key word:

'The aim of weapon-training is to KILL the enemy!'

He seemed to be the embodiment of diabolical Will, and his voice on the word 'KILL' had such intensity that even the non-liberal officer cadets visibly recoiled. That one strained syllable had in a flash destroyed whatever relevance the New Testament and the whole liberal tradition might have had to the way of life we had chosen. But this was, after all, only another moment of truth, and anyone who thought there was any other aim to weapon-training was kidding himself. In for a penny, in for a pound . . . even of flesh. But that introduction certainly inhibited me from identifying easily with my new role. And to this day, I can still hear that man's voice screaming out its message.

Apart from the difficulty of identifying with the warrior caste and the whole military myth, other things made life very difficult for me at Eaton Hall. I was no good at drill, and I was no good at either physical or psychological bullshit, both of which are the stuff of militarism. I can still hear down the long corridors of memory the rasping voice of Sergeant Horrigan (with his shaggy eyebrows and long, vulpine countenance) roaring in exasperation: 'Mr Carr, sir, you're a long streak of piss, sir!' as I shambled out of line on the barrack square. There was usually something wrong with my equipment: dirty buttons or boots, or webbing badly blanco'd, and I spent a lot of time doing jankers, parades and punishment drill.

My other difficulty was that I found it almost impossible to pretend to be a bustling, decisive leader in artificial and imaginary situations, which, of course, all situations were at Eaton Hall. So I got the reputation with the authorities of being an untidy, ill-disciplined mouse of a man. They would dearly have loved to kick me out and return me to my unit as a private soldier, but I think they felt I would do less harm as an officer than as an other rank. A few weeks previously another graduate (in economics) had arrived at Eaton Hall, and on his first morning had simply refused to get out of bed. He had said, apparently, that he felt like a lie-in! He had been visited by a series of NCOs and warrant officers, and then by officers of ascending rank, who had abused, reviled, threatened, and finally implored him to get up. But he had ignored them all, and was eventually carried off to the guard-room. A few days later he had been banished to civilian life. I think this incident had severely shaken the authorities at Eaton Hall. Anyway, even though a major told me to my face that they would like to return me to my unit, I survived. And of course they were wise: as a private I would have been a tenacious barrack-room lawyer and a pain in authority's neck.

Each officer cadet had to give a specimen talk to the rest of his class and my own lecture, which took place towards the end of the course, was something of a landmark for me. I chose the most abstract subject on the agenda (morale) and was handed the standard official sheet of notes on the subject. To my amazement, on reading these through, I found they were inept to the point of crass ignorance and stupidity. The captain who had given me the notes attended the lecture, and I took malicious pleasure in pointing out the inadequacy of the official material. It was probably this lecture more than any other single event which caused the authorities to pass me out as an officer. This taught me a useful lesson: the more abstract a problem or thought, the less confident the Army feels. It also suggested that battles are won with least cost when they are fought obliquely.

At the end of March 1957 I passed out of Eaton Hall a second-lieutenant with one pip on either shoulder, somewhat battered and shaken by the experience, but with undiminished curiosity about life and life-styles.

I had put down the Durham Light Infantry as my first choice of regiment, and the Royal Northumberland Fusiliers as my second. Why the infantry? My sepia photograph image was an infantryman, and also, having pursued the 'outsider' role for four years at college, I wanted now to experience what it was like to be inside society. The infantry is the essence of traditional militarism, and I had lived for much of my life in Durham and Northumberland. Obviously, the quintessence of 'insiderism' for me was to be in either the DLI or the RNF. It turned out to be the RNF and I was sent to Northern Ireland on the 8th April to join the first battalion at Palace Barracks, Belfast, where they were at that time attempting to contain IRA activity. I travelled by train and boat, in uniform, and, for the first time in my life, on a first-class ticket.

At Belfast station the adjutant picked me up in a landrover and took me to the barracks. During the trip, which took about ten minutes, he quizzed me about distinguished novocastrian citizens whom he thought I might know. But his every query drew a blank. His smile became thinner and he finally said:

'I hope you've got some decent civilian clothes – and a hat.' At last I could reply in the affirmative, but by now his suspicions that I might not be 'socially OK' were fully aroused, and he added: 'And I mean a decent hat – not one of those fucking silly little corduroy caps!' I hastened to reassure him, and made a private resolution to destroy the cap and buy a new hat at the earliest opportunity. His perspicacity was uncanny, though, and unnerved me considerably.

He dropped me at the officers' mess and the mess sergeant showed me to my room. After telling me that everyone fore-gathered in the ante-room at about twelve-thirty p.m. before going in to lunch, the sergeant went out, leaving me to my own devices, which at that particular moment in time were pretty meagre. Shortly after twelve-thirty I went downstairs, braced myself, and opened the ante-room door. It was like tearing the scab off a wound. The room seemed to be very crowded and was blue-grey with cigarette smoke. It buzzed with the polite snarl of genteel conversation, and through the haze I could see elegant figures in battledress languidly facing one another. Well-groomed heads and noble profiles were grouped together stylishly, glasses of gin and tonic were held at the ready like weapons, and cigarettes hung carelessly from limp fingers. This was it, then. I stepped inside and closed the door behind me.

A few eyes flitted impersonally in my direction and moved away again. Nobody came up and said: 'Ah, you must be the new man . . . I'm so-and-so, how do you do?' I stood there for a little while surveying the scene and feeling like the proverbial spare prick at a wedding. After a few minutes it became obvious that I was going to be studiously ignored, by which time my feeling of general inadequacy was beginning to turn to anger. Then I noticed a group of subalterns of my own age standing in carelessly relaxed postures round the fireplace at the far end of the room. I went up to them and said: 'Hallo. I'm Ian Carr.' A few inconsequential pleasantries were exchanged and the ice was broken. Gerald Laing, who was soon to become a close friend, was among the subalterns to whom I addressed myself, and he told me months later that they were all staggered by my effrontery in presenting myself like that. Apparently, new arrivals who were not already known or who were not the sons of famous fathers were supposed to wait until they were spoken to: and some of them had to wait quite a long time. I had, it seemed, by-passed this tribal ritual.

After lunch I had an interview with the commanding officer who told me never to be 'toffee-nosed', and informed me that I was to become a platoon commander in X company. Whether the CO had had a report from Eaton Hall which said that I was a difficult case, or whether it was pure luck, I shall probably never know, but the commander of X company, Major Freddie Ward, was the perfect boss for me. He was intelligent, a devout Roman Catholic, extremely high-principled, and at the same time he had a surrealist wit and sense of humour. A hint of riches to come was given me when I followed him around as he inspected the company latrines on my first Saturday. After peering studiously down a few lavatory bowls, he pulled one of the chains and, as the cistern gurgled and flushed, he turned to me with a wry smile and said:

'Après moi, le déluge!'

Under his guidance, I began to get to grips with the job of being a platoon commander, which meant not only concerning myself with the military efficiency of the thirty men in my platoon but also dealing with their general welfare and their domestic problems. Now, far from deliberately looking for the complexity of problems, the essential aim was to simplify all pros and cons as much as possible in order to arrive at quick and workable decisions. Logistics, the whole process of organising the feeding, clothing, equipment, and general welfare of large numbers of people, was a fascinating and valuable experience.

The first battalion was in Northern Ireland for six or seven more months until November 1957 when it was posted to Germany, and that initial period was one of intense, and sometimes traumatic, experience. There were new things to be learnt, and fresh problems, every day. At the time I was so hungry for experience that I was almost a non-political animal. And of course the grass-roots leaders (subalterns) in all wars are in exactly this state: ignorant, avidly curious, desperate to prove themselves, and greedy for experience. The fact that we were fighting Irish Catholics in Ireland did not bother me too much at the time, although I knew a fair amount about the Irish question and was aware of the 1916 rebellion.

The days were wholly taken up by very varied activities: parades, company administration, shooting on the range, sandbagging and putting barbed wire round police stations which were the main target of terrorists in those days, going on manoeuvres in the Irish countryside, visiting patrols as duty officer, going on all-night marches, and occasionally losing a night's sleep while searching for terrorists who had been observed in rural areas. My platoon never came up against any members of the IRA, though we did lose a great deal of sleep looking for them.

Despite the apparent inflexibility of the military code, the rules could occasionally be bent to fit circumstances, as they were in the bizarre saga of one private soldier who shall be referred to henceforth as Fusilier King. He was a very likeable north-countryman in his middle twenties, powerfully built, with a large red face, a square chin, and a stubby nose on which were perched a pair of regulation steel spectacles. He looked like a cross between a German scientist and an all-in wrestler. He was a devout Catholic, a very cheerful soul, and had been allocated the permanent job of keeping X company latrines in good order.

The snag was that, despite repeated attempts, he had failed to pass the Army third-class certificate of education examination, and so had never received the pay-rise to which this would entitle him. He requested an interview, expressed his dissatisfaction with this state of affairs, and said that if nothing could be done about it he wanted to leave the Army when his time was up in a couple of months. There were some fairly high-level consultations about the problem, and it was agreed that Fusilier King was a good soldier, an asset to the Army, and that in fact, given his rather simple view of life, it was decided that he really needed the kind of protection the Army afforded him. The question was mooted: What would King actually do in the big wide world outside?

I was told to liaise with the education major about the problem. 'Don't worry,' he said breezily, 'he'll get through this time . . . he'll go no further, mind you, but he'll get through this time.'

This sounded promising but, not wanting to leave too much to chance, and as I happened to be the invigilator, I told King to arrive half an hour late at the examination room. This enabled me to keep him behind alone for thirty minutes after everyone else had finished. Then, working at lightning speed, we finished most of the paper together and knocked up an amazing 75%. The major, who in fact marked the papers himself, collared me shortly after the results came out.

'I told you he'd pass,' he said darkly, 'but this is ridiculous!'

So for a while Fusilier King was happy with his pay-rise, and X company latrines shone brightly in our firmament. Shortly afterwards, I remember standing behind King as he lay on his belly firing a bren-gun on the shooting range. All his shots were thudding into the embankment about ten feet below the target frame. I peered down and saw that his sights were at zero.

'Look, King,' I said helpfully. 'You're firing from the two hundred yards line so your sights should be set at two hundred.'

He rolled on to his side and grinned at me.

'Oh, no, sir,' he said dismissively, 'I never bother with all that! . . . If I want to fire higher I just raise the front of the gun a bit!'

A week or two later, Fusilier King requested another interview. Again he gave an ultimatum: he was fed up with latrines and wanted to take driving lessons in order to become one of the battalion drivers. Lessons were arranged for him immediately, and soon the day of his test approached. I explained to the tester, Sergeant Pringle, a man with a meticulous sense of duty, that this time he must be generous in his interpretation of the rules because it was imperative that King pass his test. Sergeant Pringle gave me a searching look and a wary salute.

'I'll do my best, sir,' he said somewhat grimly.

The morning of the test arrived and the minutes dragged slowly by until just before lunch when Sergeant Pringle appeared at company HQ. I could see at once from his distraught face that something was wrong.

'What happened? Didn't you pass him?' I blurted out anxiously.

Sergeant Pringle made a weary gesture of resignation.

'Look, sir,' he said bitterly, 'he went through a red light, then he went the wrong way down a one-way street, then he nearly ran down a pedestrian, mounted the pavement and hit a lamp-post. I said to him, "OK, King, I'll take over now," and you know what he said? . . . He said, "Have I passed, Sarge?" '

A few days after failing his driving test Fusilier King was strolling in uniform in the streets of Belfast when a military policeman told him to take his hands out of his pockets. King refused to do so and told the policeman to piss off. Instead of arresting him on the spot, the policeman followed King into a café and took notes while King smashed the place up. Reinforcements arrived and King was taken to the guardroom and put into a cell where he continued giving vent to his rage and frustration by smashing anything he could lay hands on. He was so physically powerful that he even succeeded in loosening the iron bars of the window. Also, in transit, he had inflicted injuries on his captors.

Eventually, he was marched in front of the CO and a huge list of charges against him was read out. When it was over, the CO said menacingly,

'Have you got anything to say, King?'

King beamed at the CO.

'Yes, sir,' he said. 'How's your little dog, sir?'

There was a tiny, hysterical silence which was broken when the CO managed to splutter in a choking voice,

'March him out!'

King was duly taken outside until everyone had had time to wipe their eyes and pull themselves together. I forgot what punishment he was given (some days of confinement to barracks and some loss of pay) but I think it might have been a much more severe sentence if he had not asked his guileless question.

Efforts were still made to keep Fusilier King in the Army, but I heard that he managed to get his demobilisation papers signed by slipping them into a batch that were due for signature, and he disappeared without either saying goodbye or even letting anyone know he was going.

When the battalion was posted to Germany, there had to be a rear-party which stayed behind in Belfast for a week or two to see to unfinished business and to complete the handing over of the barracks to the new incumbents. Officer commanding the rear-party was considered to be a lowly and distasteful chore which no normal officer would want to do. As junior officer in the battalion, and a National Serviceman as well, I was the obvious choice for this job, and the adjutant duly assigned it to me. Although fellow-officers commiserated with me, I was overjoyed at being given an independent command and some responsibility. Organising this rear-party was extremely hard work. Although there was an orgy of greetings and happy reunions when we arrived at Münster, I felt only a drab sense of anti-climax, and after finding my room in the mess, and learning that good Scotch was only fourpence a tot, I drank myself to oblivion and went to bed.

Serving in Germany filled out the military picture considerably. In Northern Ireland we had been on semi-active service dealing with urban guerillas. In Germany we were part of an Army of Occupation in peacetime conditions: the heat was off. This was at first a welcome change, but it soon brought other problems. Sex (the absence of) and boredom soon began to preoccupy the minds of all ranks, and the battalion's alcohol consumption rose enormously. The adjutant wrung his hands and told all companies to inform their men that German beer was three times more potent than British beer. But, given that most of the 944 men in a battalion are heterosexual, that they are herded together in barbaric conditions, surrounded by wire fences and guards in a foreign country whose language they know nothing of, and with the bromide of fear removed, then the only reasonable thing to expect is drunkenness, inefficiency, and absence without leave. It didn't help to mention these points to the adjutant, or to remind him that history was on his side and that armies, from the beginning of time, had been drunk and disorderly in peacetime. He was not interested in this kind of history: he was concerned with the here and now, for which he, poor man, carried the can.

A few shows were put on in the gymnasium to entertain the troops. It seemed a humane thing to do, and it kept the men off the beer for a couple of hours. But the moment of truth came for me when we were entertained by one of the popular singers of the day, a tall, well-built girl. As usual, the first two rows of seats were occupied by the officers wearing dress uniform and their ladies in evening dress. The rest of the gym was filled with other ranks in denims. I was at the back because I happened to be in charge of that particular show. All went as planned until the singer delivered a particularly lively song during which she jigged around and wiggled her bottom a bit. Suddenly, in the middle of it, a diminutive soldier in shapeless denims rose to his feet and yelled triumphantly:

'I've come!'

A ripple of unease agitated the sartorial splendour of the first two rows and a few startled faces glanced back. A couple of military policemen bore down on the hapless testifier and removed him bodily from the hall. But it is difficult to forget the sheer delight of that man's proclamation. It was as if he had found an oasis in a desert. The only honest man in that assembly – and of course he had to be removed.

As the months slipped by in Germany, the sexual deprivation, the absence of feminine company and the kind of civilisation it brings to a society, had a profound effect on me and I began to suffer from hideous depressions. Some officers managed to achieve pleasant relationships with teachers at a local British school. These girls lived in a hostel in Münster, and threw parties on Saturdays which were famed for the kind of satisfaction they afforded. But on the whole, Germany, for an unmarried officer, was fairly barren sexually.

Some of the more enterprising other ranks simply cut a hole in the perimeter fence and under cover of darkness smuggled in the various women they had met in the local town. Patrolling the camp at night with the duty sergeant, I often had to make short detours to avoid the writhing bodies. At the time it seemed most unfair, but perhaps it was only a kind of social justice. On one occasion, having carefully avoided confronting half a dozen couples blissfully engaged in achieving orgasm, I returned to the duty-officer's room and sat down glumly, only to be further tormented by the sounds of physical intimacy coming in through the open window: some lucky fellow was enjoying a knees-tremble against the wall of battalion HQ! In a fit of uncontrollable sexual jealousy, I telephoned the duty sergeant and ordered him to search and clear the whole area.

I had been playing the trumpet intermittently as an amateur since I was at school, and in Germany the only emotional release I could get was in playing jazz. The bandmaster loaned me a cornet and when life became unbearable I would slip down to the band-room and have a blow with musicians from the regimental band. There were also a couple of officers who played guitars and so we occasionally had jam sessions in the mess. The colonel and most other senior officers lived in married quarters and so knew nothing of these activities.

One night the brigadier was a guest at a regimental dinner, and during the meal, as was customary, the regimental band, discreetly concealed from view behind a screen, played their usual selections from popular musical shows. After the meal the custom was to walk round to the door at the other end of the room and watch and listen to the band for a while before going into the ante-room to indulge in the usual boisterous parlour games. On this occasion, I arrived at the door to find the brigadier leaning languidly against the doorpost and the colonel standing beside him. The band came to the end of a piece, and instead of striking up again immediately, there was a pause and the bandmaster, offering me a cornet, said:

'Do you fancy a blow, sir?'

Avoiding the colonel's gaze, I went into the room and played 'St Louis Blues' with the rhythm section. The brigadier was delighted and the colonel, faced with the obvious pleasure of his superior, shouted with forced joviality:

'How about "Tiger Rag"?!' But I could detect a glint in his eye.

Some days later I was invited to dinner at the colonel's house, and after wining and dining me generously, he shot a question at me;

'Don't you think we should bring back flogging?'

The resulting argument was intense, and after we had arrived at an impasse, he suddenly said:

'An officer and a gentleman doesn't play the trumpet!'

I can't remember what I replied, but, in retrospect, I think he was right.

The long days and nights in Westphalia were also enlivened by some very good friends: in particular, my friendship with Gerald Laing, which had begun in Northern Ireland, ripened in Germany, and has continued ever since. My first impression of him was not particularly favourable: he looked like a typical regular officer with his stiff upperlip, his supercilious expression, and his dachshund called Andrew. But on my first regimental dinner night (St George's Day 1957) I found myself sitting next to him, and soon realised that he was a kindred spirit. At regimental dinners it is forbidden to talk about religion, politics or sex until the Queen's health has been drunk, which happens, of course, only when everyone has finished eating. Talking shop is also frowned on. This leaves precious little to talk about, but most junior officers, anxious for the approbation of their superiors, meekly accept this most uncivilised limitation on intercourse. On this occasion Gerald spent the whole meal reciting *Winnie the Pooh* in a fairly prominent voice. There was a great deal of laughter at our end of the table, and it duly attracted the attention of the colonel who barked:

'What the devil is Laing talking about?'

A captain in the centre of the table dutifully reported:
'He's saying, "And nobody
                    KNOWS-tiddely-pom
                    How cold my
                    TOES-tiddely-pom
                    Are
                    Growing."
Or words to that effect, Colonel.'

I soon learned that Gerald Laing was a man who pursued his dreams with demonic fervour. At one time the all-consuming passion had been ballet and he had taken ballet lessons. He still kept locked away with his prize possessions a pair of old ballet shoes which Belinda Wright had given him, and I believe they gave him great comfort in moments of stress. Then he had become obsessed with the romantic idea of soldiering, so he went to Sandhurst and got his commission. But the reality of Army life was tearing the dream to shreds, and when I joined the battalion Gerald was already falling out of love with this career. To add to his general frustration, he was temperamentally even less suited than I was to the celibate, all-male existence.

In Germany, the intellectual and imaginative poverty of the existence and the lack of freedom resulted in some very idiosyncratic behaviour. I have three vivid mental pictures of Gerald at this time. First, he is striding along the path outside my window and shouting in anguished tones:

'Masturbation is the only answer!' And as he disappeared round a corner, groaning once again, 'Yes, the only answer!'

Then, during a cocktail party in the mess, he suddenly dropped down on his hands and knees and scurried up and down the anteroom barking like a dog. The adjutant, his face purple with anger, hissed at him:

'For Christ's sake, Gerald! Not in front of these fucking RASC blokes, please!'

And Gerald, who was too far gone to be moved by thoughts of social propriety, bared his teeth and with a snarl tried to sink them into the adjutant's calf. With amazing agility for such a bulky man, the adjutant skipped to one side.

And the final incident occurred when I was sitting quietly in my room writing some notes. I heard the roar of an approaching motor bike. Suddenly, the door to my room burst open, and Gerald roared in on his bike, screeched to a halt in the middle of the room, and revved the engine until the place was full of blue smoke.

I tried to shout something to him, but there was so much noise my voice was inaudible, and I could see from the fury in his eyes that words were redundant anyway. As suddenly as he had appeared, he swung the handlebars round and roared out again. I got to my door just in time to see him smash through the swing doors at the end of the corridor like a bullet.

In Northern Ireland Gerald had returned to one of his earlier loves, which was painting, and in Germany he began taking lessons. As this passion grew, the Army's disapproval hardened until there seemed to be a continual ideological battle going on. Fortunately, considering that it was coming from all angles, the military rationale was pretty inept. For the assistant adjutant, a blond youth with a retroussé nose, the word 'artist' was synonymous with 'homosexual', and he cornered me one day (I was considered to be the evil influence on Gerald) and said desperately:

'Now, look here . . . I've got nothing against art, but queers are bad! . . . I mean it! . . . disgusting!'

Despite, or perhaps even because of, all this pressure, Gerald persisted in his studies. He managed to get out of the Army in 1960 and studied at St Martin's School of Art. He later became very successful in America, and now divides his life between a sixteenth-century castle in Scotland, and the front line trenches of the avante garde in New York, which seems to satisfy both ends of the spectrum of his fantasies.

A couple of lasting friendships like the one with Gerald Laing seem, in retrospect, to have been the most valuable thing the Army afforded me: but it was opposition to the military mentality which cemented them.

Early in 1958 I went on a winter-warfare course which consisted of nine days' skiing at Winterberg. On the final day I broke my ankle and spent two weeks in hospital at Münster. This gave me the quiet period I needed to get things in perspective and I realised that, though I had five more months to serve, the Army experience was over for me. I would stick it out to the end, of course, but I had to start thinking of future plans right away. Looking back over my military service as I lay in that hospital bed it seemed that there were few real villains. It was just that a lot of fairly ordinary and often not-too-bright people had simply got themselves submerged and dehumanised in a way of life which was so absurd that it bordered on the fantastic.

And as my own short life fell into perspective, I realised that I had spent all of my adolescence and adulthood to date in the protective custody of various institutions: first school, then university, and now the Army. So I wrote to the War Office and asked permission to be demobilised in Germany.

On the 8th September 1958, wearing civilian clothes, I boarded a train at Münster that took me first to Paris and then to the flesh-pots of the Mediterranean, where I spent two rich years bumming around in poverty.

MEL CALMAN

The first mistake I made was taking my moustache into the Army with me. I had had a beard at art school, and kept the moustache as a souvenir of the beard. But amongst the fresh chins of the eighteen-year-olds, my moustache could be seen at a hundred paces and marked me as if I had been painted red. Every time I footfaulted myself at drill, I was noticed immediately and the drill sergeant bellowed out:

'Who's that horrible man with a 'tache . . . stand still when I'm talking to you!'

After four years at an art school I suddenly found myself in an establishment that was half adult boarding school, half lunatic asylum. The masters were the officers, the prefects were the NCOs and the rules were rampant and completely arbitrary.

You had to polish the barrack-room bucket, knowing it would get dirty and have to be polished again the next day. You had to remove all the lettering from the lid of your boot polish tin and make it mirror-shine for inspections. (So you bought two tins: one for use, one for show.) You had to fold your sheets and blankets every morning in certain ritualised ways. You had to greet other men with special salutes that involved twisting your neck, your wrist, your dignity. You had to move by numbers: turn, two, three, breathe in, pause, two three, breathe out. You had to stop thinking 'why' and do it. You had to unlearn being an individual and become a number and put that number on all your clothes and on your soul, if told to. An Army requires instant obedience, because death requires instant obedience. You cannot say to the Angel of Death, 'I'm not coming with you. Why should I?'

After basic training, we heard rumours you were allowed to regain some of your personality. Even wear shoes sometimes instead of boots. Find some quiet niche where you could hibernate for the rest of the two years.

I had put my name down for the niche labelled 'Education Corps'. I had an Art Teacher's Certificate and a smear of education and it seemed a waste not to use any of it. But I had also learned that Education Corps sgts (and everyone in the Corps was a sgt or higher) had a room of their own. I did not like barrack-room life. The last thing a private got was any privacy.

There were others in the barracks going to the Ed. Corps and two of them became my friends. One was very large, tall, over-weight, wore thick glasses, and was called Trundle. The other was very thin, small and also bespectacled. They looked rather like an intellectual Laurel and Hardy together. We all disliked the barracks and used to sit in the NAAFI, gloomily soothing our wounded psyches with cups of tea and bitter sarcasm against the system.

I most hated the early rising. Being woken at six-thirty by a bellow from the corporal . . . hands off cocks and on socks . . . bellow . . . bellow . . . doors slamming . . . everyone cheery and awake . . . at a time when I had been used to heavy dreams of fair women. Then there was having to rush down to the freezing washroom, where forty of us scrambled for the twenty basins and washed and shaved in cold water. As my stubble was dark and tough I always looked as if I had not shaved ('Take the paper off the blade next time' was the sergeant's routine joke). Eventually the three of us bought a small heater and shaved with a cup of hot water every morning, whilst everyone else sneered at our molly-coddling ourselves.

The Army (in the upright shape of the PT sgt) soon noticed that we three were physically unfit and unlikely to pass our Physical Efficiency Tests. These had to be passed before you could complete your basic training. If you did not qualify you had to do another eight weeks. I could see myself spending the two years endlessly sweating through the same basic training.

We could not climb ropes with speed. In fact, in my case, I could not climb ropes at all. I had a strong fear of heights and had no intention of leaving ground level. We also tended to slither over the vaulting box instead of lithely leaping over it. I had a long history of physical inactivity. Natural laziness at school had combined with maternal protectiveness to produce a creature that could walk or totter, but do little else. (My mother used to say, 'Why don't clergymen fall out of trees?' And answer, 'Because they don't climb them'). At school I had carefully avoided climbing trees or ropes or anything else that involved unecessary risks. Even step ladders gave me vertigo. During games I had given an excellent imitation of someone who is keen but somehow finds himself a long way away from the action. It is no wonder I became a cartoonist: it is the ideal sedentary occupation. You might go mad, but you do not need to be physically brave.

The Army decided we needed some extra help to complete our training, and we were sent on a special course for the physically inadequate held at the PT Depot, Shornecliffe, near Folkestone. Squads of weak-kneed, round-shouldered, skinny and fat misfits were gathered there and PT sgts exhausted themselves trying to make men of us.

We went for long runs along the deserted beach in the morning. It was November and very cold. We had to go on long marches. And when we were not running or marching, we were doing PT.

Worst of all, we had special sessions called 'Confidence Training', which eroded what little confidence I had left. The climax of these sessions was a thirty-foot scaffolding, which we had to climb and then descend, from rung to rung. I managed to get up and at the top stopped to rest and shiver with fright on a tiny platform. Far below me, to the left, I could see the military hospital: to the right, the military cemetery. I thought this was carrying a joke too far. I tried to lower myself down and panic set my limbs into damp jelly. I could not move. I could hear faint shouts of encouragement from the PT sgt below, but I could not unfix myself. I closed my eyes and sweated. Eventually the sgt had to climb up, hold me round the waist, and lower me like a drunk down to ground level.

Of the three of us, one broke his leg whilst training his confidence and another had a nervous breakdown and was invalided out.

I returned alone to our unit, back to marching, drilling and bulling for eternity, as far as I could see, since I still had not learnt how to climb ropes. I always tried to run round the ropes when the sgt was not looking.

But I was reprieved. Somewhere in the machinery, a faceless cog discovered that a potential education sgt was taking twelve weeks to do his basic six weeks' training and posted me (still unconfident and unathletic) to the Depot of the Education Corps.

The Depot was at Beaconsfield, close by the Tudor-beamed and dainty tea shops. It was still the Army, but the Army ever so slightly softened; I was still a private, but the vision of three stripes and my own room glowed like an icon amongst the heathen.

One night whilst on guard duty I vomited. My stomach (always a rather delicate organ, more suited to a retired lady living in Broadstairs than an Army sgt) had decided to revolt against the strong tea and greasy fried eggs. I reported sick the next morning, which meant packing your small kit (I do not know what happened if you were too sick to do this) with regulation pyjamas prs 1, soap 1, towel 1, vest 1, socks prs 1, PT shoes (for use as slippers), pants 1, and housewife. The MO listened with apathy and pre-scribed M & D (Medicine and Duties). I was told to watch my diet: drink milk instead of tea, he said. Yes, sir, I said.

Three times a day I had to go and collect my spoonful of chalky white medicine.

'I always drink some before I go on the booze,' said the medical orderly cheerfully. 'It lines your stomach.'

In the Army you were not allowed to keep a bottle, but had to report for each dose. This suited me, as it was a pleasant walk to the MO hut, and it wasted a half hour.

I decided to avoid as many meals as possible. Instead of greasy breakfasts I had some cream crackers I kept in my locker, and water. I did not have the courage to ask the cook for weak tea (I could see him recoiling) but had asked him for milk as per MO's orders and he had said no. I cannot remember why he refused, but as a private I had learned that asking 'why?' was not the best way to make friends.

It was now December, snow had fallen and it was very cold. I found the solitary breakfasts of crackers and water (some lucky mornings I managed to scrounge hot water) poor protection against the cold and my habitual melancholy. The Army on a full stomach was depressing enough, but on cream crackers it was suicidal. I had fantasies of deserting, but the thought of glasshouse food (being a natural pessimist, I knew I would be caught) stopped me.

As soon as my duties were over, I would leave the Depot and hurry to the local beamed teashop and gorge myself on poached eggs and toast and weak tea. I began to feel even more like an old lady and less like a soldier than ever.

Christmas was coming, the goose was getting fat and I was

tucking into cream crackers and hot water. I prayed that God would try and do something about my stomach. I depended on God a great deal because I had realised the MO was not very interested in my stomach. I do not know if it was God or the doses of Mag. Trisilicate but after a few weeks my stomach stopped aching and settled down to Army food again. But I continued to treat it with respect and vetted everything I sent down.

Whilst we learned to become sgt/instructors we were watched to see if we were suitable NCO material. We knew the Army was short of ed. sgts, so we assumed that we would all pass out, provided we did not strike anyone.

One morning all the names of the promoted privates were posted up on the notice board. Everyone's name was there except for mine and one other (and he was even more unlike a potential sgt than I was).

The CO sent for me.

'I'm rather worried about you,' he said. 'We've been observing you and we feel you're not very happy in the Army.'

'Oh, no, sir,' I said, 'I've just got this miserable face. I can't help it. Even when I'm feeling very happy, I look gloomy.'

He looked unconvinced.

'You're not a Bolshie, are you?'

'Goodness, no, sir.' I desperately tried to think of something to convince him of my essential rightness as NCO material. My dreams of a room of my own were fading away.

'In fact, sir, before I joined the Army, I drew for Punch.' (I had drawn some very small headings for them but I did not think I needed to be too specific about the size at this moment.) 'Well, I wouldn't draw for Punch if I was a Bolshie, would I, sir?'

He smiled and leaned forward.

'Really . . . Punch, eh? You must do some jokes for us. Lots of material here . . . ha . . ha . . . Well, that's all right, then . . .'

And it was. The next day my promotion was announced in Part One orders and I was through to the splendours of Sergeant-hood and a room of my own.

I was posted as an education sgt (my fresh white stripes glowing on my slightly grubby battledress) to the Depot of the Veterinary Corps.

'It's a tricky posting,' said the major, 'but you're resilient.'

Am I? I thought.

The Depot was in Melton Mowbray, where they make pies and pet food, surrounded by lovely countryside and posh people hunting foxes. The Depot trained men, horses and dogs. Mainly dogs and dog handlers: the horses were remnants of the past.

The sergeants' mess was a strange mixture of dog men and horse men, both groups always telling each other of the natural superiority of their own animals. The horse men were older and nicer; some remembered the cavalry. The dog men were tougher, more like policemen.

As I knew nothing about either dogs or horses, I found it difficult to enter into the conversations. Or what passed for conversation. The talk was ritualised into mocking, sneering, swearing and joking. The dog men sneered at the horse men for having a cushy life, whilst they did the real work. The horse men mocked the others for training dogs, whilst they handled the only intelligent creatures in the Depot, horses.

I was frightened of both the enormous horses and the enormous alsatians, so I kept away from the working part of the Depot. I had a school room, a library and my own room in a hut at the far end of the Depot, and could retreat there and be forgotten.

I was called 'Schoolie', the traditional name for the education sgt, which gives some indication of the contempt the subject was held in by the rest of the Army.

I was an ersatz sergeant. The rank was given for the sake of discipline (instruction equals telling them equals rank) but everyone knew you had not earned the stripes the hard way. I was not a sgt in my bones. I did not stand up straight; I tended to sag in the middle. My clothes were crumpled, no matter how often I ironed them. My brasses glowered rather than glowed, and there were always bits of dried Brasso visible on the matted green blanco. My hair was not worn as close to the skull as that of the other sgts. I had no medals, I had fought no wars.

The real sgts bored me, and I am sure I irritated them. The mess was claustrophobic. The same jokes, the same exchanges every day. One sgt used to say to the mess waiter every night after supper, 'Serve the coffee in the drawing-room near the potted palms,' and laugh. He always called rice pudding 'Chinese wedding cake'. I used to tense myself, waiting for him to say, 'I'll have the Chinese wedding cake" and want to poison it. I used to eat quickly and escape as soon as possible.

It was like a soft prison; or an atheistic monastery.

I went to the cinema in Nottingham two or three times a week. I went to dances. I read like an addict. I wrote a little. I tried to do some cartoons for *Soldier* magazine, without any success.

I spent most of my service with the Veterinary Corps. It was my own fault that I learned nothing about animals, but I learned about people. I learned how to manage and tame the Army system. I learned how to avoid trouble.

I enjoyed teaching, organising the classes and cramming the soldiers through their Certificate of Education. The training officer and I made an unspoken pact. I would get the men their Certificates, and I would be allowed to go my own way.

I started a magazine for all the other education sgts in North Midland District. It was mostly written by myself, and run off on an old duplicator, but I did not care. It helped to keep me from falling fast asleep.

I started a film society at the camp because I wanted to see some old films from the British Film Institute, and a small huddle of soldiers who were broke and could not afford to go into Nottingham would come once a fortnight and see Buster Keaton and two free films from the Shell Film Unit.

I tried to encourage some of my pupils to read the books in the unit library, but soon gave up evangelical work as too difficult and irrelevant to their lives. I learned a lot about the problems of communicating with people: I remember spending ten minutes discussing, 'Should Capital Punishment be Abolished?' and then reading in one soldier's essay, 'Capital punishment should not be abolished. It should be made stricter.'

I used to get up too late for breakfast, so illicitly cooked for myself in my room on a tiny hotplate which I ran off the lamp. The same heater helped to warm the wooden room in winter. I had a large adaptor on the lamp, so I could have a radio, light and hotplate all on at the same time. I made tea and boiled eggs every morning until I fused all the lights, and someone got suspicious, and I had to give up cooked breakfasts.

Usually I rose only fifteen minutes before my first class at nine o'clock. A quick shave, wash, dress and next door to work.

One morning I woke at eight-thirty and was lying on the bed, thinking about getting up, when there was a loud knocking on the door. Having learnt to be cautious, I didn't shout 'fuck off', but lay still. The knocking continued louder and an officer-class voice shouted:

'Are you there, sergeant?' I carefully got up, crept to the door, and looked through the keyhole. There was the District Education Officer, on a surprise inspection visit.

I did not think he would appreciate being greeted by an undressed, unshaven education sgt, so I froze. More banging, more shouting. More trying the door handle. Fortunately I always kept the door locked at night. At last he stamped off.

I dressed, rushed out to the washroom to shave, cut myself, rushed back to my room, picked up some books to look busy, and then walked as calmly as I could across the parade ground. The officer was at the far end just by the adjutant's office.

'Sergeant!' he shouted.

'Good morning, sir,' I said.

'Where have you been? I tried your room. I tried the library.' He seemed annoyed.

'I was in the cookhouse, sir, putting up some posters for my next film show.'

I hoped he would not go and see them, because they were not there.

'Well, sergeant, come and show me your school room. You should be in your library at this time.'

He was very keen, so I did not like to tell him that I only loaned out two books a week, and certainly none at nine o'clock in the morning.

The Army was an education. It helped me to find myself in ways that I never had at art school. Being in an alien group made me define my own boundaries. At art school, at home, always surrounded by sympathetic, nice, liberal people, I had merged with them and never discovered my identity. Here, amongst all the fuck me, fuck you, fuck the expense give the cat a goldfish, I felt more myself.

There was 'them' and there was 'me'. They spoke a language that said 'cunt' instead of 'woman' and 'fuck' instead of 'love'. A landscape that was only straight lines. A country where it was a virtue not to think, not to use your imagination. If it stands still, paint it; it it moves, salute it; if it thinks, bellow at it.

I knew I was different and accepted it. At school I had felt different as a Jew, and had felt uneasy about it. Here, I was different and thanked God for it. I did not want to be a real sergeant. I was disguised as one and counted the days when I could shed it and get on with my real life.

STUART CRAMPIN

National Service was my first taste, perhaps my only taste, of complete personal freedom. In the RAF I found myself surrounded by restrictions, many of them unbelievably asinine and trivial, but, for two years, I was completely without responsibility, in any sense that mattered to me. Barring shooting the CO, or raping his wife, no matter what I did I would be out in the free world again in two years' time, not much better and not much worse for anything I might do in the RAF. I should say that it was a rather unpleasant six months before I realised that freedom was there to be taken, but, for the last year at least, I enjoyed myself and found a certain amount of satisfaction in life.

The satisfaction came because I was doing a job – repairing electronic equipment – that was essential to the operation of flying stations. This equipment was not functioning properly when we arrived at a station, and it was, more often than not, by the time we came to leave, and flying (in particular night flying) could resume again. The enjoyment came because I was given the means to have a considerable amount of control over my immediate circumstances. This was a great deal better than most other servicemen I met, of all ranks, who seemed to be much bullied by the system.

I chose to do my National Service before going up to read Maths at university. If I had taken the alternative of going to university first I would have found that the call-up had ended by the time I came to do it. This was ironic, but, having my time again,

I would make the same decision for the advantages that being a little older and a little more experienced gave me at university. I was an adult (you ought to have seen me before!) by the time I reached university and was ready to make the most of it. Poor lads straight from school spent the first years at university sloughing off their schoolboy shells, and some never succeeded.

I entered the RAF straight from school, having spent a sheltered youth in the Essex countryside. The war had largely passed me by. The planes flew over on their way to London, but only once were bombs dropped on the village. A string of six fell across the village, the last falling a tennis court away, which was the closest I got to a military happening until I joined up.

National Service was a revelation, a great force for democracy, a levelling down to the lowest level. There was I, an innocent country boy, thrust into a billet with twenty others drawn from town and country, rich and poor, articulate and inarticulate. The whole spectrum of human life was thrown at my feet: its filthy underwear, its ingrowing toe-nails, its unwashed bodies, the whole gamut of squalid personal habits. Some, admittedly, had a certain practicality, like the pyjama pocket stuffed with bits of picked toe-nail: the pieces were so much more uncomfortable to lie on if scattered around in the bed.

Some aspects of this service life had a direct and lasting effect on me. On the first day, I heard an airman use one particular seven-letter-word a hundred and eleven times in an hour; then, as I counted, I could not believe it, but after habitual usage it was many years before my own language became acceptable again. My teeth will never recover from the treatment they received then: I suppose the dentists had to train on somebody for their lucrative civvy practices, but as I patronise them now I have a certain amount of resentment and feel I have been used. One aspect at least had a strong antiseptic effect: I was turned permanently against gambling by the sight of the habitual losers handing over the bulk of their money on pay-day to satisfy their previous losses at cards (these losers invariably thought that winning at cards was a question of luck, which it so patently was not).

I had no previous knowledge of electronics, but the RAF trained me as a radio serviceman in sixteen weeks at a camp in Wiltshire. It was the first time I had been to Wiltshire, and whenever I was allowed off camp I walked over the downs, among those peaceful hill forts, white horses and barrows, dykes and stone circles. This escape into the lonely places helped me to adjust to service life.

It was exciting, too. I once had to make friends with a bull in the middle of a very large field, where I came across it suddenly in a very thick mist: the only time I felt my life might have been in danger in the RAF.

At the end of my training, by great good fortune, I was posted to RAF Chigwell to work on the emergency servicing of radio equipment at 4GRSS (I can now only guess at Fourth Ground Radio Service Squadron). Chigwell had much to recommend itself to me. It was the station within shortest hitch-hiking distance of home and cooking, it was on one end of the Central Line so I could begin to enjoy the London theatres, it was near Epping Forest, surrounded with parks and playing fields, and the local pub was the King's Head, 'with more gable ends than a lazy man would care to count on a sunny day'. The advantages were many, and included, most fortunately for us, several hospitals and nursing homes a few miles distant filled with young nurses, who, mostly being away from home for the first time like us, were only too pleased to find a large group of unattached males nearby.

The camp was small, with about two hundred airmen. Of these, thirty like myself had volunteered to be on call for emergency servicing, and were responsible for repairing any breakdown of ground radio equipment on the seventy RAF stations and installations in the south-east quarter of England (and also, oddly, Gibraltar). We thirty kindred spirits were made up of about half National Servicemen and half Regulars. The Regulars (mostly young men who had signed on as apprentices before reaching years of discretion) were probably a little unsettled by the influx of National Servicemen, who, although superficially similar in ability and outlook, had prospects in the free world so much better than the apprentice boys. One of the recurring topics of conversation of these unfortunate Regulars was how long it would be before they could buy themselves out of the RAF.

Repairing electronic equipment sounds more skilled than it actually turned out to be, although I readily admit to being not the most expert of my colleagues. All I had to do was follow a circuit diagram, and use an AVO meter. I should add that, eighteen years ago, transistors and integrated circuits had not made any general appearance, certainly not in the RAF. So there were no nasty little fiddly bits: there were great big valves which usually stopped glowing if they failed, capacitors which leaked messily if they went wrong, and resistances which could always be checked with an AVO and the colour-code mnemonic *Black Boys Rape Our*

Young Girls But Violet Goes Willingly. That was all I needed to carve out a small niche for myself as an expert in the repair of the Cathode Ray Direction Follower.

The CRDF was important to the operation of the Control Tower. It was not essential in clear visibility when pilots could find their own way down, but was used to locate and talk planes down at night and in poor visibility. In East Anglia, where there were many flying stations, visibility can change dramatically in just a few minutes if the mist descends. There was one occasion, I remember, when a flight of Hunters (or was it Vampires, or some other macabre flock?) was returning to a station in Norfolk when the mist came down, and at the last moment the CRDF failed. The planes had to be diverted elsewhere, and one or two of them did not make it. Several mischances combined, but if the CRDF had been working the crashes would not have happened. It certainly gave one a sense of accomplishing something, having arrived at a night flying station which was at a standstill because the CRDF was unserviceable, and leaving a few hours, or a few days, later as the planes were taking off again.

Most of the electronic equipment systems we serviced were comparatively straightforward (I did not service radar, although some of us did), and if something went wrong it was quite easy to see which unit was causing the trouble and easy for the station signals staff to replace it, if they had a spare. The CRDF was a little more complicated, involving a number of elements linked together: radio transmitters and receivers, a direction sensor, cathode ray tubes, and, my own particular speciality, a Heath-Robinson box, which, on a pulsed command from the Control Tower, would select a pre-tuned radio channel at the remote end. This channel selector switch worked mechanically; it dated from the nineteen-forties. It was a box eight inches square by three inches deep, containing a few hundred cogs, cams, washers, nuts, and relays. It was really very simple in principle but often troublesome in practice, as it would only function correctly when the various tensions were within fairly narrow limits. The simplicity of the principle sometimes induced stations signals to meddle (they were not supposed to) usually without any improvement, even if they were able to assemble it again. I found it added to my comfort considerably on a strange camp when the signals staff were anxious that I should not give an adverse report.

When a station cabled a breakdown we would, depending on the nature of the fault, pack a selection of tools, spare parts, and replacement units, and, if necessary, be on our way in a couple of hours. I usually went by pick-up, with a driver, but sometimes drearily alone by train, and trains in remote country districts were dreary – so much so that some have since just sunk into oblivion. The CRDF had a sensor at the remote end, usually a few miles off the runway, which picked up the direction of the incoming radio signal from an aircraft and displayed it on a cathode ray screen on the main console of the Control Tower. The main console seldom went wrong except for the havoc wrought by the Air Controllers' feet resting on the controls, and most of my time was spent working on the remote end. We could only work on the equipment when the Control Tower was not in use, so this usually meant working overnight. Some of my most pleasant memories of the RAF are of the long hours of the early morning spent in the little CRDF huts, often out of sight of the runway, but always surrounded by fields, and sometimes by trees.

These were the first times that I had regularly stayed up overnight, heard the dawn chorus and watched the lightening landscape divided by the thin stripe of early morning mist. Many of the stations were in the more remote parts of East Anglia where there were many birds, and always mist in the mornings.

The early morning is very conducive to thought, especially alone or with a sleeping companion, and I learnt a great deal about myself in those long overnight hours. I discovered by trial that previously I, like most other people, ate far too much and slept far too much. I thought very much about myself, and what I wanted to do. Of course, I wanted to paint and write, and get away from the mechanical things of life typified by the RAF; and also, for some reasons never quite clear to me, I decided that one of the things I most wanted to do was rock-climb. Thinking about university, I was partly disillusioned by the RAF. I guessed, correctly, that the awful inadequacies of the RAF probably reflected the inadequacies of other large organisations, including universities. With such inadequacies, God knows how we ever won a war: just think what the other side must have been like! In justice to the RAF, or rather to the people of Great Britain, it must be the case, it just must, that when there is a national emergency, everyone's dedication, especially the serviceman's, compensates for the inadequacies.

This vagrant life, working for a few days on one station then on another, had many advantages. To some extent, I became a manipulator, a voyeur, rather than a participant in Service life.

One was hedged around by petty restrictions; many, obviously outdated, were heirlooms of an infantry forefather. Outdated, but perforce obeyed by all except a select band, including my companions, who were able to escape the consequences of bending many of the rules. But this escape was achieved only at the cost of much hard work for the RAF in return. On our own camp, our immediate officers recognised this hard work. We could not be made to be on call twenty-four hours a day, and we could not be made to work very irregular and sometimes very lengthy hours. They recognised that we were volunteers, and were often hard-pressed, and so gave us many privileges to encourage us; or, more correctly, turned a blind eye when we took privileges for ourselves.

We usually worked through the night for one or two nights each week, for which we were accorded time-off in lieu, at the rate of about one half day off for each overnight shift. Thus, in a good week, we could accumulate about one day's leave, giving us four or five weeks' annual vacation above the standard fifteen days. In fact, in this as in so many other things, we never claimed all our rights; the system would have collapsed had we done so, and, after all, we did not wish to kill the goose . . .

There were some disadvantages to being on emergency services. The inability to forecast where we would be in five hours' time was slightly inconvenient for theatre seats (although lack of money usually forced me up to unbookable circles anyway), but was vastly inconvenient for the nurses. It was very frustrating always losing the prettiest nurses to clerks, cooks, orderlies, to anybody in fact who could make and, more importantly, keep a date.

Travelling and working irregular hours, as we did, we could easily arrange to be out of camp, or sleeping after a late return, whenever there was something unpleasant on camp we wished to avoid, such as a parade or an inspection. In fact, the only time in my blameless Service career that I was actually put on a charge was on one of these occasions. I thought the parade had started, and was just on my way to slip out of the gate for a day in town, using up some of my time-off in lieu, when I happened to bump into the CO on his way to take the salute. Had it been anyone else, my later explanations would probably have got me off, but as it was a small example was made of me for the sake of the CO. Even then, an emergency job turned up and I was on another camp within twenty-four hours, unavoidably prevented from reporting in full kit to the guard house every six hours.

On other camps, as we were for much of our time, we were able to arrange our lives to an even greater extent, and we worked, ate and slept as we liked. The only person who knew what we were supposed to be doing was the signals officer. There were exceptions, but most of the signals officers that I came across seemed to be appointed on the principle used to select government ministers: that they should be educated amateurs, and have no practical experience of what they were administrating. Signals officers were usually accommodating, partly no doubt because half the time the faults were due to the carelessness or negligence of their staff, which they were in no position to judge. On these camps we worked irregular hours to fit in with the use of the Control Tower and the urgency of the repair. We turned up at the cookhouse whenever we felt like a meal, or took packed food and a tea urn out to the CRDF hut; all with the authority of the signals officer, if authority were needed. There was considerable advantage in eating this way, for individual and freshly cooked meals were much superior to the mass-produced cookhouse nosh.

There was one particularly irritating aspect to visiting other camps on a temporary basis, as we did: we were supposed to take up residence in the Transit Billet. This limbo was intended primarily to be used by men entering or leaving the camp who had either not yet been assigned to, or who had just left, their permanent billets. It was in the charge of the station warrant officer or the drill sergeant, the one embittered by having reached the top of his particular promotional tree and being barred, by lack of a commission, from higher things, and the other de-sensitised by years of bawling at unwilling men on parade grounds. In either case an uneasy landlord, and one who felt he had to make an example of the Transit Billet. Here, where the inmates were usually not yet fully employed, he decreed that there had to be a glowing testimony of his ability to inspire airmen to polish shiny floors, clean gleaming brasswork, and whiten alabaster walls, a place where one walked on little pads of blanket to show that at all times one was ready to improve the shining hour. He would feel free to demand of anyone unfortunate enough to be found lingering in his shrine that he perform this or that little act of adoration. In addition, the inhabitants of this feudal backwater were the natural prey of anyone about the camp who needed manpower. Whenever there was an unpleasant task to be performed, those in the Transit Billet would be the customary victims, for they had not yet established, or were in the process of relinquishing, relations with a particular unit, and had nobody else to appeal to for protection. There was also the principle that everyone should be kept fully employed, and if no useful job were to hand then tasks were invented. Every day, unfortunates moved coal from A to B (unbelievably dirty: at least miners got paid better than National Servicemen), or cleaned the less accessible areas of the cookhouse, which was a disgusting experience; not so much for the actuality, but for the evidence of what one had eaten in the past and might eat in the future. I cannot remember having seen a cockroach before I joined the RAF, and very few since, but in some cookhouses I remember, vividly, floors black with them. As evening fell, cockroaches would emerge from every crevice, black heaving fingers appearing above the picture rail, and every few moments a dropout would desert the rail and join the multitudes on the floor.

And this Transit Billet, with all its unpleasant associations, was supposed to be our official residence when visiting another camp. Our officers and the signals officers on the other camps recognised that it was impossible for men to live in these surroundings and still do skilled work, but it seemed the regulations could not be changed just for us. The usual way around this hazard was to roll up our bedding before we left 4GRSS, and take it with us in the van. This also avoided the tedious procedure of drawing bedding from the Bedding Store: open 1000-1200 hrs. except by special dispensation. Whenever we wanted to sleep, the driver and I would find a pair of beds in some strange billet, unroll our bedding and fall blissfully asleep. There was sometimes a bit of a fuss when the regular inhabitants woke up to find strangers in their midst, but, if the objections were becoming too forceful, we would just roll up our bedding and disappear once more. On several occasions because of our irregular wanderings we fell foul of the station warrant officer, who would shout at us, particularly when he discovered that we did not belong to his camp. As we came from another camp, he had little authority over us, and in particular could not charge us. Occasionally these warrant officers wrote incoherent letters back to 4GRSS (incoherent, because we never volunteered any sensible information about ourselves), but we could always think up suitable stories by the time we had returned. In any case we were performing a useful service, so our officers never actually charged us for misdemeanours on other camps. In fact few of us were ever traced, or rather the offence was seldom thought serious enough to bother another camp, although, of course, such behaviour on one's own camp would have had serious consequences.

Finally, after avoiding the Transit Billets on some seventy different RAF stations, and a total of 731 days since joining up (just my rotten luck to pick a leap year) the RAF released me. I was very relieved that, despite the Suez crisis which was coming to a head, the RAF decided that it could fulfil its commitments without me. At a final interview, the officer asked me, as he was required to do, whether I would like to sign on: I said, 'No, ... sir.' He handed me my discharge papers, which said that 2732972 SAC Crampin had been a 'satisfactory' aircraftsman, and that was goodbye.

I have thought more about National Service in the last few days than I have done in the seventeen years since I was demobbed, which was unbelievably, appallingly, almost half my lifetime ago. (And how archaic the word 'demobbed' sounds nowadays!). I went up immediately to university from the RAF, and my Service memories were quickly swamped by new and more vital experiences. More vital, because, unlike the RAF, these new experiences were a direct part of a continuing existence. Today, I find that the RAF is in a separate compartment of my memory which is almost untouched; undigested. I could easily slip back into the thoughts of sixteen years ago, and perhaps some of the speech patterns as well. So much so, that many of my feelings about the RAF are, or so I like to think, similar to those I had as a teenager, not too modified by later experience. Certainly I have followed trains of thought that I have not used for a very long time, and this is how I would prefer it; yesterday – particularly seventeen years ago – is after all very much less important than tomorrow. So I have reproduced a few of my thoughts fished straight from my memory, containing the crude judgements I made as a young Serviceman. I am unable to refine these judgements: it was so long ago, and I have no better information to go on, and, quite honestly, I do not care to.

Not thinking about National Service does not mean that I value the experience any the less: perhaps even the converse may apply. National Service is one of the enormous punctuation marks in my life; it prompted, and marks very distinctly, my transition to manhood: a sort of tribal initiation rite. I was an inexperienced country schoolboy when I joined up, and a man, not quite of the world, but a man nevertheless, by the time I was demobbed, and very well prepared for what I found at university; and, most important of all, I had learnt to organise my time. I consider that my returns from university were so much greater (I enjoyed my first few years intensely) because of the experience gained while in the RAF. Perhaps the two years' complete rest from studies, and freedom from responsibility, wild oats and all that (it is difficult to avoid clichés), also has something to do with it; and I had also learnt how lucky I was to be at university. Certainly, if students today are at all like I was then (highly unlikely, I should think), they would benefit from a maturing period after school. Not so much to see the world, which is rapidly becoming more uniform and less interesting, but to meet other people whose differences, despite the increasing ease of communication, so often seem to be widening.

I speak for myself; many people's experiences of National Service were rather different from my own (isn't everyone exceptional?), but mine were valuable to me. The RAF was an organisation whose rules could be stretched, if one was recognised as a hard worker, and life made more comfortable. I had stretched rules at school, but school was a place for children, and I had not expected to find similar situations in the grown-up world. But it is a lousy, rotten, infantile world and National Service helped to form the lousy, rotten, infantile people who make it. In the RAF, I learnt how to make use of the lousy, rotten system, and this was of great service to me at university, and (say it quietly) many times since, too.

MICHAEL HOLROYD

I was shot at first while attempting to serve a writ; then I was accidentally locked, among carcasses, into a huge butcher's fridge (a huge fridge belonging to a huge butcher) which had been a subject of complaint; finally I adjourned a complicated divorce case while our solicitor was in the lavatory so that the disgruntled parties remained married a further six months. But what I remember most vividly about my deferment as an unpaid solicitors' clerk were the long afternoons, doing nothing. It seemed incredible to me that we should spend so many hours behind our desks, while outside the sun shone. It was a denial of life, the rigours of which occupied with profit so much of our working time. Occasionally I wondered why the staff did not rebel and flood out into the streets and parks. Myself, I was held in check by the sternest spirit of cowardice: in particular a fear of the open-air life that awaited me if I abandoned law: two years' National Service in the Army. This formed my chief legal incentive. If I could stick the law long enough, I thought, perhaps the Army would melt away. One trouble was that my firm of solicitors had never encountered an articled clerk before, and did not know what to do. Eventually they transferred the guilt by paying me. I learnt nothing except, prudently, some details about the law of bankruptcy and something of the law of libel, both of which were to prove 'relevant' in literature.

It took about two years to demonstrate my unfittedness for any branch of the law, after which there was no further escape from

National Service. I wrote off enquiring about the possibilities, as an alternative to military service, of coalmining in South Wales or a Russian language course conducted in Cornwall; but the replies were discouraging. There was one more hurdle to fail. I did my best. With a pair of violet-tinted spectacles and an Irish walking-stick I advanced upon Reading where I was to be examined medically. I had been up late 'he previous night recalling past illnesses and had mustered an impressive garrison of them. Water-on-the-knee and in the eye, bow-legs, an allergy to elastoplast: I revealed all, I sang. The result was a disaster. After a gruelling day I was graded 3, ensuring for myself not exemption but the choice of two years either as an Army caterer or in the Pioneer Corps, digging field latrines. Throwing away my stick and spectacles I appealed, and admitting nothing beyond Church of England, was re-graded 1.

My first month in the Army I spent at home. I had been ordered to report to a barracks in Winchester, but on arrival found that no one was expecting me or knew what should be done. They were not pleased, the sergeants and captains, and inclined, I felt, to blame me for the mistake. Fortunately there was one other person in the same predicament, a brilliant public school cricketer. He arrived an hour after I had, twirling his arms and knocking imaginary balls for six, and it was wonderful to see how everyone cheered up. Old scores were swopped in an atmosphere of great geniality, and eventually someone with rank called out: 'You two better clear off home then'.

The journey back was intensely happy.

Next time my welcome was more orthodox. I was to spend ten weeks' basic training at Winchester, but within ten minutes I knew I could not last it. I was too old, too slow, too terrified. Everything appeared to be done so loudly and at such a speed. It was astonishing to me how anyone knew what to do next: I could find no way of telling, except by watching the others and then doing fractionally later whatever they did. It is usual for 'intellectuals' comically to exaggerate their deficiences as soldiers. This would be difficult for me: I was simply no good. I could always find reasons for doing things differently, and I could see no reason for calling a tree a 'bushy top object' in order to achieve what was termed 'simplicity'. It was this quality of military simplicity that constantly foxed me. But over the ten weeks at Winchester certain changes gradually began to take place within me. I started to lose things: I lost the habit of reading, I lost all privacy and, with this, part of my own identity. At times I almost lost consciousness: at least I never felt quite all there. This was a help. I began to belong more to the platoon, to take on a corporate identity, answering, with a shout, to a number. The Michael Holroyd who had arrived at Winchester could never have got through those weeks. I was someone different.

Towards the end of this period I was sent to Andover for a War Office Selection Board Examination to discover whether or not I was 'officer material'. The answer seemed to me perfectly obvious in advance. Nevertheless, I wanted to pass. To be an officer promised, or so I imagined, an easier existence; to fail, even here, could only bruise my vanity. For it seemed to me then that the secret of all life was the courage to say the word 'yes'; whereas now I know it is the ability to say 'no'. The Army taught me the wisdom of saying nothing.

The examination at Andover lasted three days and was divided into three sections: the paper, the vocal, and the muscular. At paperwork, which was my chosen medium, I hoped to score highly. I wrestled with the tactical questions very hard, advancing what I was afterwards told were many excellent reasons for all the wrong conclusions. There was, I believe, nothing I answered correctly. For someone who knew so little of military affairs, it was astonishing this knack I had for picking the loser.

At my lecture I spoke, interminably, on 'Sense of Humour'. No one, I was later promised, understood a word. It did not matter. What did matter was that I had spoken with confidence: unintelligible, unyielding, unamusing and unanswerable confidence, attributable to the fact that every word had been borrowed from someone else. The Army, which is not badly infested with literary knowledge, failed to recognise my plagiarisms as I plundered on. People who had not actually heard my lecture warmly approved my choice of subject.

'Is a sense of humour necessary to an officer?' one major asked me, laughing, during my interview. I vigorously asserted that it was.

'Why?' The question travelled without curiosity, and I spoke, in reply, of a Sense of Proportion, of rubbing shoulders with people in all walks of life, of the fine tradition of British humour. Like languages (for which I once had some small talent) humour could take you anywhere. I spoke of Churchill and, in the pauses, I twinkled wryly. What I said contradicted almost everything I had proclaimed at my lecture, which treated humour as a means of apprehending truth. But it was the right answer.

There remained the physical problem: how to get a group of men up two trees and across a river without touching any area coloured white, and with the aid of a crowbar and two barrels – all in ten minutes: *Go!* Had my life depended upon it I could not have succeeded. But we had, among our platoon of would-be officers, a burly marine. This giant, like a cart-horse, I loaded with wood, iron and flesh. He climbed, he waded, he ran, he swam. He was the apex of an upside-down pyramid of objects. His eyes and muscles bulged with unprecedented exertion, and we just did it; not by the correct method but simply through the superhuman efforts of this one man. The examiners were incredulous. This had never been done before, being obviously impossible: but it counted. There was, however, a corollary to this feat. When it came to the marine's turn to lead our platoon over another series of hazards he failed through sheer exhaustion.

By the skin of my teeth I passed. They had given me the benefit of the doubt, but I would have to 'buck my ideas up', they said, in the future. I was as much surprised by this qualification as by the result. Another National Serviceman there was sceptical. He had been once before, told the truth, and failed. Now, quite cynically, he had lied and they had let him through. So it was all a sham. But at one level at least I disagreed with him. For surely what they were testing was our acting ability. As officers we should be called upon to act with conviction, to spread the pretence that there was no danger, the fiction that we personally hated the enemy and that they detested us. We had to act with the authority necessary to suspend people's belief in reality. As for the examination, they knew it was nonsense, we knew it was nonsense: but could we be trusted to keep the secret? That was the key question.

I returned to Winchester expecting very shortly to be posted on, like a parcel, to Eaton Hall, the officer training school near Chester. But again there was a delay. While the riflemen and corporals departed, I, together with one tuberculosis-suspect, stayed on. It was not a matter of health in my case but of loyalty. The authorities had just noticed that my mother was the native of a neutral country, Sweden: and they bristled. For months this information, copied on to countless forms, had rested harmlessly in their files, but now, in their imaginations, it sprang to life. Something would have to be done. The first thing they did was to promote me to lance-corporal; the second to confine me, as if pregnant, to the barracks until investigations could be made. The barracks were empty and there was positively nothing to do: I should have been in my element. Yet one of the things I had lost (something that had been much exercised in my legal days) was a talent for motionless inactivity. The sergeant in charge of us was a civil man and not accustomed to being a military nurse. We peppered him with questions. Did I look like a spy? Was TB contagious? He relented and, for the sake of peace, allowed us out. At once, by means I have fortunately forgotten, we acquired a landrover and, replete with Army petrol and with my new friend at the wheel, we patrolled the countryside: paddling in the sea, eating strawberries in Berkshire with my grandmother, or simply lying in the sun on St Catherine's Hill overlooking Winchester. We went occasionally to films and more occasionally to restaurants, and stared pennilessly at girls in the streets. These days and weeks, stolen from the march of time, were sweet and, being timeless, have remained with me while more 'important' events have melted away. But one morning I was sent for, told I had been cleared, and ordered to proceed to Chester: *soonest*. There was no time to say goodbye. I never discovered whether my friend had TB, and cannot now even remember his name.

The training course at Chester lasted sixteen weeks, but the atmosphere was very different. We strode about exaggeratedly swinging our arms, our chins forward, our heels biting into the tarmac, beneath the shadow of that portentous pile, Eaton Hall, an absurd and grandiose folly of a building erected specifically without purpose. Everywhere bustled bellowing sergeant-majors, effete captains with canes treading delicately on their toes, and majors with moustaches.

'Some of you will be lucky enough to see active service,' we were told. Was I the only one who found such sentiments preposterous? There seemed no way of finding out, for our ranks of officer-cadets were criss-crossed with complicated lines of snobbery, assumed rather than felt I suspected, that prevented one of us from addressing another. The Guards could not accost the line regiments who were not tolerated by the Greenjackets who were hardly recognised by the Guards: it went something like that. Though the intention had been to instil us with a lively sense of competition, the result was fatuous. We reverted to the age of ten, squabbling over matters about which we had no experience, no real feeling and up to a few months ago no knowledge. The more tedious the subject, the more controversially we treated it.

If I was exempt from this epidemic, it was probably because I had been innoculated by my extra years. Another manifestation of my great age was less welcome. At Eaton Hall I met again a number of people I had not seen since my schooldays. Then they had been my juniors: now they were senior. I had always imagined that, through ease and indolence, I had been reasonably popular at school. I had never mastered the trick of severity; I had abolished beating – could amiable inertia go further? But my smiles of recognition now went unanswered. I had become an embarrassment, and had to act the stranger with people I thought I knew: a situation that had some of the qualities of nightmare.

On the whole I do not remember Eaton Hall well. There was not the same rhythm of uniformity as at Winchester, nor any chance to be an individual: we were types. I was beginning, however, to appreciate something important: the power and value of my absence. By taking a little thought I was able within seconds partially to eclipse myself. I became the sun in the eternal night of barrack life, not missing exactly but always unseen. It became difficult to focus upon me. If I was alone in a room, that room was usually considered empty; and this pleased me well. My hand would shoot up with meticulous timing, barely too late for everything: I was the ultimate non-volunteer. On the parade ground I placed myself in the middle rank, and towards the middle of it. Since no one had learnt my name, there was almost no method of communicating with me. So they let it go. By the end I had become almost wholly invisible. In this way I slipped quietly into my role of officer and gentleman.

There was still the problem of into which regiment I should be gazetted. None of them were keen to have such an inconspicuous asset. I made investigations, my preference being to join any body of men sunning themselves peacefully on some neutral territory. I invented, Bunbury-style, an uncle who, I maintained, had served with distinction in one of these choice regiments, for this was the only way of answering, to military satisfaction, the question of why I particularly wanted to join it. Eventually, at the request of the former, I was transferred from the Greenjackets to the Royal Fusiliers whose ultimate resting-place was Sutton Coldfield.

With the rank of second lieutenant in my brand new reluctant regiment, I left Eaton Hall for three weeks' leave. It was 1956, a peaceful time for me. I led the life of a lapsed scholar, sleeping late and sleeping early, and day-dreaming through the intervals. But towards the end of my leave a suspicion had begun to invade me that all was not well. Somehow, I felt out of step. This feeling crystallised at a cinema one evening during the Pathé News, when

I noticed some faces, furtive yet familiar, staring blindly from the screen. They belonged to comrades I had seen at Eaton Hall: I was sure of it. Their brave, trapped expressions, like zoo-animals', compelled attention. The commentator, suddenly very British, described the embarkation of the Royal Fusiliers to the Suez Canal to fight the Egyptians. It might have been, so far as I was concerned, some episode from ancient history. Like most serious, responsible people who do not wish to create trouble, I took no interest whatever in politics, being deaf to their music. When I read the newspapers I confined myself of course to the arts and book pages with, occasionally, a hopeful look down the obituaries. Rumours of war reached me, but I knew it was none of my business and I had no wish to pry. But now, in this cinema, I felt obliged to do what my father had always been begging me to do: put two and two together. The answer was very alarming: I was a deserter.

'Could they shoot me?' I asked a friend who had safely completed his National Service the previous year. He considered the question far too long.

'I should think they'd grant you a court martial,' he said, 'first'.

Since nothing, militarily speaking, had the power of surprising me, I was totally credulous. Lying awake that night it did not seem impossible that they might want to encourage the others by putting a pistol to my head. At the very least I would be reduced to the ranks and given a long spell in some Army jail. Next day I telephoned my adjutant, ostensibly on a small matter connected with dress. His reaction redoubled my apprehensions of the night. Cutting across a detailed query on buttons, he demanded to know 'where the hell' I was. Did I realise I had missed the war? I was to put myself at once under close arrest, then escort myself to the Tower of London where they would be expecting me.

'What shall I wear?' I persisted hopelessly.

I had never heard the adjutant laugh before.

'It won't matter where you're going,' he said.

I arrived at the Tower of London later that morning and, standing to attention, was cross-examined by two senior officers. Why, they asked, had I not responded to the urgent telegram summoning me to active service? Because, I answered easily (grateful to have such a simple reply) I had never received it. Disbelief shone frankly in their eyes. Why had I not put two and two together? I still had no answer to that.

I spent that night in 'Napoleon's Room' at the Tower. The

following day, unexpectedly, came a reprieve. The telegram, so far sunk without trace, had now resurfaced: it appeared that the adjutant, in the heat of war, had addressed it to himself. In these circumstances there was little they could do to me, except have me up on the minor charge of being improperly dressed.

'You are wearing the wrong buttons, Mr Holroyd. Kindly take a week's Orderly Officer.'

My week at the Tower was comparatively quiet. The only irregularity came as the result of a report in the *News Chronicle* that the Union Jack there was proudly flying upside down. This crisis, which I first took to be a practical joke, was quite beyond my reach, but before it could rise to a momentous level, a new job had been found for me. I was to travel to Dover and, high up on the cliffs there, enter Connaught Barracks. These premises, which had been empty since the Royal Fusiliers set sail for Egypt, were now to be put at the disposal of the refugees arriving from Hungary after the abortive uprising. It was Saturday evening. I hurried to my aunt (a lady who had once ridden to hounds) and extracted from her garage a very old bowler hat. Crowned with this, like a small black pimple at the top of my head, I descended properly dressed upon Dover. My instructions had been to make the refugees 'feel at home' on the cliffs. This was not only vague, I discovered, but a euphemism. For my job actually consisted of juggling with inadequate supplies of light bulbs and contraceptives so as to ensure that those Hungarians occupying unlit barrack rooms were protected with French letters, while those left unprotected were bathed, like battery hens, in a permanent glare. The supplies were to be alternated each night. After a few weeks the Hungarians went forth – and multiplied.

Our battles now were ended. The regiment disembarked, flags wettened in the rain, and the band struck hopefully up. They marched, our boys, through the glistening streets of Dover; they ascended the cliffs and were greeted rather diffidently by myself in white gloves. I had drawn myself up outside the officers' mess, in which I had rapidly re-grouped all the light bulbs, and kept saluting until told ('for heavens' sake') to stop. We had suffered, while abroad, twelve casualties, all of them rather remarkably shot in the back. At stand-to someone in a forward position would stretch or clear his throat, and a comrade behind, believing that the enemy were at last showing aggressive signs of life, would loose off a volley of bullets, wounding (often quite embarrasingly) some friend. All, however, were decorated with medals. I remember

Anthony Howard showing me his a number of times before, rather ostentatiously, losing it.

The presence of Anthony Howard in the regiment was an oasis. In the law I had sighted islands of boredom; in the Army I was marooned on the vast Continent itself. The boredom seeped down the walls of the officers' mess, saturated the atmosphere, infected our very souls. We lived in a void that was never painful while we remained motionless within its circumference, but which, after only forty-eight hours' leave, would appear horrific. One officer, I remember, whose room was above my own, practised coming to a halt. Over the year I spent at Dover that was all he did over and over again. 'One! Two!' he would call out, then bring his arm smartly down to his side and his heels together, bang! bang! For a second or two he would stand there, rigid, glazed. Then off round his room again: 'One! Two! Bang! Bang!' Only in Anthony Howard did I encounter someone to whom books were a part of life, and our conversations were like a private language. There existed between us, too, I realised, an unintentional rivalry as to who was more ill-adapted to this peculiar way ot life: a contest usually settled in my favour.

What I had learnt at Eaton Hall, I perfected at Dover. At the end of my year I stood one day behind two sergeants in the same company as myself who had just read my name on a noticeboard. Was this Holroyd a new officer? they wanted to know; had he arrived yet? My technique had been simple. I acquired a board on to which I fixed some pages of blank quarto paper. Armed with this implement and an expression of the sternest vacancy, I would strut about the barracks, ostensibly from one place to another but in fact from my bed back to my bed. I dissolved into the background; I was the very substance of camouflage. According to Tolstoy, the chief attraction of military service is that it consists of 'compulsory and irreproachable idleness.' But idleness of this calibre requires energy. To appear busy is almost as demanding as actually being busy. The advantage to me was that I understood the appearance far better than the reality. My part contained two words of monologue which I left trailing in the wake behind me as I sped urgently back to my bed.

'Carry on!' I would cry. And they did. I spent so much time in bed, a damp and draughty spot overlooking the sea, that I caught lumbago and was seldom fit enough to attend sick parade.

For two months we left Dover to perform 'exercises' round Salisbury Plain. On bookish rather than military grounds, I was appointed ADC to the brigade commander, that warrior-of-letters Brigadier Sir Bernard Fergusson. He was a genial, imposing man, built like a tree but with a flashing monocle (like my grandmother used to wear), belligerent whiskers and a caravan. I was required to find out what battles were being fought that day and then arrange for him to be driven to them. Shoulder to shoulder I would sit with him in the back of the official car, a map on my knees, discussing James Elroy Flecker and from time to time jerking forward, like some oarsman, to instruct the driver. Fortunately this driver knew the area extremely well. Even so, our progress was often haphazard, and however early we started we would arrive at some interval after the last shot had been fired. I began to wonder whether we should ever see a single hostility. At last, at midnight on Salisbury Plain, lost and alone, the brigade commander's patience snapped and he set me as a punishment to practising my salutes beneath the stars.

I seemed fated where Bernard Fergusson was concerned to do the wrong thing. When he invited me to dinner the invitation went astray; another time I took along Anthony Howard who lost his hat in the house, occasioning us all manner of dreadful misadventures in attempting to recapture it.

On a third and I believe final occasion, I was put in charge of the drinks and told to 'organise' them. Everything had been poured into identical decanters and looked pale amber. I began preparing impossible beverages for the guests, all of whom were too polite to object, though their expressions were painful enough.

Suddenly Bernard Fergusson appeared before me, barked: 'I'll have my usual,' and vanished into an ambush of his visitors. I poured a stiff whisky, handed it to him: and with a gasp he spat it on to the floor.

A ring formed round us as for a fight, while Fergusson demanded to know why I had given him a brimming glass of sherry-and-soda. At that moment, tripping over the carpet, L. P. Hartley came to my rescue.

'But I heard you ask for that,' he lied. 'I distinctly heard you.' During all my time in the army, this was the greatest act of bravery I witnessed.

I passed the last four months of my military career at the War Office. These were the first days of the amalgamation of regiments and the rundown of the Army as a whole: 'streamlining' it was bravely called. In company with one other National Service subaltern, a nice intelligent man named Smout (whom I suspect of having later written a history of Scotland), I was put in charge of redundancy. We divided the country up, the two of us, and went to work. Since our recommendations were invariably accepted this was, I suppose, a taste of real power. Majors and colonels of all conditions would send us their forms giving reasons why they should stay or go. Sometimes they wrote in desperation, petitioning us not to fling them back into the civilian life they had never known; either that, or they would describe the joys of managing an egg farm in the Hebrides, a toy shop at Staines, or their qualifications for taking the cloth. It was ironic that the breed of person who had made much of one's life so uncomfortable over the past two years should apparently (and to some degree literally) be at one's mercy. But although I could appreciate the irony, the power itself was empty. As a driving force, power has never really moved me from a stationary position; and as a literary theme it seems to me less rich than love and death, in so far as it is separable from them. But at the War Office, power in all its emptiness enhaloed me: like a mirage that, seen clearly from a distance, vanished once it is reached. The style and manifestations of it, however, adhered to me like a caricature of the real thing. I was given the rank of Temporary Unpaid Acting Captain: a dizzy pinacle for a National Serviceman. And I lived up to it. On the telephone my voice was so unaccommodating that officers up to the rank of colonel felt it proper to address me as 'Sir': it was my finest hour.

Within minutes it was over: there were simply no more field officers to axe. One of the last, I noticed, had been a colonel in my own regiment, a moon-struck man with a cat, who became television critic for a fascist weekly. We had sent them all packing and now it was our own turn, Smout's and mine. For a long time I had counted off the days till my release. Now, three weeks early, it came out of the blue, taking me by surprise. I was free.

What had I gained from National Service? Time: I had certainly gained that. At twenty-three I had a little more confidence – not much, but enough to know what I did not like. I had also saved a little money to buy myself more time in which to start writing.

I believe I also learnt something of the twin relationship between dullness and danger. The two appeared to stand at opposite ends of a line that had been coiled into a circle. Those who have some imaginative life of their own will sometimes, as a form of respite, unsuccessfully seek out the plains of boredom; it is only the others with a natural supply of inner tedium who try to lose it in 'exciting' or 'important' lives. The motto of the Army, 'Service not self', seemed to me a dangerous one because it attempted to transfer to society the individual's blunted hopes of personal happiness. Since there is a tendency in every mass movement to reproduce the faults of the movement from which it is reacting, 'alternative' usually means the same. Recent radical and revolutionary groups are mostly attempts to escape from individuality into an ideal collective sphere where 'every man shifts for all the rest, and let no man take care of himself'. In all the talk, for example, about Vietnam I have listened keenly for some admission of fear. Instead there have been endless words on ethics, humanitarianism, progress, and international politics. I longed for a bit of honest cowardice, for some humour, for something personal. What I heard was truth without sincerity: the canned stuff.

If it is true that we regret only what we fail to do, then this may account for my failure to regret those two long improbable years. But at each international crisis over the following two years, a practical joker would telephone me in the early morning and pretend to be our adjutant, or some War Office official summoning me back as a reservist. Then truly, for a moment or two, I would know fear.

In more specific matters I am still waiting for opportunities to exercise my full complement of military skills. Like Lord Reith, I have not been fully stretched. I was trained as fire officer and as officer in charge of chemical warfare, but so far have held my expertise in abeyance. My inability to drive any known vehicle did not disqualify my serving as transport officer, and I understand now that I could have awarded myself a driving licence, thereby avoiding the tortured business of passing my test.

In other respects the Army did not greatly affect me. Inside the soldier had been the writer struggling not to get out. After National Service had deposited me back, like driftwood, on the slopes of civilian life, the writer began, very cautiously, to emerge. Those things I had lost in the army – privacy and the habit of reading – returned, so that I now enjoy them with greater relish. I still speak no languages; I still have difficulty over two and two, though I suspect that the right answer is often to be found by subtracting them. Responsibility and the duty and privilege of making decisions were reputed to be the special pre-requisites of an officer: in which case I may have contracted an allergy to them. I have no passion to be married to responsibility, and I have learnt to postpone most decisions until the reasons for taking them have long disappeared. My campaign in the Army was wholly defensive: it did little to prepare me for the real warfare of literary life.

BERNARD PALMER

I could not swim so it was not to be the Navy, and, as the Air Force glistened with Brylcream, I was certain about one thing only: it had to be the Army. But which unit? Not the PBI, for a start. When the time for battle came, I decided I would ride. I told my widowed mum it was to be the cavalry for her son and she looked almost pleased. The day of the medical, greatly feared, duly came and I was surprised at having to lower my trousers and cough. Something presumably jumped and I was fit for the Royal Armoured Corps.

As I set out for Catterick clutching my railway warrant I reflected how in 1939 they had tied a label round my neck and sent me to sanctuary in Lacock Abbey. With Hitler three years dead, I was on my way to the 8th Royal Tank Regiment to help keep the Russians out of Western Europe. I was innocent of all things military. Never having been in the north of England before, I grabbed a quick look at Stephenson's Rocket on the station platform before they grabbed me. They did not seem too bad. Jolly, friendly fellows: a bit rough, but not out to cow us into submission. We nig-nogs seemed a nice enough crowd but it was amazing how rapidly we sorted ourselves out: accent chimed with accent, prejudice with prejudice. I was middle-of-the-road London Grammar School. To one side was a crowd of working lads, some of whom I eyed apprehensively, envying the way they seemed to be on the same wavelength as the NCOs. Could it be that four extra years of school seemed something of a drawback? For the first time in my life education appeared to be an object of pity, not envy. To the other side, the self-conscious élite of the public schoolboys, a small minority who clearly felt the Army had been invented just for them. I studied them with curiosity. I found an ally in Terry, whose name came next to mine in the endless queues and name rosters and whose background was similar. Kitted out with all the Army's strange paraphernalia, and not a little elated, I fell asleep in a large rambling noisy set of shacks called a spider, and woke next day not a Private merely, but a Trooper.

It turned out to be very like school after all, this man's world. Life quickly resolved itself into a comfortable round of drill, instruction, talks and meals. The only novelties were expeditions to the NAAFI and commands like 'Fall out for a smoke break'. Money was a problem, though. Nobody had any on a Thursday except the naturally thrifty, and the non-smokers. It took the tender-hearted like myself at least three weeks to develop routines sufficiently convincing to repel persistent cadgers. The cry for sharing 'two's up' entered my vocabulary and the affluent threw their fag-ends to the rabble like Boyars beset by the peasantry. Although I smoked at this time I used to marvel at the lower depths of squalor of our dawn awakening. It started with crash crash, wrench wrench, and the corporal bellowing 'Rise and shine! Let's have you! I said get up, you fucking wankers!' I resented this particular slander. Wanking was impossible, I had found, beyond the confines of domestic privacy. Besides, wasn't the tea stiff with bromide? More sounds of crashing, wrenching and writhing further up the spider. No. 2 troop of C squadron lay slaughtered in their pits. Feebly beside me an arm from the next bed began groping on the locker. Fingers closed on an inch butt of fag. Spurt of match and the poor bastard sank back on to the pillow with a groan. More spurts, more groans: everywhere. Not a foot found the floor without this ritual, and I acquired a life-long aversion to nicotine before breakfast.

The barrack-room and the parade ground were the twin theatres of our lives. I was totally unprepared for both. Regimentation was alien yet tolerable, but to communal life of this intensity I was a stranger. Observation widened, wits sharpened and new social gears were cut. Bull in the barrack-room and drill on the square dominate a soldier's activity. You have to discover them for yourself but they are immense clichés and nothing new is likely to be said of them. I passed muster, more or less, in both. Being rather short, I found myself invariably at the centrally lowest point of the line and I speedily learned that the lowest like the highest tend to attract the eye. If you are five feet five inches, a point to note the next time they bring in National Service (if there is time, that is) is that the 303 rifle is about six inches longer than you are. The task of the drill sergeant is to make thirty men react and move as one. It surprised me, the odd clod apart, how easy it is to achieve this. Even the most resentful get caught up in it and after four weeks we were swinging along to the strains of 'My Boy Willie' exhibiting bags of swank. If ever I detested a concept, it was bags of swank but I got to apply it. I was at the time corresponding with a former member of the Hitler Youth, a result of the desire of my ex-form master to civilise the Nazi, and I sometimes used to think of him while apoplectic sergeants quivered millimetres from my stony eyeballs.

In the barrack-room we explored who we all were and tested our new-found experiences on each other. Only one person was on equally good terms with everybody. He fascinated and charmed lieutenant and lout alike. Slight, raven-haired and exquisite, Paul dazzled everyone with his accent, rings, long cigarette-holder and instant repartee. One night, having effortlessly creased his trousers and bulled his boots to perfection ages before everyone else, he climbed into bed, lit-up the ebony holder and, as he hurled his witty darts into his willing victims, he proceeded to do up his entire head in paper curlers. This barrack-room Noel Coward to my not entirely innocent eye displayed no trace of effeminacy. This is precisely what baffled everybody. Shortly after he disappeared to WOSB and was never, alas, seen again.

There was also Smiler. To me he represented the ultimate in depravity. He led a pack of six or so hyenas from the far end of the barrack-room. Their jargon was that of Borstal and the prison. Menace, and how easily they rattled we conformist dullards, was their forte and for obscenity HM Forces were their debtors. But they had a style as effective and coherent as that of the public schoolboys who affected not to notice them (save of course for the ineffable Paul) but who were careful not to try conclusions. After all, they would soon be leaving them behind. One night Smiler hit on a tease. Over the blanco and the brasso, talk invariably turned to cunt. The virgins present (say 98% of us) listened respectfully while our corporal (reduced, we gathered, from sergeant for unspeakable but rewarding crimes) detailed his prowess with French tarts clad de rigueur in black stockings and nothing else.

After a night or two of this, Smiler put down his boots and bulling bone and, grinning hideously to his troops, advanced to the centre of the hut, saying:

'O.K., you fuckers, let's see what you've got . . .''

He unbuttoned his fly and lay a massive but flaccid member on the wooden table.

'I can lay eight half-crowns beside that,' he leered. 'Get 'em out. Let's see yer. If it's longer, double or quits.'

There were no takers and the voice of the corporal was heard no more in the land.

Intelligence and aptitude tests were to be my salvation. It had never been explained to me that I might qualify for a National Service Commission. We wrote a few simple papers, played with some nuts and bolts and sat back for the results. So this was the way out, WOSB and the golden trail to the officers' mess. I could not believe my luck. But I failed. I was incredulous and so of course were my sixth form peers. As one by one they departed to glory I settled into a black despair nourished by years of school first prizes and an appearance on 'Top of the Form.' Smiler, *mon semblable, mon frère,* had never seemed grosser and more palpably terrifying. I actually summoned up courage to claim an interview of the adjutant. Left right left right left right: he was sorry but I must proceed to my next unit and take it up with them if I felt inclined. Meanwhile would I please get on with the job of being a wireless operator in a tank? Left right left right left right left right.

I joined the 8th King's Royal Irish Hussars on a deserted aerodrome near Leicester. O brave new world. At first I thought we were being delivered into some foreign mercenary Army. Why were the officers caparisoned in this foreign headgear? Polish, it seemed. In fact it was Spanish. The 8th KRIH is the only British regiment whose officers are permitted to wear an enemy forage cap. In the Peninsular War they stripped a hostile army and took to themselves their crossbelts and a dark green cap like the one with tassels usually seen on General Franco. The Irish Hussars of course embroidered the brilliant gold V-bands that edge their cap with shamrock. These living symbolic contacts with history text-books were awe-inspiring. Not only that, but these Hussars had even charged with the Light Brigade. And were we schoolboy National Servicemen to follow the six hundred into the valley of death? Curious to learn that this regiment, then in armoured cars, had been overrun by Rommel in the Western desert and taken lock,

stock and barrel into prison camp. PRISTINAE VIRTUTIS MEMORES –
Mindful of former valour was its motto.

The unit was recently back in Britain after a generation spent
abroad. Its attitudes and atmosphere were totally different to the
8th RTR. It had a kind of family feel. The senior officers were
battle-scarred cavalry men of the old school: charming, kindly,
faintly academic even. The young officers, especially the subalterns
whom I learned with interest were titled 'Cornets of Horse', were
languid, polished and casual. The NCOs did not bully or lecture.
Discipline tended to run in fits and starts. I had the feeling that this
distinguished regiment dating back to 1693 was somewhat baffled
by its new-found task of training bulk intakes of National Servicemen in peace time. At Catterick I had been trained as a wireless
operator but it had all been classroom stuff. Radio net exercises
had been conducted in lorries dashing about the Yorkshire moors
and County Durham. Now I found myself in the turret of a thirty-
ton Comet tank fighting to keep the damn thing on tune and strain-
ing to interpret the crackling, fading orders.

The first time I peered into the turret of a Comet I felt there
must be some mistake. How could anybody possibly fit into the
minute amount of space left around the gun? Now my size became
an advantage: I could easily scramble in and out of the turret,
and inside even found an inch or two to spare. Comets carried a
crew of five: driver, co-driver, gunner, wireless-operator and
commander, usually a sergeant or above. Life in a tank depends
on the rapport between commander and driver. Without it, you
lurch and lunge wildly over the terrain, bashed around like the
balls in a pin-table machine. Mine fortunately was a good crew
and our commander, Cornet Alexander, was the nephew of the
field-marshal. (He subsequently went with the regiment to Korea,
and there met his death.) On the aerodrome at Oadby there was
little scope for crashing around. There were hours of maintenance
on the tank and occasionally we ground about on the deserted
runways like stately processions of prehistoric monsters. Then
came the day for range practice.

For this we trundled off to Warcop in Westmorland. Until
conscription I had never seen the north of England. The moorland
oppressed me as it does so many southerners and the only form of
life that seemed natural to it was the tank. Out on the hills lay our
targets. I shall never forget the first time we fired a live round.
I had always been pleased with my status as a wireless-operator
but had not appreciated that when the action started I was the one

who had to heave the shells out of the racks and into the breach. On the command *Fire* my eardrums caved in, my eyes seared to blindness, my skin scorched in the sheet of flame and my ribs collapsed under the shattering recoil of the gun. The enormity of the assault on the senses was beyond my comprehension. Either I was now dead or somebody had crammed my head into a biscuit tin and lit a thunderflash. Slowly it was borne in on me that I was supposed to produce another shell from my back pocket and that we were going to commit suicide again. And again and again and again. A day or two later, still deaf but hardened and enjoying the game of soldiers like nothing since the toy fort on the hearthrug, I was delighted to have my place taken in the turret by a visiting brasshat. As the gun fired, his loosely-fitting headgear shot out of the turret in the blast followed rapidly by its stunned owner. The occasional hour snatched by some tinkling hill stream where the black and white dipper walked incredibly beneath the water, the wheatear bobbed on the dry stone walls and the curlew with its incomparable cry slanted overhead, belonged to paradise by comparison.

B Squadron of the 8th KRIH were the tops in the regiment at everything from fornication to football (the latter was practised mainly by the National Servicemen and the former by the Regulars) and so naturally Cornet Alexander's troop was picked as the demonstration team for the War Office displays of tank technique held on the Thetford battle area in Norfolk. It was all part of the fun of playing soldiers. We learned how tanks were said to 'brew up' in the war when hit by a shell, and heard ghastly stories from our veteran NCOs of the very real horrors that lay in their experience. Yet it was always difficult to relate what we were doing to the deadly facts of war. But I got an inkling. Our set piece was to lie up in some conifers with orders to destroy 'enemy' tanks, guns or emplacements two or three miles away. Slowly we manoeuvred our way over the ground, using hillocks, hedges and available cover till within striking distance. Then in a hull-down position, we would poke up our camouflaged turret and loose the opening rounds on our target. These moves were so practised on this given piece of ground that our demonstrations took on the character of a well-rehearsed play with tanks as *dramatis personae*. But, as actors will, we occasionally fluffed our lines: Able Charlie would fire too soon; Bravo Dogo would take a wrong turn in the wood, show himself too soon and be pronounced *hors de combat* by an umpire (umpire of all things). For the grand finale, we would creep to about half a mile from our target and then get the order to advance at full speed. This was a moment of both exhilaration and dread. Here the ground was more or less level. We lurched forward, crashing gears on surging Rolls-Royce engines faster and faster. To be inside thirty tons of metal shifting flat out at thirty miles an hour is dire: the sense of power races in the blood, the thudding, juddering racket is so extreme the teeth grow loose in the head, through bush, through briar you charge like a mastodon berserk. Hedges crash flat, trees splinter and snap, earth leaps off like foam, walls cascade in showers of fragments. To leap a yard across a ditch in such a mass of metal at such a speed is to know the impact of a meteor on the moon. It is insupportable, but somehow on command you brace yourself to load and fire a series of smoke bombs from your own private mortar in the turret. They arc away and spurt rapidly one after another into a dense curtain of billowing white smoke. More tanks are racing forward from the rear under your cover, and behind them are infantry. Slowly the roar subsides: the battering slackens at last and you grind to a halt. As the dull ache of bruises begins its own relentless crescendo, you fall out for a smoke break . . .

In camp, barrack-room life was like home from home. Now we polished a crowned harp of Ireland for cap badge and not the trainee's generalised mailed fist of the RAC. 8th KRIH glittered on our shoulders while our officers dripped epaulettes of silver chain mail to save them from the sabre slashes of long-vanished enemies. The Liverpool and not the bog Irish were the mainstay of our regulars and I learned to interpret Scouse. Their piss-ups were epic. One bunch of late revellers, finding handles too much to cope with, simply beat our barrack-room door flat in the middle of the night. I do not think they got so much as an extra guard duty for it. They inspired comradeship and affection and I never feared them for a second as I did the evil guys from my own home town. Sex was where they found it on a Saturday night and presented no problems. The NS boys were altogether prim and proper. Avid listeners to the exploits of others, they recounted nothing themselves because they went on leave to girlfriends of their schooldays who would not mind the occasional hand up their knickers but who switched the light on the moment you tried to get your tongue between their cherry-red lips. In 1948 Vera Lynn was still next to Godliness. Buggery was a constant theme of jest but honoured entirely in the breach. And yet the regiment, a small one, included a long-established male marriage, apparently connived at and condoned by all, from the colonel down. A certain NCO was in speech and manner clearly feminine in disposition. He was nonetheless a respected and sharply efficient campaigner. He lived in special quarters adjacent to the stores and so did another regular NCO, an Irish tank driver who had been decorated. They had taken up together in the war, and never since separated; the regiment, in its quiet monotonous way, saw to it that their relationship survived. Nobody seemed to see anything in the least incongruous about this.

As a result of working in a tank demonstration troop, I got promoted lance-corporal. Somehow the rank seemed pettier than trooper and its associations with Cromwellian cavalry in the Civil War, so ambition revived. Envy, not fame, I fear was the spur: envy of the effortless supremacy of our aristocratic officers whose passions centred on points-to-point and vintage cars. So I applied again for WOSB and this time my request was encouraged, not blocked. Down at Limpsfield in Surrey I joined candidates fresh from basic training a seasoned veteran. For three days one mysteriously became an officer cadet and *ipso facto* a gent. We played the usual games, figuring out how to get absurd objects through impossible obstacles, and I gave what was reckoned to be the winning talk on the history of photography inspired by the Fox Talbot who had invented it in Lacock Abbey, and to my intense joy I was through. In the summer of 1949 I joined no 12 Platoon of C company at Mons Officer Cadet School, Aldershot.

I remember this period of my life for one person only. We did all the usual things: I bounced back on to the square and was driven ferociously to and fro, I got beaten up in a boxing ring by an extraordinary flailing Maltese with a heavy moustache, thrown into a swimming pool and left for dead on the bottom (I still could not swim), all this while trying to square my ridiculous pretensions with the fact that gentle bookish me did not really square very easily with the keenness and aggressive spirit continually demanded of officer cadets. I was not, however, alone in this. Some tended to come to me for advice about the Army as a whole, others for how to stay out of trouble or to double blanco webbing, merely because I was a relatively old sweat by, say, six months. I was able to help one chap who was on the point of collapse through a vital cross-country run, and another oafish lad with his weapon drill. This was to no avail, as it happened, because when we marched off the square at our passing-out parade his was the rifle that remained hopelessly behind on the ground. But one of our number will remain with me always. Peter was the outstanding cadet of our platoon and for some reason we became friends. He was grand without a trace of side. He lived for the Army and adored everything about it. He and the Army were made for each other. He spoke modestly of his father, a distinguished officer, and of his mother, who had been a concert pianist; and they lived in a big house in Shropshire. He dazzled everybody with his natural superiority and his equally natural charm. No one was surprised when he passed out Best Cadet and received the sword of honour. It seemed only natural, too, that he should decide to go on to Sandhurst for a regular commission. Some months later, a commissioned officer myself, I was sitting at home over tea with my mother back in the same two rooms in which I had grown up. She was reading the evening paper when she suddenly asked me what had been the name of my friend at Mons. At my reply she handed me the paper. It appeared Peter had got into financial difficulties and had uttered a couple of forged cheques for no great sums. His parents, we learned, were neither rich, nor distinguished, but were ordinary folk who lived in a semi-detached. When detectives arrived at the Royal Military Academy to ask him some questions, he had slipped into the next room and fired a final bullet into his brain. I never felt quite the same about officerdom after that.

I was commissioned into the Royal Army Service Corps, which I dimly, and no doubt justly, felt to be a judgement on my merits. Somehow life among the sacks of flour and the petrol pumps, even as an officer, did not quite make up for the excitements of the 8th KRIH, and I found myself posted back to a Command Supply Depot at Thetford. A captain was in command who had a bungalow and lived like a civilian. There was no mess, so I took up residence in a hotel. Boredom and disillusion set in and I took to Spanish by correspondence. East Anglia is an agreeable place and I saw a good deal of it. My duties mostly consisted of signing forms that I did not clearly understand. Now and again somebody would salute me in a kind of frenzy of absentmindedness to which I used to reply vaguely, 'Oh, hello there.' Back home it was now a different story: the girl I had always longed for, her pale skin and auburn hair set off by a black velvet New-Look dress, now came effortlessly to my arm. None but the brave tinkled complacently in my head, but how dull it all was. There was a spell attached to a gunners' unit at Stiffkey when I shared properly in the life of an officers' mess. Rowdiness, massive drinking bouts and a batman to pull your boots off. There was even the mess night the buggers slid the table section into my belly until they pushed me with a crash through the double doors at the end of the dining-room, an oft-repeated trick. I continued to toy with Spanish irregular verbs and pursue my bird-watching out on Scolt Head. And then suddenly I was out and back on the street. All I had to show for it was a fawn riding mac, a little officer cadets' green pork pie hat, and a swagger stick.

Certainly because of National Service one was harder and fitter and none the worse for that; had learned more rapidly the ways of men – though some, like myself, had been in arrears; had acquired the rudiments of some specialised skills (the Army failed completely to teach me to drive, and there was not enough time to teach myself); and the Army expanded my vocabulary. Yet as a soldier I had been a fearful prig, and curbed my tongue from obscenity: the moment I left I could not stop effing and blinding. I doubt if the prospect of war even in those queasy post-Hiroshima days ever seemed to me much more than a remote lark. We heard nothing of nuclear warfare and trained as though it had never come about.

I knew I had finally got the whole thing in perspective the day I joined the BBC:

'Now, Mr. Palmer,' said the sprog personnel officer, 'during your National Service I see you were commissioned. Tell me, as an officer, didn't you find your lack of inches a disadvantage to you . . .?'

JOHN FURNIVAL

I had to report to the Tower of London to do my basic training with the Royal Fusiliers: that was their depot. But my first day in the Army I was sent to hospital, to Greenwich, with a poisoned finger. It was a very minor thing, but they kept me in there for a month because it would have been awkward to have gone back halfway through an intake; so I spent a month at Greenwich doing virtually nothing.

This was quite a good way to go into the Army because you saw the other end of it, people who were waiting for discharge, and you got to know what the Army was really like, if it was really like anything. And it was the first time I had ever seen a bullet wound. There was someone in my ward, a National Serviceman, who had been shot in the arm in Malaya. He was due to come home and on his last day out there he was wounded. It had shattered his elbow so that for the rest of his life he had to wear this device to help him move his arm. That was quite an experience. Later on, when we went out on the ranges for rifle practice and everyone treated it as a sporting event, I used to think of that guy's elbow.

There were also some wounded from the Korean war still in there, though that must have been over a long time then. One bloke had bullet wounds in his back and he used to have these terrible nightmares, screaming out in the night.

It could have been very depressing, but there were lighter moments. There were a couple of guys in there being circumcised for some reason. They were both northerners and they used to work this comedy act, singing George Formby songs with their pricks hanging out, all wrapped up in bandages.

After the month I went back to the Tower and joined the next intake for basic training. Normally National Servicemen were completely cut off in places like Catterick and so on, but we were totally exposed to the tourists. We were not allowed out of the Tower for eight weeks, but it was not as bad as being shut right away like most recruits. I remember we had to do our five mile run around the moat: about twelve times round.

The ravens were quite amusing. They were in the Army, too, they had numbers and drew rations; and they were just like old sweats, you know, the eighty-year-old storekeepers they have on every camp, just kept on the strength to take the piss out of the nig nogs. They specialised in creeping up on you. In the morning you had to go on fatigues, picking up leaves and rubbish around the Tower, and the ravens would stalk up behind you and let out these terrible squawks. Frighten you out of your life.

There were quite a number of east-enders in the Fusiliers because the regiment used to recruit a lot from around Stepney and Bow. I remember we had these feathers to stick behind your cap-badge called 'ackles; we used to be issued with clean ones every two or three weeks, and they were never called a cockade or feathers, they were always 'ackles.

Something that surprised me was the amount of anti-semitism that persisted. I thought all that had disappeared. They said Jews were dirty and things like that, which was a bit unpleasant because we had several Jews in the intake.

I suppose the most memorable thing that happened to me there was falling down one of the spiral staircases. We always wore hobnail boots and I was clattering down one of these stone staircases carrying a fixed bayonet when I met an officer coming up. Of course I had to salute this guy. The whole operation was impossible and I fell all the way down and landed on my left thumb, so I have a permanent injury to my wrist, which is very feeble. Perhaps it has given my drawing a more sensitive line. I suppose I was lucky to miss the bayonet, otherwise my drawing might be even feebler than it is now.

At the end of the basic training you had these interviews, if you had any educational qualifications, to see if you were officer material. I had my interview and we both decided that I was not fit to be an officer. I happened to know there was this linguists' course, so I suggested that. They were quite relieved, really, to get rid of me. It was certainly a relief to me. I could not think of anything else to do in the Army, and at least I would be learning something. Anyway, I went with another bloke from the intake, who was actually one of the Jews, down to Bodmin, to an establishment called the Joint Services School for Linguists, which was in an old war-time camp out in the country, with a very peaceful atmosphere.

The whole course lasted about nine months and we were only about half the time there. Unfortunately the commandant was a very keen golfer and he was not getting any golf in Cornwall: that, combined with the fact that the living was very easy for us, persuaded him to move the whole camp up to Scotland, to a place near St Andrews.

We were nearly all doing Russian; we had to reach 'A' level in nine months from scratch. It sounds pretty impressive, but considering we did nothing else and we had it drummed into us from nine to five every day, it was nothing spectacular really. I actually read the dictionary through several times. It might sound tedious, but I really enjoyed it.

The teachers were very interesting. They were all civilians, emigrés. They were rather sad people. They obviously missed Russia and hated being stuck in Scotland. Some of them were Polish, actually. Our teacher was a Pole, which was a slight disadvantage because they have this peculiar pronunciation: they pronounce all Russian l's as w's, it is a sort of affectation. I suppose we must have picked this up because I failed to get on the interpreters' course at Oxford, which I really wanted to do, so I had to finish my training as a translator.

I have not made much use of Russian since. I did not really keep it up, although I have used it in my art work. Visually it is a very beautiful language, and at one stage of my work I used quite a lot of cross-language puns.

Anyway, I was transferred to the Intelligence Corps and at the end of the course I was posted to the War Office. That was more or less like a civilian job. We just worked office hours and I was able to live in my own flat. In fact the only time I wore a uniform was once a week to get paid. I was very grateful for that. I mean, apart from it being very itchy, I always felt uncomfortable in uniform. I think some uniforms make people feel stronger, but I reckon ours was designed to make you feel weaker. The tunic was always riding up and the trousers slipping down, leaving you sort of split in the middle with a great webbing belt stuck round your waist. You felt very vulnerable and not at all aggressive. Psychologically I should think it was a complete failure – and a good thing too. I expect that is why they have changed it.

Obviously I cannot say much about the work I was doing at the War Office. What it consisted of mainly was systematically reading through *Pravda* and *Izvestia* and *Krokodil*. The general idea was to note the names of any Russian servicemen in a filing system so that we could gradually build up a picture of where various units were based. It was a pretty primitive form of intelligence. Of course there were other sources: there was actually a department called 'Dirty Documents' that dealt with scraps of letters found on rubbish dumps in East Berlin and so on, and somebody had to make some sense of them.

Apart from translating duties we had to act as cloakroom attendants whenever they had a big international conference at the War Office. It gave you a close-up look at the people who held the fate of the West in their hands. Most of them seemed pretty stupid to me. I remember one evening at the end of one of these conferences. Of course they all came in mufti. The American officers and the French and so on wore individual styles – snap-brims, tweedy check trilbies, whatever – but every British officer wore a bowler hat. We must have had about a hundred bowlers hanging on this hatstand in the middle of the cloakroom. Everyone had been drinking heavily so they were pretty well oiled. At the end of the conference they all came barging in to collect their gear, and someone knocked the hatstand over. There was the general staff, pissed out of their minds, all grovelling about on the floor and trying on these bowler hats to see which one would fit. I think if Russian Intelligence could have seen them they probably would not have bothered any more.

Apart from little diversions like that my second year was pretty unexciting. I had been counting the days to demob ever since I was called up, but when it came it was rather an anti-climax.

Looking back I do not think I regret the experience. It was good to have that two-year break between art school and going to the Royal College. I suppose I resented the waste of time then, but it brought me up against all sorts of people I would not otherwise have met. It did not figure in the official purpose of National Service at all, but that was probably the one good thing that came out of it. You had two years with nothing to do really except getting to know other people, or at least getting to know about them. Perhaps we made some use of it.

BILL TYLER

'The General would like to see you at four-thirty tomorrow,' his secretary informed me over the telephone.

I might never have been a National Serviceman but for a (some would say misplaced) social conscience. Five years at architectural college and two jobs later I was, at the age of twenty-five, working in the architect's department of a world-famous organisation just about to start a rebuilding programme under the guidance of 'The General'. Golden-bowlered by a nation feeling less threatened than at any time for twenty years, he had spent the greater part of his life dedicated to a purpose that, suddenly, was discredited and now disillusion with things military no doubt made the task easier for him.

Still, it stuck in his gullet even to have to suggest that I (evidently being an important member of the construction team) could obtain permanent deferment, and that it could be arranged through his friends in Whitehall. No sooner was the proposition made than I knew that any mutual respect would be gone if I accepted, and what of my friends and colleagues who had no string-puller? They would never forgive me two years of professional advancement and domestic comfort, gained not even through the conviction of a conscience nor the discomfort of a disability but simply by having access to the Whitehall ear.

For me there was no great fear of Army life, having been embraced by the khaki cloth as a schoolboy and achieving the exalted rank of corporal in the Cadet Force. Exercises in Totteridge Fields and in Richmond Park during term time and summer camps at Pirbright, Shorncliffe and Fingringhoe (and how we boys did!) kindled the military flame in me that had already blazed in thousands of other young hearts in the napalm and splintered images of Korea. National Service was a duty avoided only by conchie cowards and the helplessly halt.

The General was visibly relieved and muttered, 'Well done, my boy,' when I replied that I did not particularly object to my two-year stint, and almost apologetically asked if I would mind postponement for three months more to enable the current project to be completed. July seemed to me an infinitely better month in which to start basic training, and in the blazing summer of '59 I found myself a (probationary) member of the 'finest club in the world'.

During those super-heated days of July, August and September, 3 TR.RE (the Army seemed obsessed by abbreviations) at Cove near Farnborough became the focal point of the initiation training that had been devised with the expertise born of thousands of exactly similar intakes of recruits. Those directed into the Royal Engineers generally had a background of employment in the construction industry, and traditionally architects were leaders of the building team. That I was somewhat older than the majority of recruits, and academically qualified, gave me an unenviable authority within the barrack-room, enhanced by the lessons in bulling boots, blancoing webbing, cleaning a rifle, or pressing trousers that had been learned so well as a cadet.

I soon became an arbitrator in all sorts of arguments, adjudicating on matters temporal and spiritual, advising on techniques military, and averting open clashes that were all too likely to erupt in the close confinement of our barrack life. To some I became a father-confessor and confidant, listening to problems about mum, sister with two bastard kids, the girl who was pregnant (and then joyfully was not) and the wife who was thought to be having it off with anyone. Scribe to two out of thirty almost justified the unofficial Army claim that ten per cent of recruits were illiterate, although both could, and did with difficulty, manage to read letters from home, aided occasionally where handwriting or spelling were almost incomprehensible. For two or three pages of simple word combinations I would get half my webbing blancoed or a pair of boots bulled in exchange.

Returning to camp after our first leave during August Bank

Holiday weekend, I found a considerable change in the attitude of the room NCOs and soon discovered that this was because I was one of only four who had brought their cars back. Allowed to keep it on the camp with the CO's permission only for use as leave transport, it nevertheless quickly became the regular evening bus to Aldershot, Woking, Camberley, and Guildford. No longer in possession of civilian clothes, and not allowed out of camp officially except on rare weekend passes, I wore a chauffeur's uniform donated, in part, by each of the passengers for that particular evening. Departures from camp were carefully timed to coincide with contrived emergencies in the guard room, but the return procedure was always somewhat more hazardous after a stop-vomit-start journey and a pious hope that someone would be sober enough to negotiate the guard room in the reverse direction.

Rapidly going bald, I had invested £25 in an organic hair treatment course using different ointments each night of the week and which I applied in the seclusion of a lavatory, normally after lights-out. Following one particularly drunken expedition, I succeeded in massaging a tube of secret formula shampoo into my scalp and the next morning, during drill, I became aware of a stench suggesting that either the adjutant's dog had crapped on the parade ground, or one of the squad had in his pants. Whichever way we marched made no difference, and when eventually my head started itching terribly I realised (and confirmed at tea break) that the combination of sun and beret had created the ideal conditions for instant fermentation.

Fraternising with our wardens and tormentors was hardly popular with the other recruits, although most of them appreciated my dilemma. For the NCOs it was probably worse; not daring to show favouritism in any way, but knowing that if they pushed me too hard I might well not be taximan. Their frustration was no doubt even greater when I passed WOSB (what, incidentally, did the Whorehouse make of character references from a retired general and a communist ex-tutor?) if their treatment of other would-be officers was any guide. There were, of course, some particularly sadistic corporals who seemed about as popular with their fellows as with us, and the more often they were refused a lift the more violent their reaction. I should, even now, be doing extra duties were it not for the efforts of my travelling companions to make sure that their slag was not kept waiting for the nightly screw.

165

Petrol simply could not be afforded out of pay of a few shillings a week, but this never became a problem thanks to some unknown benefactors who always kept the tank topped up. A source of replenishment came to light rather unexpectedly and almost put me in the glasshouse. During a period of camp fatigue duties I was attached to the ration truck party and on one trip the driver suddenly swung up a narrow lane that was certainly not on the normal inter-camp run. We bumped to a halt in a clearing just off the roadway and, grabbing a jerrican from under the seat, he hurriedly explained that he was just going to borrow a couple of gallons. Reeking of petrol after sucking at the syphon pipe, he clambered back into the cab and promptly reversed the truck into a three foot deep ditch. Help was summoned from camp in the form of a mate driving a three-tonner, which toppled over with agonising slowness as it tried to winch us out of the ditch at anything but a straight pull. A heavy dumper truck was brought up next and, manoeuvring in a part of the clearing that had never seen wheels before, it began to disappear into a swamp patch to the great consternation of the driver who was to remain marooned for some time to come. Admitting defeat, the duty officer was informed and arrived complete with mobile Coles crane and a posse of military policemen. We were eventually marched off for interrogation. That someone blew the gaff was clear, for trips round darkest Surrey in the car were no more; neither were some of our NCOs.

Passing-out day was cold, wet and windy and had a splendidly funereal feel about it as the family gathered for the last time, in mourning for the parting of the ways. It contrasted oddly with the brilliant days during which we had drilled, scrubbed, polished, fought mock battles, built bridges and rafts, laid minefields and booby-traps, and had finally survived unscathed. It was a portent of the grey world of the Officer Cadet School at Mons, the end of perhaps the longest period of freedom I had had. For three months I had enjoyed always being told what to do, of never thinking for myself, of having no responsibilities and no reputation to live up to.

Attitudes now changed dramatically. No longer the camaraderie born of a common discomfort or challenge defeated, but each one for himself in the scramble to be cock of the dung heap. Initiative was now the byword, with the least intelligent always contriving to be at the front, or the top or the back or wherever it was that they would be noticed most. What a bloody waste of effort when almost never being in the right place, but having a good excuse, was every bit as effective!

The altered circumstances of personal relationships was rudely brought home when all new officer cadets were matched in an inter-company boxing tournament. My opponent had been a room-mate throughout basic training, but I remember little of the encounter as it happened, except that the world turned red, and the floor kept coming up to meet me. For two and a half rounds I struggled to fend off punches, trying to remember whether it was a right or left hand that should be leading. Eventually the fight was stopped, and what had seemed to be a well-earned win eventually became a pyrrhic victory, for what no one knew beforehand was that a novice had been matched against a one-time junior ABA area champion. The bastard had kept it quiet and for that he was never forgiven!

Bloody and bruised, I was given three days' sick leave ending in time for instruction in the new self-loading rifle, only to be in front of the MO again, totally deaf from the combination of punchbag and recoil noise. Off all but light duties for three weeks, I happily lay on my bunk listening to the stentorian commands of the sergeant-major shatter the frost-laden air of December mornings, or to the crackle of blank-firing rifles in the dusk of a dank, rain-sodden day.

Perhaps the trouble with Mons was that we were not all from one corps but were rivals divided by ambition as well as loyalty in a half-way house between the ranks and a commission. The thought of a further three months of hard graft seemed, at times, a prize hardly worth competing for, and yet no one was prepared to admit defeat and opt for the simple life. With something less than enthusiasm I survived the Basic Officer Training Course and so was posted to Gordon Barracks at Chatham as an officer-cadet RE.

Technical lectures, demonstrations and practical exercises, as well as the inevitable drill periods, made those three months a strange mixture of almost academic college life and draconian military discipline. There were perhaps four or five non-technical members of the cadre, but all the other twenty or so were architects, surveyors or engineers. Our common expertise quickly established a complementary outlook that never entirely accepted the regimentation of the Army, although there were some who, seeking a short-term commission, took life rather more seriously.

The night before the pass-out parade dress rehearsal three of us had the hilarious idea of removing all the toilet rolls in the ablution block and locking the cubicle doors from the inside. The chaos that ensued the following morning surpassed all expectation, as beer drinkers with the runs and normal regular guys found their evacuation thwarted. The parade eventually got under way somewhat late, and, blackmailed by the possible relegation of the entire company, we presented ourselves to the OC as the offenders. Threatened with a report to the Commandant, stern disciplinary measures and return to the ranks, our commissions seemed to have vanished at the eleventh hour. Then, at the end of the tirade, there came just the slightest admission that initiative and non-conformity were qualities that, after all, the Army did grudgingly appreciate.

A dance was held on the eve of the parade and by tradition those about to be commissioned put on a short revue, the high spot of our show being a ballet sequence performed by two of our largest men and the smallest. This ended up with the stage collapsing under a *pas de trois* totalling over five hundredweight and which perfectly set the scene for a thoroughly boisterous evening. That night we were privileged to have our own rooms (now being gentlemen) and I happened to be in one isolated in a separate wing of the hut. It was not until the parade had formed up that someone realised I was absent, and fast asleep in new-found comfort and an alcoholic haze I was rudely awakened with just ten minutes to go. Frantically struggling into BD and boots I remembered that some time the previous evening I had lost my beret. I borrowed one a size or two too large from someone not on parade, hurriedly tied a new knot in the tape band and made for the parade ground at rather more than a gentlemanly pace. As time went on the beret became ever more loose, with the ends of the knot eventually fluttering in the breeze like a couple of bloody pennants. My panic at what might happen when it finally dropped over my eyes was equalled only by the pain of silent belly-laughter suffered by those marching behind. Thank God for the short-sightedness of the general who inspected us and took the salute!

Out of training at last, in mid-April 1960 I was posted to the Deputy Commander Royal Engineers at Minden in Germany. It had taken nine months of sweat and taxpayers' money to train me for a job that was hardly removed from the one I had had in civvy street.

A major, myself, a staff-sergeant, sergeant, two corporals and a couple of sappers were the military members of the unit, administratively responsible for the maintenance of Army buildings. Attached to us were a number of Germans (including a particularly bouncily-bosomed clerk) whose function was to oversee the various contracts that were carried out for redecoration or repair work on barracks, stores and married quarters. The Germans had a canteen in the attic of one part of our accommodation and this had a certain notoriety in the garrison. My instant introduction to beer and schnapps lasted well into the night, and it was several days before my greenish-round-the-gills appearance finally wore off. Our OC was an engineer of exceptional merit, greatly given to beer and women, and his caravan was, by repute, frequently to be found in a field or lay-by rocking on its springs. Certainly it was often out of the compound on Bouncy Boosy's days off.

More or less a civilian in uniform, I was billeted in the garrison mess, run rather as a residential hostel for civilians of officer status who worked for the Army, as well as for visiting officers and those attached to units where no mess existed. The civilians were a motley bunch of mostly female school teachers, Army Kinema Corps personnel and NAAFI representatives. Communal rooms were in a splendidly Germanic house, perhaps built by a banker just before World War I. Most of the residents' rooms were in a new two-storey block, with women segregated on the first floor.

There were only two other National Servicemen in the mess and together with a middle-aged major we made up the entire military complement. These three had established a well-entrenched relationship with a particular group of teachers, and it was not long before I joined their company. We visited places of interest at weekends, dined and danced at local restaurants, went for picnics on fine Sundays, played tennis, arranged mess dinners and dances and somehow contrived to enjoy every minute of leisure as fully as possible.

As a non-combative unit, we never had parades (and anyway there were not enough of us even to look as if we were on parade) nor had special duties, nor went on exercises. Routines were geared to those of the civilian work force and consisted of checking work dockets and indentures, and running the rather limited number of Volkswagens used for visits to the various jobs needing supervision. Not long after my arrival at Minden the run-down in direct military involvement in buildings commenced, with the Civil Service Directorate of Works gradually taking responsibility from the CREs. Eventually we were informed that the unit would be disbanded and many weeks were spent in endlessly checking our stores and equipment and in justifying what could not be accounted for. There were many items surplus to the inventory which we shared out, but at the end of the day a good deal of valuable equipment was still missing. The staff-sergeant, who could always be relied on to obtain anything that anyone ever needed, was supposed to be doing a very nice line in NAAFI duty-free cigarettes and spirits for the Germans, and probably in WD property too.

Elizabeth and I usually partnered each other during the summer social round, and what had started as purely physical attraction to five feet four inches of shapely blonde teacher became rather deeper as we spent more and more time together. The exodus of the BFES contingent during the school holidays cast a gloom over the mess, which none of us felt able to dispel. Two trips to Holland and four days in Berlin did liven things up a little, though.

Berlin was an extraordinary experience. Our special passes for the Eastern Zone were examined behind a shuttered window by the Russian Frontier Guards, and with every passing minute the waiting room took on a more cell-like appearance. At last we were rubber-stamped out, with our time of leaving noted by a British military policeman. If we did not check in within two and three-quarter hours, at the end of the one hundred and ten or so miles of autobahn, then a search would be started just in case the Russians, or more likely the East Germans, were again in an abductive mood. The city seemed to be on the knife-edge of existence; isolated and unsure of the future, one could sense the tension in peoples' mannerisms, in the bustle and haste of ordinary events, and in the wildness of the night clubs. The Kurfurstendamm was too obviously a showcase for the West German economic miracle, and the cardboard-front architecture of Stalin Allee in the Eastern sector, standing white-elephantine in the middle of acres of rubble, would have been more appropriate in the West. As an outpost from which the Western allies could flag-wave Berlin served a purpose: as a city it had no reason to exist.

Elizabeth was back in September, and the mess took on a new lease of life with Scottish dancing once a week, cards, slide shows of holidays, coffee parties and mess dinners. A mild attack of tonsilitis kept me in bed for a few days in October and Elizabeth was a ministering angel. One night she came to my room in her dressing gown, bringing a promised toddy that she had forgotten about earlier. We made love for the first time that night; not for want of my trying earlier, but now she really did want it too, and how!

Within days came the blow that DCRE was to be disbanded and I would be posted elsewhere. Handing over to the Garrison Works Office involved vast numbers of forms being distributed all over the place, most of them probably ending up unread and misfiled but at least received. The final party in the attic was something of an orgy, although I have no clear recollection of anything after the first hour or so. The aftermath I do know about; at ten shillings a bottle, whisky was cheap enough to drown in (we used it to pay off night club and restaurant bills at a rate of about £4 a bottle) and since then I have never touched a drop of the stuff. Embarrassed by my military presence, the Command Works Office decided that I could be usefully employed winding up another DCRE some thirty miles from Minden. Mess facilities were offered at Bielefeld or I could travel daily up and down the autobahn. Elizabeth gave me no choice, even if it was more expensive in contraceptives!

The liberal-minded Germans helpfully provided vending machines in public toilets and in many bars and restaurants, and I doubt whether having asked a chemist for *Gummiwaren* I could have coped with something like *'was vorlage, bitte?'* The machines were not without their dangers however: 1DM (then one shilling and eightpence) would buy a single condom packed in a round flat tin or a thin cardboard pack, and a friend was greatly frustrated, and so was his woman, to discover that one had inexplicably sold him aspirin!

The new unit was efficient and friendly and most of my time was spent not in helping to wind-up affairs but in supervising the construction of a new school, to be used by BFES. This was designed and built by the Germans to their own standards on the assumption that one day it would be handed back to them with the departure of BAOR. We fairly easily won the CWO rifle team trophy as there were then only four other DCREs, and that was the only time that I touched a rifle in fifteen months' service.

Loving Elizabeth needed a certain amount of stealth as she was naturally anxious that our affair remained private, and others' rooms were anyway supposed to be out-of-bounds after midnight. Neither of us wished to be the subject of malicious tale-telling by frustrated fifty-year-olds. One guest night we left the hard-core drinkers round the bar, and retired to Elizabeth's bed. Just on the point of orgasm, our rhythm was rudely broken by shouting and swearing from somewhere out in the garden. Doors and windows were flung open to see who was fighting, and, expecting a knock at the door any moment, I hurriedly withdrew, pulled on my trousers, and quickly made my way back to my room. The noise outside subsided, and in getting undressed for bed I realised I was no longer wearing the french letter I had just had on. Creeping up the now dark stairs I felt every inch of every tread for that bit of rubber, and crawling on hands and knees along the corridor I still could not find it. Maybe someone had picked it up and perhaps from just outside Elizabeth's door! A second search drew a blank and my anxiety was only relieved the next morning when Elizabeth told me she had found it on the right side of the door.

Early in December I received notice of posting to the CWO at BAOR HQ at Rheindalen, near München Gladbach. Rheindalen was also the HQ of NATO Northern Group and was a small township built entirely to house the administrative personnel responsible for a vast number of military installations throughout the whole of North Germany. Quite close to the Dutch border, and within easy reach of Dusseldorf and Cologne, the whole set-up had a cosmopolitan flavour, helped enormously by the internationalists in NATO. A vast office block, eventually to become a civilian hospital, dominated the complex, which consisted of a shopping centre and NAAFI supermarket, two cinemas, a Garrison theatre (excellently equipped), gymnasium, swimming pool, married quarters for officers and other ranks, mess buildings, barrack-rooms, sports fields and a nine-hole golf course.

CWO was now almost completely civilianised and I shared an office with a number of ex-military men who had either been retired early or had been taken on as local staff at the end of their term of service. One or two had spent many years in Germany and knew the whole system inside out. The more recently retired clung to their military background, still calling themselves major or captain and doing things in a precise military way according to the book. Given the job of liaison officer on an Anglo-German housing scheme (the Germans were again to take over eventually), site meetings were somewhat protracted affairs as every technical word was translated for my benefit. I also designed a scheme for the phased alteration of a barrack dining-hall, so carefully planned that everyone, except me, was frightened it would go wrong. When it came to it, attention to detail was only sometimes appreciated.

Having explored Northern Germany from the Baltic to the

Hertz Mountains I could now turn my attention to the southern half. Many weekends and leave days were spent on the roads between the Eiffel Mountains and Bavaria, interspersed with trips to Minden and Elizabeth ostensibly visiting Rheindahlen so that we could stay together in a quiet little *gasthof* in some picturesque village. The Germans were always early risers, it seemed; making love in the morning meant that we missed breakfast and on one occasion were oblivious to a chamber-maid who came to tidy the room until she fled, shrieking apologies, at the discovery of two naked bodies.

As demob came ever closer I thought quite seriously about signing on, or even joining the Directorate of Works as a civilian, rather than re-enter the rat race where I had left it two years before. But the fun of not conforming, of enjoying the privileges conferred by BD without suffering the strictures of military discipline would soon end; and then there would be only an old soldier's memories of cheap booze and fags, of sightseeing and the social life, of warmth and love with Elizabeth.

Strolling across the golf course to the office one morning towards the end of June, I realised that I had worn boots for only twelve days during my time in Germany; two of those were on the rifle range, and the remainder whilst skiing at the BAOR leave centre at Winterberg, a magnificent group of sports facilities that Hitler had built as the training headquarters for the German 1936 Olympic team. Boots seemed to symbolise the pedantry of the Army, the lead weights that made sure there was no break-out. But my escape had been almost complete, I had been a fugitive from military duties sucking at the udder of Army beneficence.

I never did hand in any of my kit. I still have it all.

ALAN MARSHFIELD

For two years I had Sergeant Strychnine on my back. I was in three camps and he was there waiting. Not the same face, not the same number of stripes, but there: a larynx that filed vowels out of hate and a brain of cork round a hypothalamus like a pea. I should explain that about his voice. An NCO who bawled raw recruits into shape was as proud of his voice production as an opera singer:

'You have to bring it up,' he would say in off-hand moments when he treated nignogs as something nearly human, and he would slap his blanco'd belt and swell the wind in his belly, 'From here. When you're shouting on the square you have to save your throat. You throw it up from your stomach.'

Throw up is the word. I had enough orders thrown up at me to convince me I might really be doing some good, relieving the bad cooking and worse beer in the sergeants' messes of cold war England, England in repair.

Which gave me the status of fatty pork. Greasy and horrible. I felt like it, often.

But Strychnine. I first met him in basic training, where the buffos of Aldershot ruled our lives with step callipers and a time-table of terrifying rigour. Strychnine was a corporal then, an anaemic National Service *capo* who got us on to breakfast parade by seven-thirty every day in a memorable July of heat and drought. Marching down to bacon and beans, mess-tin clanking, stride easy, the bloody birds singing over the huts, I had moments of almost pleasurable private thought. Would I get a letter from home, or from the girl who was drunk on Merrydown in that fashionable pub near the Sallyport of Old Portsmouth harbour?

'Fall out!' barked Strychnine, when we reached the canteen.

Food put some life in him, revived the adrenalin in us. I forget the exact schedule, except that the hot square, like a simmering airstrip, was for more than half the time our only horizon. Bacon and beans made Strychnine jumpy, and he would start us off with a tart reminder that we could forget any hope that life in basic was meant to be worth living. He had many endearing ways on the square. Two minutes of double-march would make us gasp for the normality of about turn and open order. A slow march was near to manna. I dreamed of slow marching behind Strychnine's stringy little corpse on a gun carriage. There were some poor sods who could not get the hang of even that, of left, slide, right, slide, and Strychnine would be at them, harrying them with his skinny obscenities.

'Get in step, you bloody ijit! You got your feet caught in your mother's cunt. You're bloody tripping like a constipated bloody fairy!'

I thanked God for ballroom practice.

I have three recallable episodes with Strychnine in basic. Your luck was holding if you fell in in the middle file. The back one was tricky but out front was murder. I had an innocent, sardonic look that to drill-corporals was the world's most detestable expression. I felt on the next notch to lowest anyway, but out front I learnt there were some notches to go, and I would go all right if I did not grow a better face quickly. I was looking at Strychnine one day, sadly and philosophically, I thought, wondering what kind of neglect at home had made him, a National Serviceman like ourselves, so greedy to insult and punish. He caught my eye. He came over. His whitey-yellow, untanned face jutted up into mine, a sickle of known forehead and chin made alien by power and insecurity. There was a small scab by his lip where a farmboy had planted a homegrown fist two weeks earlier. Pity it had not been on bayonet practice.

'What you looking at me for, soldier?'

I stood rigid.

Everyone had been looking at him. Why me? There were few of us, in fact, he did not pick on sooner or later. When it came to your turn, boy, you had a special relationship with him.

'Am I a bloody oil-painting, soldier?'

The good answer was yes. A modern painter would have done that face, a thin sliver of bowel covered in white ulcers, very well indeed. But I did not think of that. A shot of fear had given me the stumbles. What could I say? No, sir? To say he was no oil-painting would have spelled out what every man in the squad was screaming in the tight silence of his lungs, that he was the ugliest bastard in creation. To have told him he was an oil-painting would have been calling him a Botticelli beauty, a Rotherhithe fairy. Two hours of hot sun and new boots made one think quickly. No answer was not only also an answer, but eyeball to eyeball with Strychnine it was the only answer. I answered with silence. The most undignified silence I could manage. A decrepit and capitulating silence. I was not really terrified but I got together the features of utter, watery fear. Strychnine back-marched the right distance to resume command. A retreat? He had made his point. He may have been glad that I was not cockier. It was a hot after-noon for him too. We had another half-hour to kill with this malarkey.

The other time he put me on a spot, though God knows I was the last one to make a drill-corporal suspect insubordination, was prior to a church parade. We were going to be buffed up and marched to the local chapel the coming Sunday to celebrate a prehistoric contract between heaven and the garrison. Strychnine stood us at ease. The tarmac of the barrack square was boiling up through our boots. He stood easy himself, sallow in shirt-sleeve order and nervously fit. Filling in time. If I had only known what every old sweat knows: do not stand out when they are bored and slow and filling in time. Later, when they are in a hurry, you can get away with murder.

'Does anyone think he doesn't want to go on church parade for some reason?'

I did not think. I just knocked my feet to attention. Strychnine strolled over to me.

'Oh, yes, soldier, and why don't you want to be on this church parade?'

I picked around for a formula.

'Conscientious reasons, corporal.'

'What does that mean, soldier?'

'I don't believe in it, sir.'

'Corporal!'

'Corporal.'

'What don't you believe in, soldier?'

It was funny, I had not questioned up to then why I should allow myself to be in the Army, though later I rationalised even that, I remember. But I did know about the Almighty.

'In God, corporal.'

'You don't believe in God, soldier?'

'No, sir – corporal.'

He hauled my eyes down towards his pure blue Aryan pupils, and they puked into mine their pure blue lines of disgust and dismissal.

'You don't believe in God, soldier?'

I nodded. On such momentous subjects, even on the gluey tar of a drill square, I reckoned that men could resort to the more tactful signals.

'Who do you think, soldier,' he began, and awled me with his bully's blue eyes, 'who do you think makes the fucking flowers grow?'

To this day I do not know the answer.

I went to chapel. All through the service I sat in my pew while Strychnine and two hundred other men in khaki, heads bowed, knelt to the god who made the flowers grow.

My last brush with him in basic training came on a night sortie. We were spread out over a couple of miles of sandy scrub under a summer moon of extraordinarily delicate warmth and unreal candour, our rifles loaded with blanks. Strychnine was looking at his watch all the time, and for some unaccountable reason flares were popping in the selene sky behind and before us. It felt like on holiday. I pulled my trigger.

The world went deaf and motionless and the warm night air hove to around me. The faces of my fellow conscripts froze, or fell back regretful, sensing that lanky what's-his-name had boobed. Some even looked around for the corporal to come in and take control – which he did.

'What the hell are you up to, you silly bugger?' he barked in a whisper.

'It just went off.' I was not aware that my finger had been that eager to get in under the guard.

'You could have blown somebody's eyes out!'

'I'm sorry.'

'Bloody sorry! See me in the morning. Scatter!'

Soon after that, squirming through the brush towards the enemy bangs, I was tapped on the shoulder by an adjudicating officer.

'You're dead.'

And I had to stroll back to base before the game was over. I was more upset at being dead than at being the man who had given away our position.

Next morning I fetched up at Strychnine's bedside where he sat polishing his boots.

'What do you want?'

'You told me to see you, corporal.'

'Why?'

'I let my gun off last night.'

He looked puzzled.

'By mistake. You told me to see you.'

'Oh, yes.' He was finding the devil in him hard to stoke up that early. 'You bloody fool, you could have shot somebody's eyes out!'

'Yes, corporal. Sorry.'

He got up and strode out into the corridor yelling, 'Everyone into B Room!' There was too much that morning to cope with evidently, so I shrank out of sight. He got us together and, fed up and tired, tried to sound angry as he went on about some mucky sod who had been making love to a hole in the wash-house woodwork.

I had a rest from him then. My medical record had me down as LOC, Lines of Communication. That meant no front-line stuff. LOC is not so hot, when you think about it: what else do the enemy bomb if not the communications? But I thought I was lucky. They were sending me on a clerk's course. Surely Strychnine could not type, or know that form TFL2 and not FL2T was the one for telling widows their husbands would be long absent, with or without leave.

But he could type, and he did. He had three stripes now and Educational Corps flashes. Still an NS man, blond and good-looking and more poetic. This was a lull. Strychnine as saccharine, joking at the typewriter keys at the better use we could doubtless put two fingers to. He singled me out only once, sweetly. To pass the time. How unkillable was scheduled time! He had us writing essays on autumn. There was no run-up to the subject, as there had been before the chapel parade. He did not say, 'Who do you think shrivels the fucking leaves?' I think he had been reading some poetry. We had found him on his back looking up at the sky when we arrived for his tutorial. Very few camps have an obvious purpose, an educational camp even less so: it is just full of people glad they are nowhere worse. Nothing much happened there. There was one rumour about a colleague of Strychnine's buggering a cook, or a NAAFI orderly, and getting busted, but generally the place was cooler (it was September) and less dramatic. I cannot remember where we ate. Anyway, Strychnine liked my essay and read it to the class. The poets he had read were not the ones I had been reading, evidently, since I had lifted nearly every phrase. He smiled as he gave me back my paper, but did not try to talk to me. Who would have been the shyer? We were both nineteen. Not a good age for neutralising the taboo fortified by three stripes on a man's arm. Perhaps he was a little jealous of my essay.

There had to be some explanation. The next time I met him, two months later, he had aged twenty years, was taller, and loathed everything about me. This, too, after ten days of sloppy lull in a transit camp, where the beans were cold, the webbing notched loose like gunbelts, the sheets as black as if every man slept with his boots on, and where the only thing of rank on the unshaven horizon was a neurotic corporal who flapped around in black-Kiwi'd plimsols.

Transit camps should not be allowed. They are a deceit. They open up vistas of a cushy job at the end of every posting, of two years of cold beans and easy squalor.

But at the end of my permanent posting was Sergeant Strychnine. He was not evident at first, but he was before long. I was a fully-fledged clerk by this time, which meant a job in out of the cold. And it got cold enough on Salisbury Plain, especially when I was on guard. I made my debut in the Tidworth Regiment with a guard duty. A day and a half of panic, then I was standing in the guardline, everyone else dapper and me in denims. I had thought that sergeant in the office was such a nice guy.

I had not caught his name properly. Stricks or something – or Sphynx – something like that. I was one of three new clerks drafted into the squadron. Stricks or Sphynx was the sergeant in charge of the office. He would decide what we were to do, put us in our places. He had a nice face: solid, sympathetic. Not that he said, 'You'll like it here, boys!' He didn't, being a man who said little. But he made us feel the office was a good place to be in. Look around. It was. Desks and filing cabinets slotted at right-angles like bits of Lego. No belts or berets. An informal, unhurried, tidy sort of place. Officers popping in, polite. No one shouting. Not a cushy number, no. Parade at eight-thirty with the rest of the boys; a fair amount of bullshit and swank. That I could see. But you could belong in that office.

I do not know who drew up the guard lists. Stricks? Very possibly. My second night too. I still have nightmares about half-unpacking, being called away, not having the right kit, being inspected. In my anxiety I asked everyone in the office how I was to turn out for guard, and when, and where . . . Best or second best? Some said best, some second. Were these sods having me on? These, my future mates!

'Oh, and you've got to have your denims!'

What for? How? Wear them?

'Yes,' Sphynx put in, 'wear them over your best.'

That is how I turned up on guard, and minus my rifle. I got three days up before the regimental sergeant-major in marching order for that error of judgment. I suppose Stricks did not like the look of me. Soon afterwards a request came from the quartermaster for a clerk. They sent me.

My new master, the Q, was, however, more recognisably the same stack of commanding poison I thouhgt I had evaded. But he had aged terribly.

He was a foot taller, too. His face was red and bloated as if a century ago he had slipped head first into a pig-trough and decided he liked the flavour. And he hated me. I was tall, ungainly, and I read books. He was my height, hard-packed and retarded. He had to hate me. There was a bomb over his stripes and he hoped to be an officer before he died, though he knew what hell of ignominy awaited the 'ranker'.

He was new to his office, and what an office! The Q-block was a line of stores under a veranda stretching the length of the barrack square. It contained the armoury, bedding store, tool store, and a few other repositories, closed most of the time, containing things like bedsteads and Windsor chairs for the use of. There were three storemen. When Strychnine arrived on the scene the Q-block was a shambles. The previous quartermaster had spent all his time playing darts with his storemen behind his office door. The bedding was mixed up with the shovels, and an assignment of cartridge cases was wedged under the bedsteads. There was one broom of which the head would not stay on, so that it had seen little service. Chits and ledgers were stacked up in one corner of the stores office for the old Q to use as an armrest. The floor was crusted with mud. All this Strychnine had been appointed to put right.

The old Q had been busted and would probably take three months to crawl back to sergeants' mess level. I saw him around only infrequently, a worn, uncertain, evening sort of creature in black plimsolls.

First of all Strychnine put me right. I was his clerk, right? But I was in a store-block, right? So I would wear denims like the other storemen, right? Right, monkey. If he did me one favour it was that one: no pressing of second-best uniform! He meant to humble me. Not that he did not have other ways. Most of them more obvious. One was making me get the office tidy, starting on the floor. Wash that mud off. Put some polish down. Bump it up. He stood, six foot plus in his studded boots, as gross as a bison and as companionable as a snake. I went down on my knees in my denim overalls and plied bucket and brush. No doubt he felt like some sort of colossus.

Strychnine sensed something that he had to get the better of in the first round. I was nineteen and not in the Army from choice. He was about forty and in it because he had chosen it and had nowhere to go outside it. He had to hit me hard. I would have to work out the ledgers and compose the letters. Beyond that, there was no room for a rival. He had to make it clear who ran that office.

I had no ambition to be his rival. As cold and hard as last week's bread pudding in my lower gut for two years was the dread of being put on a charge. Everyone knew what a full bull session entailed. Blancoing webbing, cleaning brasses, pressing creases, cleaning a rifle, bolt and barrel: it could take all night until lights out. Everyone did it before big parades and kit inspections. But doing it alone, every night, so that you could be up for charge inspection straight after work, missing your tea, for a week, would be no fun. Not even for those who had lots of mates to help them.

I was a loner. The Army was my monastery. When I had got used to the Tidworth camp I got into the habit during winter of going to the boilerhouse to read. I would sit on a dustbin in smoky light and sulphurous fumes, the only place to be alone and quiet. Perversely, I often found this monastic life inadequate. I went into Andover and joined a play-reading group. In Andover too I met two elderly Esperantists who put me in touch with a young man in the States who had majored in Spanish. Twenty years later I am still writing to Jim Donalson. He now owns a motel in Florida, is still as keen a linguist as ever, and this year I am going to St Augustine to see him for the first time. From our first exchange of letters Jim and I took to each other.

But Strychnine could not take to me at all. He came from the

Gorbals and was mortally afraid of emotion. Which made him good at discipline but a trifle inflexible. He was ignorant but just shrewd enough to frighten others into doing the brainwork for him. From time to time he had to take stick from above too: from the adjutant, who was a thin captain with a label and no presence at all; from the major, who was squireish and jumpy; from the colonel, a man with a moustache and a stiff cough between phrases to keep him in touch with the dark brown voice that officers liked to affect in those days. Strychnine could take stick; he had enough of the rat in him to do that. And then he would pass it on.

There was none of this stuff about work being passed down from controller to deputies to assistants who would leave it to itself. When the work got to us, the assistants, Strychnine would see that we did it. In Army terms, he was an improvement on the old Q.

But no one liked him; he was too obtuse to be forgiven. He made me clean lavatories once. Another time he relegated me to the boilerhouse to do the stoking and promised me I would be on a charge – for reading a history book during office hours, or for fooling with a little Latin, I forget. The tool-store corporal usually did the boilers. He was called in to take charge of the typing and I was sent to shovel. That lasted a day. Strychnine had discovered that he needed me. I needed him, as they say, like electrical terminals stuck in my testicles.

Somehow, though, we were a duo. It was getting around that the stores were a funny place. More efficient than before, yes, but bloody peculiar. Strychnine and Marshfield Ltd. Strychnine for the tyranny and fuck-up, Marshfield for eccentricity and brains. Compared to the squadron office, stores were a lower order of life. But we were becoming respectable. People dropped in to see us. A doughy lieutenant from the workshops once clapped his cane on our office counter.

'Marshfield, we're painting a name on a personnel carrier. How do you spell ghost?'

They made him a captain soon after. I even had the major in.

'Marshfield, the Old Man just said "a number of men *was* on parade" – that's not right, is it? Shouldn't it be *were*?'

To keep the peace I told him you could say either.

But it was not just English as she was seldom spoke that made us known. They really did say that the stores were efficient. I did not see it that way. Over and over I just kept saying to myself, 'Does he have to be so unlovely?'

For I was having some lovely experiences out of camp at that time. I would row for a rowing club in Southsea at weekends. I went to France for a holiday. I had a girlfriend in Waterlooville. And in Salisbury I had discovered Anna. Her name was Jeannette but she did not like that, it did not suit her flamboyant nature. She was serving in a dry cleaner's and reading Kant and James Joyce, and with her Polish husband lived in a caravan. We read poetry to each other. Played chess. Talked about life and art and ambition. I would write and she would paint: we encouraged each other.

In Waterlooville I was making my first gropings towards sex: which in 1953 was not without a lot of hot fuss among the cow-cakes and wood spurge. Sex seemed important but really was not, then. What I got from Anna and her husband in the Salisbury caravan, and from long-distance Jim in America, was far more significant: lots of talk and intelligent excitement. It was an age in my life when I first conjured with sounds and ideas, and often I went to my iron bed with mind tingling.

In the morning there was Strychnine. Our relationship came to a head on manoeuvres. The regiment was kept in a fair state of preparedness. In the twenty-one months I was with it we had one go on the ranges, one public display of fieldwork, one forced march, one sports day, and one weekend of manoeuvres. At the display I watched from a hillside. But in that weekend of manoeuvres on the plains of Wiltshire I played my part.

The stores department was wired for sound. I was radio operator. If our army on the move wanted ammunition, spares and hotplates, it had to know where to locate us. Which was soon more than we could do ourselves. Strychnine was perched in the front lorry of our stores convoy. I was at the back of the line, out of touch and out of mind, nursing a radio which I had had one week to learn about, crouched in an armoured half-track. One of my luxuries was stopping. Just stopping. It gave me chance to rest from the ironclad rattle that was going right through to my skeleton. It also gave me a chance to try and tune in to one or two other sections of the operation. What operation? Not to reason. Anyway, stops were few. Strychnine was reading the map and if we had stopped too often it would have spoilt our faith in him.

But in the end we did stop in earnest, about four o'clock tea-time, and he came back to me.

'What the Christ's wrong with this map, Marshfield?'

'Where are we?'

'We're here, for Chrisake!'

I thought for a moment he was being droll but he was stabbing the map with one of his boiled fingers.

We had stopped by a pub and a tree and a church and a few shops that gave promise of being a locatable village. He was pointing to something five miles north of Amesbury.

It was more than my life was worth to ask an inhabitant where we were, but over a grocer's was a telephone number.

'Don't they say where we are on that bloody radio?' He stomped up and down the pavement, his red face bulging.

'Where *we* are?' I did not labour the point. 'Q, can we have some tea?'

'You find out what the fuck's wrong with that map.'

The drivers had wandered off to a teashop but the storemen were not moving. It took me five minutes to find our village: about as near to Amesbury as Huddersfield was. What next? Tell Strychnine he was wrong? He would like that. But he would like it less if I did not locate us. I did not even know where we were heading.

'Well, for Chrisake, where are we?'

'Where are we going, Q?'

He put his hard, full, sweating face close to mine. 'We have to rendezvous with HQ where that bloody fucking cross is.'

'Ah. At what time, Q?'

'Eighteen hundred hours.'

I thought a little. We were more than two hours away from the place marked X. There was also the matter of avoiding telling him we were not north of Amesbury.

'I think, Q, if we keep going up this road we'll reach this spot here.' I put a pencil cross. 'Then you turn left and go on and you'll reach here. Then you turn left again and you'll be on this main road, which you see goes right past the rendezvous point.'

He ripped the map from me.

'Corporal Lomax!' he barked as he went past his equipment storeman. 'Tell those drivers to shake their fucking arses out of that café!'

We were on the move.

We rendezvous'd at seven o'clock, an hour late, in twilight in a field that looked like a camouflaged fairground. Full of clowns I did not recognise.

'My fucking radio operator got us fucking lost!' he told his buddy, the squadron sergeant-major.

'Put the fucker on a charge!'

'I fucking will.'

Life seemed pretty meaningless then. Two more days in a sardine can and then a fizzer. That night the storemen tucked into an orgy of spam and tea at ten o'clock by oil-lamp in one of the lorries. I was allowed to collect a messtin of stewed tea and a hunk of bread, which I had to carry back to my half-track and torch-lit radio. I did not dare ask for bedding. There had been colder nights in my service of crown and country, but none so hard as that one in a two-foot wide metal groove down the middle of a half-track.

Strychnine and his pal probably got drunk. In their normal nasty sanity they would not have bashed on the door of the half-track at one in the morning and bawled,

'Keep awake in there, soldier! We're expecting a message!'

With the smell of autumn in the ferns and two moons dangling overhead, the camp and the oaktrees quiet, the day's work done, I doubt if life had ever offered Strychnine a more gratifying moment than that one. Life was a fuck-up and he was overweight, over-looked and hated. But he was on top. Bullshit baffled brains, if only because those higher up were at it too and would never ask questions.

Next day a lot of things happened. All the trucks and equipment ducked into the trees and put on green hairnets. Walking around was like being on a filmset waiting for Japanese commandos. Strychnine jostled us a bit, but he had bowel trouble and we did not see much of him. I strolled down the line looking for aerials and trying to find out what wavelength we were on. Two or three bands seemed to have the consensus and I made a note of them.

At tea-time Strychnine came out again. He trod delicately. I was away from my radio, squatting under damp spruce trees with the storemen. He lowered himself beside us, like a shuddery old man joining a picnic.

'What's going to happen, Q?'

'We're going to be attacked.' He hunched his knees up painfully.

'We can take it, can't we?'

'I bleeding well can't.'

'Have some spam, Q.'

Strychnine shivered.

'Who's going to attack us?' I asked.

'How the fuck d'you think I know? You lot had better stick to your wagons tonight. Marshfield, I'll be coming in with the radio.'

I gulped. All night with Strychnine in a torchlit half-track. Me threatened with a charge. Him in his condition. He might fall ill,

I might have to nurse him. That would be terrible. He might even feel better and crack a few of his ropey jokes. That would be catastrophic.

He came in all the same, as the equinoctial sun went down over the gigantic land shelving westward to Stonehenge.

'Shift your arse over, Marshfield.'

I fiddled with a few dials.

'Are we in touch with everyone?'

'They're a short walk away.'

'On that fucking thing, I mean.'

'I think I know the channels.'

'You'd better fucking know.'

Confusion set in sooner than I expected. I do not know if we were attacked or not. Perhaps in the nature of things the Tidworth Regiment was not supposed to be attacked. I never knew. There were explosions (they went on all night) and flares, and voices outside, and a lot of static on the radio. Really it was all very boring. Strychnine was as restless as a bull outside an abattoir:

'You keep us tuned in. I'm going out for a minute.'

An hour passed and he had still not come back. I sat with headphones on reading medieval history by torchlight. A bang on the door. I opened it. A National Service officer poked his head in. 'How are things?'

'What?' I asked abruptly.

He looked at my book and grinned. 'Studying the manual?'

'You might say.' I grinned back.

'Stores?'

'That's right.'

'This lot is to move forward. Can you get out and guide the driver to that black clump two hundred yards over there? He'll never see it through that slit of his.'

I got out and led the half-track through the night. It was quite exhilarating, crossing the fields at two in the morning, lit by enemy flares, reciting Shakespeare aloud to myself. I learnt a lot of Shakespeare in the Army. Walking backwards I saw other lorries following. I trusted they were ours.

Once in the black clump our job was over. I locked on to what seemed like HQ's band but heard nothing of significance. I slept.

After breakfast we were on our way home to Tidworth. Back at camp Strychnine was unusually docile. Rumour had it that he had been caught short in the crisis. The only man in the latrines when the camp was abandoned. He did not press the charge against me and there must have been a reason.

Some time after that episode I was asked to design a screen for the major, and I was allowed to work on it in office time. That was enjoyable: the screen developed some fancy curves I was proud of, but what took the time was the painting. With oil-paints borrowed from Anna I worked a French poem down one side (Verlaine's *Il pleure dans mon coeur*) and illustrated it with a girl in a lit doorway in a dark, rain-sodden street. When I was half-way through, Strychnine glanced at it.

'Looks a fucking mess.'

I think he was pleased I was doing it. There were times when he even tried to relax and confide in me.

'The men don't like me, you know.'

'Oh? Why is that, Q?'

'I don't know. You got to be fucking hard in this game. Look what happened to the old Q.'

He was mortally afraid of becoming like that lost creature, busted down to corporal, flitting about between NAAFIs at night in black plimsolls.

Today? I imagine that today Strychnine might be running a sweetshop or an off-licence. I have been a little more successful. But I am his age now and I sometimes suspect I might exude a little of the same poison.

MICHAEL BAKEWELL

Nobody could say that I had the aspect of a military man. My father had been an RSM on the Somme in the First World War. My uncles had been in the Navy and the RASC. I even had a second cousin who had been in the Royal Flying Corps, but none of this background had been absorbed. During the blitz I used to sit and listen to my father and his fellow air raid wardens talking about the First War. It seemed to be the only time they had ever known any real happiness. They sat in the back room with a crate of Guinness night after night talking on and on about the war. Father had been in the Ordnance Corps in charge of a great horde of baffled and reluctant Chinamen who had been brought in through some unlikely alliance. His most treasured possession was a pile of note-books, finely drawn and neatly coloured, in which he had put down the characteristics of various shells and other kinds of explosive devices. He had a passion about explosives. Even at the height of the war the garage was full of mills bombs and incendiaries.

Sometime in the early forties I joined the School Cadet Corps – not out of any particular conviction, but simply because I did not want to be a Boy Scout. My uncle was Chief Scout for Warwickshire, my Coventry cousins adept and enthusiastic scouts. I knew that I would never be able to compete and the Cadet Corps at Sutton Coldfield seemed the safest way out. We wore old First

War uniforms with puttees and had rifles that fired single rounds inserted with difficulty into the breech. We drilled endlessly, went on wet and muddy expeditions in Sutton Park and prepared for weeks for the annual inspection – an occasion on which I invariably ended up with chronic hay fever. Eventually I became a field telephonist, laying lines across miles of wilderness, trailing the vital threads across tiny streams, plugging the whole lot together and trying vainly to communicate with distant co-telephonists through long hot summer afternoons.

My father of course wanted me to go into the Army. I settled for the RAF, partly because I knew that I could never match up to what he had done and partly because most of us at school thought that we would have an easier time of it. Most of our friends who had served in the RAF had had an easy war and there seemed no reason why this should not be so in peacetime. Flying never entered into my calculations. Most of the people I knew who had joined had never seen an aeroplane.

I did of course do my best to keep out of it altogether. There were friends who had discovered painless but useful ailments like perforated ear drums or ingrowing finger nails. I hoped that hay fever might stand me in good stead, but no one was impressed. Everyone I knew had only one desire – to secure the cushiest possible job for the shortest possible time. There was no glamour or pride or sense of duty or purpose. It seemed to hold nothing but mind-consuming inanity.

I was sent for basic training to West Kirby on the Wirral peninsula. It was the first time I had ever been away anywhere by myself apart from odd holidays in youth hostels. Everyone seemed lonely, frightened and inadequate. West Kirby was reputed to be the most ferocious of the training camps, although in the end I came to realise that the worst was always the one you were sent to. Basic training lasted for eight weeks, but we were continually harried by rumours of having to stay on seemingly for ever if we failed any of the final tests. There were tales of men who had been there for months, broken in body and spirit, permanently on jankers. One man in my hut, a God-made scapegoat if ever there was one, did fail basic training and was kept on for a second term, but he went to enormous lengths to do so – always late on parade, uniform in wild disarray, rifle clogged, brass unpolished. The rest of us were helped, cajoled or bullied through the whole process. There was an assault course where I had to keep going back because at every obstacle I lost my hat. No one seemed to care. It was more important to keep one's gear intact than to master the subtle crafts of war.

We drilled endlessly under enormous cold skies full of screaming seagulls. We polished and painted everything and underwent the whole process of inductionary intimidation through mindless discipline familiar to all of us who had been reared on Brian Donlevy's performance in *Beau Geste*. Some of us rose magnificently to the occasion. There were those whose best boots were polished to a degree where they became works of art, and were proudly displayed as such at the foot of a perfectly displayed kit. One poor lad whose boots had acquired an hallucinatory brightness that would have won them a place in an exhibition of pop art fell foul of the corporal in charge of the hut. His boots were picked up and hurled across the room at the wall. The precious patina was cracked and he was put on a charge for dirty boots. It was impossible to win in such a situation. The only way in which the boots could be brought to the required degree of shine was to burn polish into the surface with a red hot spoon. Mere brushing was not enough. But if you were seen applying the fatal spoon you were charged with damaging government property. The patina was too fragile to survive actual use. The boots were brought to their high degree of perfection to be worn for the first time on the passing-out parade. They were lucky if they survived one inspection. My particular intake passed out in the middle of a violent blizzard. Boots cracked everywhere. The inspecting much-braided officer trotted between the ranks while the band played excerpts from Meyerbeer.

'It must be breaking your heart what this beastly snow is doing to your boots,' he said.

To my surprise I was listed as POM – Potential Officer Material. This rather threw me off balance, since this had never entered into my calculations. National Service was, as I have said, something to be endured and not exploited. I dutifully went through the tests and interviews and against my better judgement the whole notion began to grow on me. For the final meeting I arrived clutching, for reasons I have never been able satisfactorily to explain to myself, a copy of the *Daily Telegraph*. The young Flight Lieutenant commended me on my choice and the whole conversation began to go very smoothly indeed. Fortunately, at last, the question of politics came up: what did I think about the Communist government of China? I said that I thought it was an ideal system for the people of that country after years of misery and suffering. And what did I think should happen to Formosa and the government of Chiang Kai-Shek? Formosa should be handed over instantly to mainland China and the cosseted General should seek political asylum in the USA. The interview terminated sharply. Looking back now on those years denied the pleasures of the officers' mess and the privileges of rank I am astounded by my lack of guile on that occasion, but not ungrateful.

I found myself increasingly uncertain as to what kind of person I was, or was becoming. At first I tried to cling on to shreds of culture like some kind of protective clothing. I used to seek out remote lavatories where I could sit and read Racine. When I did go to bed I would try and blot out the sounds of the hut by filling my skull with music; Rossini's *Semiramide* overture was a firm favourite, I remember. But always underneath it all was a ground bass of words, a kind of drowsing flyting from one end of the hut to the other: 'Fuck off . . . Bollocks . . . Fuck off . . . Bollocks . . . Fuck off . . . . Bollocks . . . . . Fuck off . . . . . . Bollocks . . . . Fuck off . . . . Bollocks . . . . fuck off . . . . Bollocks . . .' Very soon these turned out to be a better soporific than the Rossini.

Withdrawal was for officers. I gave myself up to the life of the hut. I became part of a generalised drill movement. Even the drill itself began to impose a kind of rough shape and unity upon us, for the time being at least. I went to pubs in Liverpool and dance-halls in New Brighton and tried to make myself indistinguishable from the others.

I was much impressed by the Londoners, a species I had not encountered before. They seemed a cunning and inventive lot. One night they took one of the country boys down to the local. While he was out in the bog they filled his beer mug with urine. He returned and drained it happily. 'Trouble with this beer,' he said, 'it tastes like piss.'

Sex dominated most of the conversation. They all seemed to have terrible anxieties. They were worried about what their girls were doing and who they were doing it with, they were worried about the size and volume of their pricks when erect (one boy even ran a bulletin board on the subject), they were worried about the weight of their balls when they did not masturbate and the possible dire consequences when they did. Beds were known as wanking chariots. One lad was so worried about the possibility of his deflowering his girl before marriage that he masturbated daily in his bath to keep his desires in check.

For the most part our whole life centred on the camp, which

seemed so vast that I never worked out where it ended. There was the gymnasium where I vainly tried to throw the medicine ball the required distance for pass-out, there was the hospital which I passed on nightly sentry duty but mercifully never entered, there were the canteens which I associated largely with long spells of enforced potato peeling. There was a weapons range where we were inadequately instructed in the technique of firing various guns. I particularly remember the stens, lethal to the user, likely to come to pieces in your hands, and, as far as I could judge, harmless to the enemy. Occasionally route marches took us out on to the Wirral. The feeling of freedom was wonderful. We marched whistling wartime tunes past the cottage of a dear white-haired old lady. She stood at her gate waving her handkerchief and blowing us kisses. I think she thought we were off to Passchendaele.

'God bless you, boys. I love you all,' she called out again and again.

'She'd have her fuckin' work cut out,' muttered one of the surlier spirits.

In the middle of basic training, Christmas took place. I had been out of the camp from time to time at weekends to Liverpool and New Brighton, but somehow this was still part of the training experience. Liverpool seemed merely an extension of the camp, a kind of glorified NAAFI, part of the same basic reality. Home, on the other hand seemed totally unreal. There was so much light, so much comfort, so much food, so much wellbeing. In the end it proved to be meaningless, a kind of mirage. Real life was out there on the Wirral under the seagulls, with uncooked herrings for breakfast and standing to attention and bawling out 'NCO!' every time the corporal came into the hut. Real life was blanco and polish and gleaming floors and foot drill and the endless repetition of the march past and general salute. I was very relieved when the buses drove us back to camp and put an end to the confusion in my mind.

We returned from leave hardened campaigners. The latest intake of recruits looked very new and very frightened. The corporal in charge of the hut who had seemed a creature of mindless misdirected malice now incessantly told us how proud he was of us and how well we would acquit ourselves on pass-out. He was a wiry little Irishman whose great passion was weightlifting. He used to invite groups in to watch him and basked in what he supposed was their mute admiration. The one thing that did not please him was a successful POM. He did not like his National

Service lads to become officers. The day after one brightly shining youth was selected for officer training he trampled on his impeccably creased trousers and threw him against the wall. Shortly before pass-out the corporal was abruptly taken from us. There had been some particularly spectacular punch-up somewhere off Lime Street. He had broken his wrist and been grabbed by the RAF Police. Weightlifting and authority vanished overnight.

Most of the time was occupied by rehearsals for pass-out parade. For these we were joined by the station band. I was particularly impressed by the General Salute to the tune of which some distant folk-hero had attached the words:

> Stand by your beds
> Here comes the Air Chief Marshal
> He's got lots of rings
> But he's only got one arsehole.

As I said earlier, the parade itself took place in a blizzard. We were specially commended for our drill and spent the remainder of the day in a state of military exaltation. God knows what it must have felt like to win a battle.

After ceasing to be POM I had filled up a form listing the trades I wished to be considered for in my service career. None of the categories seemed to fit. All seemed equally irrelevant. I filled in a few occupations at random. As things turned out it made very little difference.

While on leave after basic training I was told that I was to be a telephonist and to report to a base in Lincolnshire. Telephonist was not one of the trades I had put down on my form, and I was not very sure what it involved, but I remembered those happy days in Sutton Park laying lines with the Cadets Corps and set out for Stamford.

I was based at a station called Wittering, between Stamford and Peterborough. The buildings were redbrick, covered in ivy and rather handsome. There was a feeling of faded nobility about the place as if somewhere in a remote corner of the airfield the Battle of Britain was still going on. One day on a cross-country run I came across a group of empty huts falling slowly into decay. They seemed to have been left like that since the last fighters had gone up eight years previously. Somewhere or other Anton Walbrook was still playing the Warsaw Concerto and the cast of *One of Our Aircraft is Missing* were having their final briefing. I wandered into the barrack block where I was to live. It felt very much like my first day at school except that I was the only new pupil. On entering I was given a pair of skids cut out of old blanket so as not to damage the shining surface of the floor, and slowly skated my way over to my bed. A few weary souls were listening to the Light Programme on the tannoy. A corporal entered. I sprang vigorously to attention and screamed out 'NCO!' No one stirred. The Light Programme droned on. The corporal told me to forget all that bullshit and go out and have a cup of tea in the café on the road.

Wittering was only the base camp. The real working area lay deep in the fens some twenty miles beyond Stamford, a radar and plotting station. I was driven out there by lorry through Stamford and out across the fens. This was a journey I was to do daily for many months and of which I never tired. There was Stamford itself, now almost wholly by-passed, but then part of the A1. Lorries slowly heaved their way through the greystone buildings and the fantastic churches; the whole thing was like something out of a gothic fairy tale.

At the radar station they were rather surprised. No one had warned them that they were to receive a new telephonist, nor was there really need for one. The sergeant in charge calculated the number of teabreaks that my arrival would make possible, and was happy. The job itself was easy. Most of the work was purely routine: coping with local station calls, occasionally routing calls through an RAF network system and (which was where life became adventurous and exotic) connecting with the GPO system. There were only five of us. We lived a life apart from those concerned with the basic functioning of the radar station, took our meals together and constituted something of an elite. Life was calm and reassuring. I can recall only one disturbing incident.

The adjutant rang through and asked to be connected with a station in the Midlands. A few minutes later the CO, an unknown figure but a switchboard position outlined in red, asked to be put through to the adjutant. I was alone on duty. I told him the adjutant was engaged. To whom was he speaking? I named the station.

'Right, laddie. I want to listen in to his conversation and I don't want him to know I'm there. Fix that up for me, will you?'

I sat there in a state of paralysis gazing helplessly at the switchboard. Even if I had been prepared to go along with his monstrous request I had no idea how to accomplish it. I had visions of being shot at dawn or at the least undergoing a lifetime of fatigues.

The CO audibly fumed. The sergeant returned like a God in a machine. Instantly he disconnected the adjutant and told the CO the call had been somehow cut off. Did he wish to speak to the adjutant? The CO hung up.

Some days later I put through a call from West Kirby about the misposting of a fighter plotter. The flight sergeant had expected fifteen new trainees. He had received only fourteen. Had someone gone missing? I had nothing better to do and left the line open. The missing fighter plotter was a certain AC Bakewell, who had vanished without trace. Desertion even in peacetime I remembered was a considerable offence. I hastened to make myself known. Fighter plotting was one of the trades I had put down on my form. I was received into my new trade without enthusiasm. The record had been put straight. The sergeant in charge of the telephone system reorganised his teabreaks.

The trade of fighter plotting is fairly well known from old films. You stand on the edge of a vast map of a sector of the British Isles. You listen intently through headphones to a man hunched over a radar scanner who reads off map references and ancillary information about the height and speed of individual or groups of aircraft. In your hand you hold a magnetised pole and pick up and move about a figure group corresponding to the aircraft. The magnets are mostly tired and the plaques fall with a heavy crash in the middle of the map. You lean over or crawl your way across England to replace the plaque, by which time you have missed the relevant information for five other aircraft. If you are lucky, the aircraft moves out of your sector before any real damage is done.

There were far too many fighter plotters. It was a way of disposing of the dubious intellectuals or the misguided lefties. I felt a distinct sense of awe at joining their ranks. They constituted a hardened break-away movement. I first met them in the rest-room after I had been expelled from the telephone exchange. There was one who talked only of Finnegan's Wake and New Orleans jazz, another who had taken Wyndham Lewis as his province and another who sat in a corner and read I. A. Richards, of whom I had never heard. I longed for the telephone exchange. Where I had previously clung to art as a private consolation, I now realised how publicly inadequate I was.

Fighter plotting was carried out on a nine-to-five basis, which seemed to imply that East Anglia was left undefended through the hours of darkness. There were occasional night flying exercises depending upon energy and enthusiasm. Yet we were never left

in doubt about the terrible realities surrounding us and the pre-
cariousness of peace. This was the time when the cold war was at
its most intense. We were rounded up for indoctrination lectures.
'When the balloon goes up – and, mark my words, it's going to go
up pretty soon now – ' was how most of them started. We were
read harrowing descriptions of atrocities in Belsen and Dachau –
'And there's one thing you can be sure of, the Russians will be
much worse.' National Service seemed some kind of trap out of
which we would never escape. We had been handed over to a bunch
of maniacs to fight their cold war for them.

Fighting seemed to play precious little part in our daily activity.
Because the trade was so grotesquely overmanned we only ever
saw the operations room once or twice a week. The rest of our
time was spent on fatigues – potatoes again or scrubbing a night-
marish succession of cooking implements in the tin room. In the
mornings I generally had the job of cleaning out the sergeants'
mess. The smell of stale beer and old cigarette ends has stayed with
me ever since. The job took about ten minutes but I was expected
to spin it out for two hours so that they would not have to think
up anything else for me to do. I had a copy of Milton's minor
poems. I memorised *Lycidas, L'Allegro* and *Il Penseroso*. It is not
Milton's fault but his lines now only convey to me just how sticky
table tops got through having beer spilt over them.

'Misemployment' was as I remember the technical phrase for it.
In theory an airman could not be misemployed for longer than
three months but I passed virtually my whole RAF existence in
misemployment. Some of it was mildly interesting – drawing up
weather charts so that the adjutant would know what he could
expect on his long weekends, monitoring intercom chatter during
night fighter exercises. Most of it was meaningless jargon delivered
through heavy distortion at top speed, but it somehow gave me
the excitement of remotely being involved in the process of actually
flying.

It was as near as I ever came to it. There were schemes for taking
us up in rusting old Dakotas to demonstrate what flying was really
like, but mercifully these never came to anything. There were so
many schemes that never ever came to anything. We spent weeks
preparing for an elaborate exercise in which we were all to be
carted off blindfold in dead of night and dumped in distant parts
of the country. We had twenty four hours in which to find our
way back, escaping the vigilance of the police and the military who
would be out to get us. Some of us felt quite limp with excitement

at the prospect, but the whole thing was abandoned at the last moment.

What we were sent on was courses and attachments. I learned to fire every weapon in existence, gained some sketchy notion of unarmed combat and fought off successfully a free course in Moral Rearmament which at that stage was looked at with a kindly eye by the Forces. Some of the attachments were quite extraordinarily pointless. I was packed off for a couple of weeks to serve as a firefighter somewhere outside Nottingham. The first few days were hysterical, letting off various shapes and varieties of fire extinguisher, struggling into heavy asbestos clothing complete with space helmet and roaring off across the airfield clinging to the side of the fire tender, massive axes at the ready for cutting heroic pilots out of blazing aircraft. But very soon it became a matter of dreary routine, sitting in the fire tender helping the corporal do the *Daily Mirror* crossword, waiting for something to crash. In the evenings there was fire picket duty at the station cinema. I saw Ingrid Bergman as Joan of Arc and a marvellous movie called *Man and his Mate* which had no dialogue but grunts, and Carole Landis in a bear skin pursued by monstrous lizards through the jungle. On my last day a jet overshot and touched down with very little runway left. The fire tender would not start. I was struggling into my asbestos gear and a flying-officer was dancing about on the Control Tower balcony screaming at us to get the thing moving. It juddered forwards and stalled. The plane somehow stopped before hitting a hedge. I was told that the following week the fire tender failed again. A Tiger-Moth crashed in the middle of the field and the pilot walked over and helped them to get the engine going. But that may have been apocryphal.

Leave was merely confusing. Like that first Christmas it disturbed my sense of reality and was more pain and trouble than it was worth. As time went on I made the journey home less and less frequently. Stamford and Peterborough were both very attractive places, and I came to like the countryside of the fens. I did have one week in Bournemouth. My father was ill and depressed after a prostate operation and it seemed possible this would be his last holiday. I wandered round miserably not knowing what to do with myself, desperately conscious of a hot sticky uniform, wondering how to spend the precious hours of freedom, feeling that I belonged nowhere. Later that year my father died and I went on a long spell of compassionate leave.

When I returned to Stamford everything had changed. The camp had virtually been put on a war footing. The operations room was manned twenty four hours a day and maximum security had been imposed. The Korean War had escalated. My period of Service had already been increased in the summer from eighteen months to two years. I felt that I might have to spend the rest of my life defending the fens from the yellow peril. A kind of panic had set in about the security of the base. We guarded it like Fort Knox. We prowled about at night, climbed up and down the radar masts making sure they harboured no Koreans or vigilant young pilot officers putting us to the test. By day we paced up and down on the roof of the operations block looking at the clouds. The English genius for compromise was put to great effect. We were to shoot at anything that did not reply satisfactorily when challenged, but to give ourselves time to reflect on the situation we had to keep our rounds in our pocket. Mine were generally inextricably interleaved with a Penguin copy of John Donne. After a time we were replaced by guard dogs.

The intensification of the war brought about a period of frantic, pointless activity. We were taken on visits to other stations, driving for miles through tulip fields and dykes. We took part in elaborate exercises of simulated invasion. On one of these, somewhere outside Grimsby, the use of something mysterious called 'window' and various other anti-radar devices produced a situation of total chaos. We stood over the table, rods at the ready, plotting aircraft that never were. The only reliable reports came in from the Royal Observer Corps, old gentlemen lying back in their deck chairs scanning the skies with binoculars. After a massive raid by fifty aircraft turned out to be a particularly dense piece of cloud a despairing flight-sergeant sent a couple of us to sit on the roof of the operations block and report to him any planes that passed over. Shortly after this the station was put out of action, and, as far as we were concerned, the exercise was over.

In early spring six of us were sent off to Bentwaters, a disused airfield in Suffolk. Although initially there may have been some hope that someone would eventually find us fighter plotting to do, it soon became clear that we were simply a labour squad who had been sent out to make the place inhabitable for an American fighter force which were going to take it over. Life was relaxed and pleasantly disorganised. We lived in a hut in the woods, found our own fuel, ate at a make-shift canteen, and tried to strike up some kind of relationship with the hordes of nightingales who kept us awake all night with their incessant jabber. We built store rooms, painted neat lines on the roads, drove round and round the airfield picking up fuel tanks jettisoned during the war, founded a modest library and awaited with some interest the arrival of the Americans. Every few weeks they would send a delegation down to look at us, pronounce the place unfit for human inhabitation, and depart.

The camp was so vast that we were given bicycles, and Suffolk opened up before us. The pubs in the nearby villages seemed still to be held in a kind of golden age, with redfaced yokels singing ethnic ballads. Vast lustful girls ran screaming after us down country lanes and tried to drag us off our bicycles. One member of the hut was unlucky enough to be caught. It proved a singularly unrewarding experience – 'Like fucking a sack of potatoes,' he said. The following week he went down with VD.

Life suddenly seemed to expand. Visits home were now almost totally abandoned. I wandered happily round Woodbridge and Ipswich, cycled to Lowestoft and Yarmouth and one strange evening trekked across country to find the Persian Rose growing (with some difficulty) on Edward Fitzgerald's grave. National Service virtually ceased to exist. The work was mindless and totally undemanding. No one cared very much whether it was done or not. I read a great deal, but now no longer in the lavatories. There were problems. We had a running war on with the cooks, which took the form mainly of epic inter-billet battles with fire extinguishers. More disconcertingly, two of my friends were made acting RAF policemen, because the whole place was so desperately short-staffed. They went through a personality change so total as to be unrecognisable: instant mean-mouthed bastards they became.

Eventually the Americans arrived. We had all been expecting something like the good old days of the war, cheap beer and packets of monster cigarettes. By what seemed a massive error of judgement we were strictly segregated. We were barred from their PX, worked and lived in separate areas of the base and never met them at all except in the pubs. This scarcely helped matters. The pubs were packed out with drunken transatlantic airmen. Wealth poured across the bars. The interiors were fantastically and odiously redecorated, as were the barmaids. In some dismay we began to cycle farther and farther afield to find pubs that the Americans had not discovered. We tried Woodbridge and Orford and Aldeburgh. The nightly treks grew longer and longer. On my way back one night my lights packed up and I ran into a village policeman.

I stood trial in Woodbridge's ornate seventeenth-century court-house and was fined fifteen shillings. It seemed remarkably good value for money.

Once the Americans were established and their fighters were streaking down the runway frightening the skylarks to death and waking up the nightingales, there really was no reason for us to stay on any longer, but no one seemed to be able to think of anything to do with us. Some of the more ardent spirits tried to insist on their rights and be returned to their proper trade. I was full of gloom at this idea. I had just managed to get myself permanently attached to the dustcart run, which meant that I spent the morning emptying the Americans' dustbins (including those of the PX), loading up and driving off to a dump a few miles away. There was a good pub close by and the afternoons were free. I used to go to a place called Shingle Street and sit on the beach reading (for reasons now obscure) *Also Spracht Zarathustra* and watch the boys from the local Borstal institution being exercised.

My only anxiety was whether I would be released in time to go to Cambridge. The war continued but the Koreans had not landed and East Anglia seemed secure. After a good many forms and letters the RAF agreed to let me go a month early. One by one the other members of my hut were posted to real radar stations. In the end there remained only me and an amiable Welshman. We had so little time to serve that I suppose it was not worth the rail fare to move us. There was nothing at all to do. Even the dust cart had been taken over by a civilian contractor. We were told not to let anybody notice us. After two years we had become expert in this. The only problem was that we were faced with handing in our kit. Mine had long since disintegrated and been dispersed. I spent days wandering round stores trying to find a spare mess tin and buying other odd items of equipment from an army surplus stores in Ipswich. Right up to the last minute I was still worried that they might find some way to keep me in.

On the last night the two of us went down for a quiet drink at the pub by the rubbish tip. When we walked back to the hut the nightingales were still at it and all the surrounding huts were now occupied by the Americans. We went round pulling the fuses out of the boxes on the outside of the huts, a kind of farewell symphony. We wisely plunged ourselves into darkness as a last gesture. The following morning I caught a train to London and spent my first day of freedom looking, very slowly, at the Festival of Britain.

RICHARD KEY

In many ways I was lucky. Although I had no really positive feelings about National Service, I certainly did not resent giving up two years, nor did I feel it was a waste of time.

I arrived at the Royal Naval Barracks, Portsmouth on 11th February 1957, to start my National Service as an ordinary seaman at the age of eighteen and a half. I had wanted to serve in the Navy, and in order to guarantee entry I had taken the precaution of joining the Royal Naval Volunteer Reserve six months before my call-up was due. I knew it was expected of me to obtain a commission, mainly because this, together with my public-school education, would go a long way towards assuring my future after National Service. This too was in my mind when I joined the RNVR. At the time the Navy was cutting down on its intake, and was mainly taking only ex-RNVR conscripts.

As I walked through the gate at Portsmouth, all I really knew (although I did not think about it consciously) was that National Service was part of my life-pattern, just as school and taking my first job (as a trainee sales representative at Fry's chocolate factory near Bristol) were part of the same pattern.

The security of this continuity was reinforced during my first two weeks in Portsmouth, for most of my fellow National Service-men were from similar backgrounds and we all went through the same kitting-out and basic training procedures. The fortnight we had done of RNVR training counted as the first part of our real training, and we then went on to HMS *Ocean,* an aircraft carrier which was then the centre of National Service training operations, and in harbour at Rosyth, in Scotland.

Ocean was docking just as we arrived, and there was a serious accident. In order to pull the ship up to the wall, a two-inch wire hawser is put over a bollard on the dock, and the other end is wrapped round a winch inside the ship; it is not fixed to the winch, but there are about four or five men pulling it and keeping it tight. For some reason it got to a point where this hawser just snapped, and on an aircraft carrier the winch is in an enclosed space, not in the open like on most ships, and the hawser just flayed around in there, hitting these men's legs and breaking their arms, causing great cuts and so on. When a wire goes it is terrifying, because it is like a great snake flailing around. We came on board just after this had happened. We walked below deck through the aircraft hangers and so on, and as we came to the forward lift that takes the aircraft up on to the flight deck, there were these three men laid out on stretchers, ready to be carted off to hospital. And that frightened me, I know. I had a healthy respect for wires after that.

Basic training was nothing like as rough as one has heard it was in the Army, people being driven to string themselves up and so on. In *Ocean* we were divided up into classes of about twenty and each had an instructor. In our case it was a cheerful petty-officer who had quite obviously seen some service. The way he talked to us was very rough indeed, but he let us see the twinkle in his eye and he was always making jokes. He gave us all our instruction in seamanship and drill. One day he caught me telling a joke to my neighbour during a seamanship lecture and demanded to know what it was. I replied, with attempted innocence:

'Nothing, sir.'

'I know your sort,' he replied, 'as the actress said to the stage-door johnnie – you've got love in your eyes and murder in your trousers!'

I did not find the discipline particularly tough throughout the whole of my National Service. It was always there, but in ordinary everyday life it was not applied as inhumanely as I have heard it was in the Army. There was hardly any need for bull, for finding people jobs to do. When I was an ordinary seaman, the jobs I had to do on board ship had a purpose, and I knew they had a purpose.

Towards the end of our period of training on *Ocean* we left Rosyth and sailed on a courtesy visit to Antwerp. On arrival our petty-officer told us that during the visit we would be allowed shore leave as usual until midnight, but he warned us of the dangers to young sailors in foreign ports, and particularly stressed that on no account should we venture into the red light district near the docks.

I decided to go ashore with a friend for the evening. We wandered around and looked at the town and after a meal and some beers we started to wander back to the ship, bored and cold sober. We were approached by a Swedish merchant seaman, who although slightly drunk persuaded us in excellent English to let him show us the red light district. As we walked down the street we saw the houses on both sides had quite large windows at ground floor level: most of these were brightly lit and occupied by women who were just sitting waiting or leaning out and calling for custom.

As we walked by, our Swedish guide made derogatory comments about the women, who were mostly between thirty to forty, with bleached blonde hair, overtly buxom, and all had very hard expressions. Slightly horrified by the experience, we were taken into a bar at the end of the street by our guide for a quick drink before returning to the ship. As we entered we saw our petty-officer, drunk, and dancing clumsily with one of the street women. Next day he denied all knowledge of either our meeting him or the incident.

At the end of the four-day visit we sailed to Plymouth and our course came to an end. Most were sent to other ships while myself and a few others were considered suitable to attempt a National Service Officers' Board back at Portsmouth. The Board process took a month, and during that time we felt we were being watched closely. We did our best to please up to the final event which was a detailed and gruelling day of initiative tests, discussion groups, lectures, and a detailed interview with the examining board. I failed. The course broke up; those who were successful went to start their training and the failures returned to thir ships. Not having a ship, I was moved across to the general barracks to wait for a draft to a ship.

The move to the barracks began a decisive chapter in my life, and looking back it was the start of a rather hurried maturing process. It was the first time I had been away from the protection of my middle-class environment and even during basic training and the hardships which occurred on HMS *Ocean* I drew comfort from the fact that the others were all similar people with the same middle-class consciousness. Once in the barracks I was just another sailor, and one in a minority. I was faced with having to survive and co-exist in a world which was not of the making of anyone I knew and in which I felt at a distinct disadvantage.

Natural shyness and basic fear prompted me to keep myself to myself. I was helped in this by being given a rather individual task until my draft came through. It was called 'Recess Messman' and this meant serving food to the men who were locked up in the barracks recess; that is, the prison cells or brig. Serious naval crimes were dealt with at the main naval centres because they could provide the proper punishment facilities. The barracks recess consisted of two separate areas: one was a large general cell where the men waiting for court martial sentences were kept, sleeping on reasonable bunks and eating normal barracks food; and the other was the cell block, which was for the most serious offenders.

Cell block offenders were in solitary confinement, slept on hard wooden bunks with only one coarse blanket, and had to exist on a diet of bread, potatoes and unsweetened tea and cocoa. To occupy inmates during the day and to make sure they spent their time usefully they were given six-pound lumps of old rope hawser which was cut into short pieces, and by every evening they had had to separate by hand each individual fibre. This, in theory, gave a six-pound bag of oakum, soft material suitable for stuffing mattresses, pillows, and so on. Any man not completing his six pounds was given the residue the next day in addition to a new six-pound load.

I had never known anything like this situation, and it affected me deeply. Not only did I feel that these ordinary human beings were treated inhumanly, but my middle-class veneer was beginning to crack and I felt I was becoming depersonalised by my involvement in the situation. On reflection, this was the first time I had had any inkling of the depths of the human condition, and I found it very distressing.

However, living in the barracks had some advantages. In contrast to the work I was doing I found that the sailors with whom I messed were beginning to accept me. I was chatting one evening to one particular long-serving able seaman when he said to me:

'Always remember, lad, if ever you're out with a party and you're not getting anywhere, whip it out and wap it in her hand. She may scream, but she'll hang on for grim death.'

In due course, I heard I had been drafted to HMS *Striker,* an LST (landing ship tanks) which was part of the Amphibious Warfare Squadron based on Malta. My reaction to this posting was mixed. I was happy to travel, but apprehensive as to the ship I was joining;

particularly as to what I would find on the lower deck of a ship in contrast to the barracks at Portsmouth.

The nine months I was to spend on the lower deck of *Striker* were to be the most critical in my life. It was during this time that I felt myself change, that I developed some personality outside the pattern I had conformed to for most of my life, and at the end of that time I really felt as if I had been de-conditioned. This period was a watershed for me, and, although I certainly knew something was happening at the time, the full realisation of its importance did not come till much later.

I was the only National Serviceman among one hundred and forty regulars, and certainly the only public schoolboy. I was completely on my own among these people from a totally different background, and I was judged solely on who I was, not on where I had been to school, where I had worked or who my parents knew. I was well away from home, completely cut off from any middle-class influences, apart from the officers. It could have been a period of military humiliation, and I have heard terrible stories about other people in similar circumstances in other ships and other services. But after the usual initiation of letting my hammock down, and trying to goad me in the traditional ways, I found I was gradually accepted. I think the fact that I liked to keep myself to myself helped, and also that I started to laugh with them at their jokes on me and was never drawn. But (perhaps because it was a small, closely-knit community) I was spared the brutalisation which some people went through.

During the nine months I became more and more detached from my background as I thought more and more for myself rather than relying on stock class conditioning for the answers to my problems. One of these was having to live and get on with other people at close quarters. Although I lived away from home when I was at school, conditions were not similar. My mess was in the stern of the ship on the starboard side within an area which measured about thirty by twelve feet. There were two rows of metal lockers, giving three messes spaced eight feet by twelve. I shared with ten to twelve other men. We slept at night in hammocks slung from pipes just under the deck head.

I was the first National Serviceman to be allowed on that ship for some time. The last Commanding Officer, who had just left the ship, had been efficient but eccentric. He objected to National Servicemen joining his ship, being trained up, and then moving on to take commissions on other ships. He also felt it was healthier to shave his legs regularly, and had unsuccessfully tried to persuade the crew to do this as well.

Once I was on board I easily settled into the routine. When we were in harbour it was generally maintenance work. This consisted of scrubbing the decks, and painting and cleaning the sides of the structure and superstructure. When we were at sea the work was all the manual tasks involved in actually operating the ship. Gradually, during the nine months I was with the ship and through the familiarity of living so closely with the rest of the crew I became assimilated into the ship's company. With this acceptance came a certain amount of respect for what they considered my superior education. I was approached by one able seaman who had completed more than eight years' service and asked to help with his correspondence course in horology. He was the only rating I met during my two years who seemed to have any concern for his future employment.

I had never really had (or been allowed) to think about the lives of anyone lower than the middle class. I should like to think that this was due to my conditioning. However, it was almost as if one day on *Striker* I took off my blinkers and found that I had human beings all around me. These people had hopes, fears, dreams and sometimes tragedy in their lives, yet there was always humour, too. The more I lived with them and talked to them, the more I realised the size of the economic gulf between our backgrounds and how unjust and immoral it all was.

Yet there was another and even larger gulf between us and the vast majority in the civilian populations of the Mediterranean ports we visited. Soon after I arrived on *Striker,* I saw the small son of a Maltese boatman (who was contracted to remove our rubbish) pick out a slice of bread floating in a mixture of waste food, dog-ends and tealeaves in one of the uncovered dustbins on deck, and quite openly eat it. I also noticed how Britain exploited the island, and how the Maltese accepted it because the alternative, the rule of the Catholic church, was even worse.

HMS *Striker* was built during the Second World War in Canada, of welded construction, and specifically for the Normandy landings, I believe. It was still going in 1957, though in some places on board there was now about a quarter of an inch of rust to half an inch of plate; sometimes we just used to paint over the rust, and hope it held together.

Striker used to take part in mock amphibious assaults on beachheads in Malta or, mostly, Sardinia, together with Royal Marine

Commandos and our NATO allies. Some of these exercises were quite big, clearing a beach area then pounding it with high explosive and god knows what else from cruisers and destroyers, with air support as well. I used to be stern anchorman on our ship. That is, after we had put the Commandos ashore from small boats the LST would drive up the beach, open its bow doors, lower its ramp and all the other equipment, tanks and so on, would drive out of the belly of the ship. As the ship went in, you would drop a stern anchor so that you could winch the thing off again, and that is what I used to operate.

LSTs had to be flatbottomed, of course, and if we were going into a beam sea the thing became just like a cork. And when we were going head into it, the bow would just bounce off the top of the waves and down with a bang, again and again. As she went down, the stern came out of the water and the screw would race. As our mess deck was in the stern, the whole thing used to shake with the vibration. Then it would settle again in the water, and it would be a little more steady; then up again, and so on. I was never seasick; I had discovered when I was about fifteen on a cross-channel ferry, where there were only two or three of us who were not sick, that I was a good sailor. I felt a bit queasy a couple of times, but I was never sick.

I enjoyed the life, working in the open air, and it was all the more pleasant because it was in a warm climate, of course. When we were working we used to wear just hats, shorts, and sandals, with a knife strung round our waists. I found the full uniform cumbersome and uncomfortable; I could never be relaxed in it, just from a physical point of view. But while you had to be presentable to go ashore, there was not really any bull, you did not have to have a mirror shine on your shoes or knife-edges in the seven horizontal creases of your trousers, just as long as you were presentable. You were only sort of half-inspected before you went ashore.

The Navy's attitude to sex I thought was very sensible. They realised that if men were going to be cooped up in the ship for weeks at a time then when they got to a port it was more than likely that they would go looking for women; and that anyone who is in a place for only a couple of days is not going to develop any sort of relationship with a woman who is straight. So they accept the fact that some people are going ashore and are going to pay for it, and that the chances of them picking up something nasty in the circumstances are pretty high. So they made it clear to anyone going ashore that they should go along to the sick bay beforehand

and ask for what was known as 'sports gear', and they would then be issued with contraceptives. There seemed to be no limit, if you went along the next night and asked for half-a-dozen more then you were given them without any question. They also tried to develop the attitude that if you did pick up something (and they told you the symptoms) then you should go to the sick bay and talk about it. As a result of this, nobody was worried about anything, nobody was worried that if they got a dose then they had to keep it quiet; they just went along to the sick bay and were given injections and so on that would clear it up.

During that nine months in Malta I visited Cagliari in Sardinia, Palermo and Port Augusta in Sicily, Calvi in Corsica, Leghorn, Famagusta, Tripoli, and four times I went to Naples. That must seem a pretty good trip round the central Mediterranean, but the truth was I did not see very much. Since I went to Naples four times, I really should have gone to Pompeii, but I didn't; and I could have gone across to Capri, but I didn't. What stopped me firstly was the strangeness, the foreignness, not speaking the language, and secondly I just did not have the money to do anything like that. Once you had paid for a few dutyfree fags and some sweets, there was not much left from a National Service seaman's pay to go tripping round foreign ports.

I found that I gradually became less reserved during that nine month period on *Striker*. I was the only National Serviceman on board for about six of those nine months and when three more arrived they did not realise for at least two days that I was not a regular member of the crew, which quite pleased me.

The night they arrived on board was the night we returned to Malta from an exercise off Sardinia. Normally in Grand Harbour, Malta, the ship was moored to head and stern buoys. It is manoeuvred up close to the head buoy and a boat is lowered to carry a 'buoy-jumper' and a line from the ship to the buoy. The buoy-jumper takes the line, jumps on to the buoy and passes the line through the ring of the buoy and hands it back to the boat which then carries it to the ship, leaving the jumper standing on the buoy. He has to remain there until the crew on board ship can attach the wire hawser to the line and pull it through the eye and back again on board. Having secured the bow hawser, the process is repeated at the stern. The most frightening part of the buoy-jumper's job is when he is standing cold and alone on a curved, wet and rusty surface while 3,000 tons of ship manoeuvres itself into position very close to him. This can be particularly dangerous at the stern as the propellers may be churning around uncomfortably close to him. The only time I ever did this was the night these three National Servicemen arrived and I came back absolutely filthy, cold, furious I had been given the job, and stormed, cursing like a true matelot, into the mess and took no notice of the three new faces. Nor did I really for two or three days until someone must have told them that I was a National Serviceman too and one approached me and asked if it were true. I would like to think that their eventual assimilation into the crew was somewhat easier due to the groundwork I had done.

After seven months in the Mediterranean on *Striker* I still felt I had to have ambitions to be an officer, although these were considerably reduced by my experiences. I managed to get what was called a Mediterranean Fleet Board which was expected to discover whether I was good enough to go back to England to take a proper Board again. I passed that, and went back to England and I then passed my second National Service OSB, but by that time they were accepting so few for training that they sent me back to the ship. There was an unwritten rule that if you were left with nine months to do of your National Service they would not recall you for officer training. But two months later the pass mark of the succeeding candidates was so low that my mark was higher, and they recalled me to HMS *Raleigh* to train as an officer for sixteen weeks. I was back with the kind of people I went into the Navy with, people from the same background. I just slipped back into a middle-class situation but was never as involved as I would have been if I had gone on the officers' training course straight away.

My final five months of National Service were spent as an officer on a coastal minesweeper based in Scotland with various trips around the English coast and across to Europe. I was one of only three officers, and there were twenty-seven crew; so everyone knew everyone, and it was a very happy ship. The Captain was marvellous. He was a lieutenant-commander who had won medals in the war as a submarine skipper, but had made one mistake and been passed over for further promotion. He was a fantastic seaman; he could handle that ship on a sixpence, he knew her so well.

When I joined I took over from another National Serviceman as navigating officer, gunnery officer, wardroom wine caterer and correspondence officer. I found that the man before me had been cooking the wardroom wine accounts, not on the fiddle but because he did not know what he was doing. I knew little enough about book-keeping so I went to see the skipper, who helped me fill the gaping hole ahead of the audit the following week.

I enjoyed this period enormously, particularly the seamanship part. My attitude towards the crew was obviously affected by the time I had spent on the lower deck of the *Striker*. I tried to treat them fairly, and I think they respected me for my fairness. I do not think I ever had to do anything particularly unpopular, like give anyone punishment or report them. My confidence improved, and my knowledge of the way people worked. I will not say I wished to sign on, but my National Service certainly ended on a high note.

For me National Service was two years of enforced growing up, and looking back on it I think it was probably better for me than if I had gone to university because I was confronted with a wider spectrum of life. I was lucky in that I managed to get away, and did not spend two years in Catterick or on the top of a hill somewhere. I was very lucky in that I managed to pass an officers' training course, but even more in that I spent nine months on the lower deck of a ship in the Mediterranean, travelling about and living with a hundred and forty other people with whom it is unlikely that in the normal run of my life I would have had any close contact. The experience enabled me to think for myself and set the pattern for my social and political development thereafter. I often feel that I would still be a Tory-voting chocolate salesman working my way up through the management system if it were not for National Service.

I still have an ambivalent attitude to it; for although I am opposed to compulsory military service on principle, nevertheless I benefited from it. The only thing National Service did for me was to give me a chance to be confronted by life in a raw state before it became too late. But given the option I think I would do away with public school education and the whole middle-class conditioning of the educational system rather than re-introduce National Service so that people like myself could become 'deconditioned'.

LES WILES

Milling around on Devizes Station, nervous, expectant and mainly silent, we were herded politely on to trucks and driven to the camp for processing, documenting, kitting and feeding. At six hundred hours next morning the shouting and bullying started to train us to fight (and maybe die) in the interests of freedom and the maintenance of colonial privilege.

History shows that men all too willingly accept an ordered system of society which imposes discipline and organisation irrespective of the validity or brutality of its controlling caucuses and their motives. It is a salutary lesson to find that, faced with the conflicts, even when at their most naked, one stays as firmly silent as the mass. Admittedly, to take immature youths and bully them in a controlled situation with the intensity and ferocity that is applied in basic training (or more correctly, basic conditioning), and to use members of their own class to effect the programme, is a calculated policy with a guaranteed success factor.

In a situation where the antagonist holds all the aces the only answers are confrontation or silence. It is seldom that one hears the sound even of the proverbial pin. Like the time, during training, that the RSM, on that fatuous daily exercise 'any complaints', bellowed for silence and then demanded that if anyone wished to do so he should 'Stand up and let us all see who you are!' It was not only the food we had no stomach for.

These conditioning tactics are part of every minute of one's training life in one form or another. They successfully persuade one, in a very short time, to at least partially accept the inherent superiority of the system, the class appointed to effect its requirements and the gospel quality of its pronouncements.

When my intake's training came to an end the number of volunteers for overseas service did not measure up to requirements. For reasons best known to the establishment it was decided to assemble those persons who had so far failed to respond to the number of requests put in the previous six weeks. We were dutifully assembled on the Square, gently cajoled for our intransigence and then given a fulsome exposition of the duty demanded by our Queen and Country. The brief determination of our responsibilities was followed by a tantalising glimpse of the delights we would enjoy should we see the light: better pay, better conditions, and eulogies on greater leisure time to be spent on surf-washed, sun-drenched beaches, with more than one suggestion of beautiful dusky maidens crowding the quayside eager to welcome us warmly to their shores.

The appeal for volunteers that followed was conducted on the same basis as a fund-raising dutch auction: *who'll be in the first ten for sun-drenched beaches – last ten for dusky maidens – only five more – then you may break to the NAAFI.* And over it all the threat in the very first sentences: If we don't get enough we'll draft anyway. They got their volunteers.

The need for conformity of the spirit as well as the body permeated every aspect of the relationship between military machine and men. In that first confused, but relatively civilised, day we were classified according to belief and in my papers there appeared, following an arbitrary, dismissive clerical analysis and interpretation of my philosophical views, the legend 'Atheist' in the space donated to 'Religious Denomination'. I am an agnostic.

At the end of training I was jeeped to the Hampshire camp of their choice at which I would spend the rest of my time. In the Pay Corps the overloading at the top end of the establishment structure was relatively absurd. Our camp, with a total of only about two hundred and forty souls, had both a full- and half-colonel, more majors and captains than any field regiment could hope to muster, and lieutenants vied with privates for numerical supremacy.

I was immediately taken to the second-in-command on arrival. Our lieutenant-colonel was living proof that Napoleon was only half right. A professional soldier, he had risen from the ranks by way of hard and dedicated work to the pinnacle of promotion open to one of such basically inferior stock. His perfunctory welcome was followed by a close questioning of my religious beliefs, and although I explained that I thought it dishonest to admit the ritual 'C of E', because anyway I was not clear on the sectarian differences, and had been singularly unimpressed by what I had seen and understood of organised religion so far. He was most disconcerted by my answers and dismissed them by explaining that as the Queen and Winston Churchill were members of the Church of England he could see no reason why I was not as well, and went on to say that the colonel himself would be speaking to me very soon on the subject.

Learning from my new-found colleagues that the 'Old Man' was a religious nut did little for my confidence, seeing that I had to spend the next twenty-two months there, and it was with something approaching terror that I eventually marched into the presence. I was told, with something less than Christian charity, that I was the first person of my type he had ever met and that I would not, unless I changed my views, 'get on well here'. I was told to see the chaplain – a suggestion to which, in cowardice and fear, I succumbed.

It being a small camp, the chaplain turned out to be the local vicar who habitually carried decaying food in the crevices of his teeth: presumably a recent affectation as no decay was visible. He told me he found it impossible to discuss such matters with unbelievers, and exhibited a most disconcerting embarrassment over the whole affair. He introduced me to a local who claimed to be a Socialist but had subsequently seen the light. We had one chat over tea and buns and the whole thing faded out from there.

My position was helped by the fact that a week later I was followed by another recruit with similar but better articulated views. The colonel, poor old fellow, nearly had a heart attack and railed against the new permissiveness. In a way I hope he has passed peacefully on as life in the seventies would be a living agony for him. The pressures in these circumstances were greatly mollified and soon afterwards our leader was promoted to brigadier, presumably for services rendered to something or other.

I am convinced that Machiavelli is required reading for every graduate of Sandhurst and WOSB. Their ability to manipulate groups of people with well-chosen words into believing that to return half of what has already been taken away is a gesture of generosity defeats the logic of credibility.

A beautiful example of this occurred when the Army pay system was restructured. It was the practice that at each weekend a thirty-six-hour pass was given, with a forty-eight every, I think, six weeks – subject, of course, to guard duty commitments. The introduction of an entirely new pay system for the Army meant that a vast amount of work was involved. For over three months we worked twelve to fourteen hours per day, six and seven days per week, without relief from other duties. Exhausted, deflated, writers-cramped and punchdrunk, our task was finally concluded. We were called together, addressed in terms of fulsome praise for our diligence, and the major delegated to perform the task moved from congratulation to adulation of us and of our efforts. His crescendo of praise culminated in a grandiose gesture, delivered with oratorical expertise: for our labours an extra forty-eight was to be our lucky gift. Some of the silly bastards actually cheered!

A valuable product of the experience derived from being thrown together with an arbitrary group of people from widely varying backgrounds and different geographical areas; in my case it opened wide the eyes of someone who had gone through childhood and adolescence in the fond belief that London and South-East England was the centre of the world. I had heard of Scots and Welshmen, of course, but had met precious few; knew of country bumpkins who used 'oo-aar' with every phrase: but they were remote and of little account. On the radio at the time there was a popular comedy programme that featured a female by the name of Marlene whose principal humorous affectation was a broad Birmingham accent. Shortly after joining, in the course of a group conversation a fellow interjected with what I believed to be a humorous comment. My response in similar style was met by profound hostility. After the initial shock at this unwarranted agressiveness I realised, to my astonishment and embarrassment that there were people who *actually* spoke that way.

That fellow, though, had nothing on the trooper I once spent a week with at Netley Hospital. In a bed opposite me was a Geordie with an accent broad enough to run a motorway down. Incidentally, his presence was the product of a too-vigorous romp with his bride-to-be who had succeeded in rupturing the tip from the rest of the only weapon the Army had not issued him with, and had set it wandering around at will. The cure prescribed was ether packs thrice a day and his squeals rent the ward, much to our sadistic amusement. I digress. The point of the story is that one afternoon we were allowed, both being mobile, to take a trip together into

Southampton. During the whole course of our expedition of something like four to five hours' duration, I can truthfully say I understood not one sentence he spoke and was reduced to answering through a system of guesswork based on the inflection and context of his remarks. His language could just as well have been that of an obscure Mongolian tribe, for all I understood of it. I have been fascinated by accents and dialects ever since.

The number of recruits who actually believed in the purpose and validity of their situation was fairly small. Being Pay Corps we had a goodly sprinkling of bourgeois, accountants in the main, who were commissioned (or if they were real dead-heads and failed WOSB were nevertheless rapidly promoted to sergeant) and therefore professed allegiance to the system. The number of others so aligned could be counted on two hands.

The rest were divided into two camps. The majority group was the 'let's make the most of it' type who accepted the situation; some even worked hard at making the grade, coveting the stripes that would make mum proud of her success-story son, classical cannon fodder.

The rest of us resented the deprivation of our rights and the enforced service imposed upon us and, lacking the sophistication, maturity and consequential courage to put up a direct and sustained confrontation to the system, resorted to less dangerous but suitably satisfying substitutes. Sadly, despite our anarchic gestures, we too would most probably have ended up as cannon fodder if the call had ever come.

On arriving at my ultimate posting I was temporarily lodged in some barrack-room or other, but one week later was delighted to learn that I was being permanently assigned to Number Three Platoon. Three Platoon had the reputation of being the most indisciplined of the camp. This reputation was either revered or despised, according to attitude, but there were precious few conscripts who had less than a sneaking admiration for this motley crew. Most of the platoon members worked hard at sustaining our image and we could be reasonably guaranteed to be the last on parade, have the scruffiest of turnouts and to be generally bottom of the poll on all counts that the system regards most highly.

Our NCOs were always, for some reason or other, of the type who either did not care or were quite unable to cope. This was probably due to the generally inefficient system of allocation, but we fondly believed it was because with us they had given up hope and had made us the dumping ground for all their misfits.

This general atmosphere of anarchy, which never actually created a breakdown in the system as such, was tolerated for the simple reason it was contained, and, in the generally relaxed atmosphere of a regimental pay office, to endeavour to make any radical changes was not worth the effort. About once a year there was a purge and a few fellows got jankers, but that was all. Real individual acts of rebellion were in fact rare and, in my experience, all occurred outside the camp.

At the time of the Suez Crisis, with Z-reservists all over the place, a general atmosphere of dissent and barely-suppressed rebellion existed amongst those who had been recalled. Conscripts in the office next to mine had sent out the call-up papers for these reservists, and some of them had come back with one word scrawled across them: BOLLOCKS. At that time I was sentenced to twenty-eight days' detention and as no facilities existed at our camp I was, as was usual, sent to serve my time in the guard room of the Artillery Paras at Barton Stacey. This was usually hell for those concerned, but for me and another bloke who had been caught the timing was most fortunate. The guard room and cells were packed with reservists who had failed to report or had gone absent from the camp or Germany and had been hauled back to await trial. A constant stream of miscreants went through the guard room and the necessity to control them (and many were belligerently hostile) meant that we were tucked away and by and large forgotten.

During our stay we had the pleasure of a visit for seven days from a fellow who we knew as Woodsy. A recalled reservist, he had requested whilst on parade that he be excused to perform a common natural function. The RSM, purple of face and neanderthal of intellect, responded by bellowing, 'Well, piss on the square!' Woodsy, respecting the order of a superior, dutifully did so. The seven days? Section 40, 'Conduct prejudicial to good order and military discipline'.

The man who impressed me most, however, was the one I met in a pub in Winchester, the garrison headquarters of the KRRC. He had first been called up as a National Serviceman nine years previously, but his accountable service ran to approximately six months. Very shortly after joining he had gone AWOL and, as detention and periods of absence did not count as service, almost all his time had been accrued whilst on remand awaiting courts martial and his periods in detention had always been followed by almost immediate absence. He had been let out for the evening by a friendly sergeant whilst awaiting his court martial, on his promise that he would return. Everyone expected his ambition, a Discharge with Ignominy, was certain this time, so there was no fear that he would absent himself. All the real hard cases were apparently either Scot or Scouse and this Glaswegian was no exception. He swore that if he was not given his DI this time he would leap the table and assault the Court President, thereby achieving with certainty the desired result.

I never did discover what happened. We are all very much products of circumstance and situation and who can say for certain what is a truly independent act as opposed to a conditioned response? In different circumstances the courage and tenacity displayed by that man would grade him in the hero class, but our values only permit such epithets for conformists. Conformism provides moral support even when the subject is isolated. Such courage and tenacity of purpose in the face of every obstacle and recognised social mores shows a strength of character that can only be looked on with awe and even fear. I heard tell of others in similar circumstances, and have often idly wondered what the time-serving record is for a National Serviceman.

Humour is the antidote for most discomforts and if one removes the steamy glasses of nostalgia the military reality is little different to civilian life in this respect. With a large group of young men of the same age and multitudinous backgrounds it tends to be unsophisticated, boisterous, vulgar, not infrequently somewhat cruel, and punctuated by long periods of boredom which are so easily forgotten.

There was the time when the Army was making its first few fumbling steps towards the humanisation of conditions as the spectre of the end of conscription was rising on the political horizon. On the food front genuine attempts were being made to vary menus, but unfortunately the senior officers and NCOs of the Catering Corps were far too old sweats to grasp the new concepts, and their efforts were little more than pathetic gestures.

Bunny was one of a group of us who worked, sat, and ate together. He was a Notting Hill Londoner as long as the proverbial streak, and he could talk his way into and out of almost anything if he chose to; he had a great line in patter. Now my mother is a good, down-to-earth English cook, roast beef and Yorkshire and none of your foreign rubbish. Digging into my stew one day, to my astonishment I found this piece of herbage the like of which I had never seen before. I immediately complained to all and sundry in the vicinity that the cookhouse wallahs had no doubt been putting the yard sweepings into the food. Bunny took up my indignation with comradely approbation. Suppressing with a flourish one or two half-hearted interjections from weaker souls, he strongly recommended I make full use of this God-sent opportunity. True to the traditions of Three Platoon, I pounced upon the orderly officer on his round and complained loud and long at this unwarranted adulteration. His crushing response I shall remember to this day, not so much for the technical rendition as the astonishment with which he contemplated my ignorance. I can seldom look a bay-leaf in the eye without remembering his expression – and Bunny's treachery.

Shortly after (but not for this reason) I was elected to serve as platoon representative on the newly-conceived Catering Committee. This attempt at democracy was inhibited by the total absence of power and effect accorded to it. Every soldier, for instance, will remember Pom. It is that insipid slush that pretends to assume under certain conditions a similarity to the staple food of the Irish and currently postures under various instantly recognisable proprietary brand names. My first attendance at the committee meeting elicited the information from the Catering Corps officer that certain funds were available (administered solely by him) for supplementing the standard issue of provisions from the military authorities. I immediately strongly recommended that we sold all our stocks of Pom to the pig farmer down the road and used the proceeds, supplemented by the funds, to buy real potatoes. Following a shocked silence the officer informed me we would all be court martialled (to this day I cannot see why) and proceeded to ignore me for the rest of the meeting. I was totally ostracised at the next meeting and reported back to my platoon that I was resigning.

As far as I and Three Platoon know the committee is still meeting and is still being ignored by the Catering Corps officer.

The tedium and boredom of an undemanding job in constrained circumstances gave considerable time for reflection upon the nature of the organisation to which one was unwillingly, albeit temporarily, espoused. It was not until the Suez crisis, however, that the realities struck home. Being concerned with the accounts of the Special Air Services, paratroop regiments and Tank Corps meant of course that we took the brunt of the organisational problems in our area because these were the very people who were recalled. After the war had got under way some of the paybooks we had so hurriedly issued just a few weeks before were abruptly and prematurely returned to us. It was the job of the War Office to advise the next of kin of the loss of their son or husband in our last pathetic, futile, blimpish escapade: and our job to work out the widow's mite. To handle the blood-encrusted documents of a young man who had so recently been earning his civilian crust and had ended his days pumping his lifeblood into the gutters of Port Said was sufficiently close a physical contact with the geographically remote events in Egypt to impress upon one the fearsome lines between life and death and bring close to home the very short odds that separated one from a similar fate.

To try and determine the benefits, if any, that accrued to the individual from the experience is well nigh impossible. Did it 'make a man' of one? Did it broaden experience, provide otherwise unobtainable opportunities, teach a respect for authority, encourage personal discipline and give all those attributes to the lucky recruits its committed apologists claim?

For my part, as with all others, how the hell do I know? The pattern of my life before, during and after, would without question have been planned and lived quite differently.

Much of the experience, particularly the sense of community in the barrack-room, was pleasurable and I will remember forever the joy and peacefulness of the times spent poaching huge and beautiful trout from one of Hampshire's most magnificent chalk rivers – that I had better not name.

But I remember too the eyes and actions of little men with large powers. I remember the first-hand stories of what ordinary men did in cold blood to other ordinary men when on active service or occupation duty, and I shudder because I know that the German experience was not a unique national aberration and given the appropriate circumstances all men are capable of the grossest of excesses.

So maybe I did learn a lot.

Regrets? Well, I never did believe the dusky maidens come-on, but I doubt if now I shall ever again get the opportunity of seeing Singapore or Africa.

ALAN SILLITOE

To begin with, I didn't think of it as National Service. It was conscription, a fact of life.

Since the age of eleven there had been a war on, which meant that sooner or later I would have to go and get shot at. Such was the state of morale in working-class Nottingham anyway that most people expected to get bombed and shot at, rather than to shoot at others – the enemy – in any aggressive fashion.

Somehow, call-up seemed to promise a continuation of life in Nottingham. I lived in a house only a hundred yards from a vast factory engaged on full war production, which the Germans constantly attempted to bomb and machine-gun. So in that sense I had already been shot at. Fortunately, being so close to the factory, inside it almost, we were safer than those who lived a mile away where most of the bombs fell.

Going to war was expected of everybody, if you were a teenager, that is. Otherwise you were already there, or stayed behind and enjoyed the general prosperity that it seemed only a war could bring.

My friends and cousins were constantly deserting from the Army, but I viewed their escapades without any moral condemnation whatever. They were, after all, only exercising the same sort of free will as those who went willingly. I was prepared to go, because it was obvious that the German Nazis had to be put down. In other words, you had to die fighting before they walked over you. As for really winning the war, only the Red Army was doing that. The Germans made political realities terrifyingly simple – which was one of the costs of fighting Nazism.

I decided early on that when I was called up I would go into the Air Force as a navigator. I had studied the theory and practice of map-reading from a young age but, on thumbing through *The Complete Air Navigator* in the public library, I saw that trigonometry must also be learned.

Having left school at fourteen, my education would not help me to attain such a specialised post, and the only way to make up for it was to join the Air Training Corps as a cadet. I am going into this matter of early indoctrinal training because as far as I am concerned the four years I spent at it were also part of my National Service. One was obliged, in any case, to join some sort of youth or cadet organisation during the war. Only Britain and the USSR attained such 'total' mobilisation.

I went along to the local group while still underage at fourteen, to enrol with a couple of friends. There I met Mr Pink the adjutant of the squadron, Flying Officer Pink as he then was, pink indeed in the face and on the top of his head, a man of fortyish who bullied us with much humour at the thought perhaps that though we were not the most promising of material we were nevertheless to be taken seriously.

We stood in a line in the assembly hall of a local school, and when he asked those who cleaned their teeth to put up their hands, mine stayed down. The gist of his speech that followed was that there could be no life in his squadron for anyone who did not clean his teeth. He spoke as if civilisation began with the cleaning of teeth. Those who did not do so had not yet come out of the caves. So there was nothing else to do, I saw, except buy the necessary implements and start scrubbing away – night and morning.

The commander of the squadron was Flt/Lt Hales, husband of the poet Madge Hales. He had been an officer in the Royal Flying Corps in the First World War. There were meetings and parades two or three evenings a week, and from the beginning I took my training seriously simply because most of it was 'learning'. It was, to a limited extent, a furtherance of my education, and I saw straight away that there was much to take in.

Basically it was a matter of mathematics (algebra and trigonometry), elementary navigation (the triangle of velocities), theory of flight (lift, weight, thrust and drag), aero engines (the four stroke or Otto cycle), morse code and meteorlogy and so on.

I learned to recognise star constellations in the sky at night, and the silhouettes of a few score planes, as well as to write clear English in the various tests.

I went occasionally to aerodromes for a week or a fortnight and clocked up dozens of hours flying time in many sorts of aircraft. Military training began there, firing a three-o-three rifle, elementary tactics, street-fighting. I also met boys from all over the country, several of whom were members of the Young Communist League as well.

Being a factory worker, and a member of the Transport and General Workers Union, I was extremely left-wing in my views and my interest in the socialist system of the USSR. So I went through the obvious military side of my training in the knowledge that it would be useful indeed when I was called up into the fight against fascism.

After the day's work I looked forward to study at home so as to catch up with those boys from grammar schools who found the tests somewhat easier to pass. My feeling as a cadet was one of slight embarrassment at being in a factory instead of still at school. And in the factory I was occasionally secretive about being a cadet in case any of my mates or acquaintances might imagine I was too 'keen' to get into the services.

Was it really as clear cut as this? It was certainly true that conscription was in the offing, and that the war would go on forever.

I reached top rank and passed all possible tests in the ATC, but when it was obvious towards the end of 1944 that the RAF would need no more aircrew, I decided to try to get into the Fleet Air Arm, which still wanted pilots because the war against the Japanese promised to go on even after the Germans were defeated.

I went to Crewe a little after my seventeenth birthday to take intelligence and aptitude tests. The papers were simple IQ questions, and then some naval officer asked me a few easy algebraic conundrums. He also wanted to know if I was interested in sport, and I told him I was very fond of it, that I played cricket and football whenever I got the chance – which was a lie because I hated anything to do with sport.

To my surprise I was handed two days' pay as a naval airman and told that I had been accepted to train as a pilot, with the possibility one day of getting a commission – though I would have to wait some months before being called up for the actual training. I certainly felt a different person than the boy who had gone along to the ATC three years before. What is more I had a number: FX643714 – which I still remember, as well as the anger of my father when he saw that I had virtually joined up.

The war ended in Europe and in the Pacific, but National Service did not. This was an injustice in fact (a National Injustice instead of National Service) and I would have been more than justified in joining the ranks of the deserters, but for a long time I had geared myself to accepting it. I had trapped myself by latching onto the means of widening my horizon in some way. The extra 'education' I had received made it impossible for me to stay out of National Service. At the same time it confused my innate nature. I had been man enough to go to work at fourteen, but not man enough to fight free of fate when it finally caught up with me. Everything has its price, and at the time I explained it by saying that, not knowing what to do with my life, I 'went in' out of curiosity and inanition.

The Fleet Air Arm informed me that they would not now be requiring my services as a pilot, so I 'got my papers' to train as a wireless operator in the RAF. Real military life began, three years of barking dogs, of an existence I was not used to and would never get used to.

I remember the first day at RAF Padgate – how many do not? – where the issuing of uniforms and kit took place. Going along the line with outstretched arms the various items of equipment were draped over them, and for the first time in my life I acquired vests and pants, sophisticated garments I had never worn before, so that for a moment or two I was puzzled as to how I would get them on. That was another important thing for me in my National Service, if I think back on it. First – toothbrush and toothpaste, and then underwear.

It was a rule that one never talked about politics or religion, a clear sign that nothing else was worth discussing. I met IRA supporters and communists, anarchists and rebels and nihilists. I was torn between hatred of the life, of those blinkered barbaric swine who tried to make everything unnecessarily difficult and whom we generally regarded as the scum of the earth, and what I found of interest in talking to youths from all over the country, getting to know about their lives, and in many cases puzzling out their accents, and relishing the different slang and dialect words flying around.

One advantage of the first year was that while being trained as a radio operator (during seven months of it) I was taught to touch type, a skill which helped when I later became a writer. I also liked learning about electricity and how to operate transmitters and receivers, how to send and take down fast morse on short wave sets that could reach places several thousand miles away. It was something in harmony with that part of my temperament which responds to mechanics and machinery.

The first winter at the radio school in Wiltshire was the awful time of 1946-47, one of the worst seasons on record. During icy blizzards the school stayed open when others had sensibly closed down and sent the men home. There was no fuel, and we were forced to thieve and loot for our existence. I remember one youth in the hut suddenly bending over his bed and coughing a pint of blood on to the floor. He was sent into hospital with tuberculosis. Everyone was lethargic, grumbling, bad-tempered, and hungry. We heard later that the Commanding Officer of the camp was decorated for his devotion to duty in keeping the place open in impossible conditions. Every medal is earned at somebody's expense.

As an aircraftsman-second-class wireless operator/teleprinter operator I went on the troopship *Ranchi* to Malaya. I do not think travelling conditions had altered much since the Crimean War. The ship of ten thousand tons had three-and-a-half thousand people on board. I shared a mess deck with two hundred others, at night sleeping in hammocks in the same space that during the day served as a dining room.

I found the food quite good, but after a while I gave up sleeping below and cornered a place for myself on deck in the open air where, despite the hard boards, I was comfortable. It took four weeks to reach Singapore, where we disembarked.

There was a library of sorts on the boat, and I got hold of a paperback copy of *The Mutiny on the Elsinore* by Jack London. I had not read any of his work before (and very little of anybody else's work, come to that), and disliked this one, so that I have not been induced to read much by him since. It was full of fascist ideas about the innate superiority of the Nordic race. The other book I read was *A Room With a View* by E. M. Forster, a work which intrigued me, though the style seemed a bit dense compared with what I had up to then been used to.

Life in Malaya was almost pleasant for a while. I flew in an Avro 19 to the RAF staging post at Butterworth, in North Malaya. From then on I hardly ever wore a uniform. My work place was beyond the far end of the single runway, in a small hut set on a piece of raised land in the middle of a paddy field, and squared in by four tall aerials. By these I communicated to aircraft, receiving coded weather messages, and sending out bearings to help in their navigation. It was interesting work, for I could chat with radio operators in Saigon, Bangkok, Karachi and Ceylon.

At that time members of the RAF were being demobbed by groups, and every month the numbers of the current groups bound for home would be clandestinely tapped into the ether by radio operators straight from Uxbridge where such issues were decided, and passed to all stations in the world by the direction-finding channels, so that the ordinary airmen knew when they were going to get demobbed even days before the commanding officers of the various aerodromes could tell them.

Consequently when I went to the cookhouse for a late meal after coming off duty the cooks would heap up my plate with the choicest food, while I in return, from the corner of my mouth, would say: '65, 66, and 67' – and watch them smile with relief and delight if their exit number was on the list.

Working the D/F aerials was a heavy responsibility, for I often had to navigate civilian passenger-carrying aircraft. I would sometimes be 'on watch' as much as fourteen hours, and on one occasion I gave radio bearings on my complicated Marconi machinery to a Lancastrian which had just taken off from Darwin in Australia, and guided him over the stormy Java seas into Singapore. My ears and fingers had the light touch, and if it was technically possible to get a good bearing I was able to do it.

My abilities in this direction were called upon when the so-called State of Emergency was declared in June 1948. A squadron of heavy Lincoln bombers was sent from England to try and hunt out the communist guerrillas in the jungle. This increased my work to a hectic degree, work indeed that now went strongly against my political beliefs.

The bombers roamed around the jungle dropping their loads, and when they asked me for bearings in order to check their positions the angles I sent began to lack their accustomed accuracy. Even as much as half a degree out – something which could not be proved one way or the other – meant that they missed their targets (which often could not be seen under the massively thick coating of forest) by many miles.

A clandestine communist transmitter began broadcasting to the people of Malaya, exhorting them to rise against their British imperialist oppressors, and it was decided to locate it by direction finding, and then either bomb it if it was in too inaccessible an area, or send troops if it were close to some road or trail.

The D/F operator at Singapore, and myself at Butterworth, were given the time and frequency, and told to take cross bearings on it. I tuned in, and got a fairly clean reading, but somehow my hand became sweaty and slipped on the goniometer, and accidentally, shall we say, two degrees were subtracted from the angle. How accurate the Singapore operator was I have no way of knowing, but it would not have made much difference, since mine must have been far enough out for another load of bombs to be wasted on empty forest.

The war against the communists had nothing to do with us. We were only waiting to get back to England. I lived from day to day and did not know what my life held for the future. I had no thought of going back into a factory, not because I did not like it or felt it was below me, but simply because I knew that it was finished as far as I was concerned. I vaguely played with the idea of going to a radio school and, after a few months' conversion training, getting a City and Guilds certificate which would enable me to find a job as a radio officer in the Merchant Navy. This seemed the most suitable thing. But in general the future was like a wide empty sky.

During my stay in Butterworth I was part of a group whose job it was to go out into the jungle if a plane crashed, and look for survivors. This was something I volunteered for, because getting away from the camp on any pretext whatsoever was always a bonus to me, especially if it took me up into the forests.

I wanted to see what it was like, and find out whether I could physically survive there. In any case I needed the occasional hike or expedition to get used to such terrain. One such journey took us on an attempt to scale Gunong Jerai in Kedah state, a mountain of four thousand feet just by the coast. I wrote an account of this trip and sent it to Flt/Lt Hales in Nottingham. He showed it to Mr Pink and one of them (I am not sure who) kindly got a secretary to type it for me.

Seeing something of mine in typescript for the first time made it look so clear and close to print that I read it in a rather bemused way. It was my first long piece of writing, and I was so pleased by it that I did not notice its naivety and clumsiness. In a way it was almost as important to me as my first published work. I put it by, and several chapters of a novel which was published thirteen years later were subsequently based on it.

I also wrote odd poems and other bits and pieces to pass away the long hours of isolation in my radio hut, when often for much of the shift there would be no aircraft to occupy me. These scraps of prose were generally concerned with the beauties of the scenery.

My time in Malaya came to an end, and I set out on the journey back to England. I felt fit and happy at the thought of getting free of the Air Force, though still without any fixed idea of what I was going to do. All I knew was that I would be demobilised with the rest of my group, and have a few weeks of idleness before deciding.

I lived from minute to minute, the future perhaps hidden and wrapped up in each one of them, enjoying the rough seas of the Bay of Bengal and the Indian Ocean. In Biscay the sea was so turbulent that many of my mess mates could not eat or do their turn at handing out the buckets of stew for meals. I was quite happy to do more than my share. In between times I smoked cheroots and heavy tobacco, and walked on the highest decks to get the best view of the swelling sea. I was lit up because the present was so uncertain, and nothing seemed to matter. I had worked years in a factory and done my turn in the Air Force, and it already seemed as if I had lived several times over. The only vision I had before me, apart from the stormy and cold sea, was one of freedom, of throwing off a hated uniform. But it was impossible to see beyond that act.

The slow troop train trundled out of Southampton docks and up through the drizzle of England – which smelt sweet enough to me – to the demob centre on the Lancashire coast.

Things do not become clear only when I look back on them. They were quite clear enough at the time. As my friends one by one were called to have an X-ray (to prove that they were going out as physically fit as when they came in) and then sent home on leave with sufficient back pay to have a good time, the questions that had bothered me on the troopship no longer seemed important. The future would look after itself, as long as I got *out*.

After my X-ray I was not given money and a rail-pass, but was asked back into the medical office. The MO was not happy, he said, about my X-ray. In fact it was not very good at all, with so many black and pitted marks down the left side. I would need to have treatment.

'How long?' I asked, choking on even those two words as I tried to take in what he meant.

'That depends.'

I had tuberculosis, and that was a fact. I could go home on leave for a few days, if I liked (if I liked!) but then I would have to come back to hospital for further tests, and then be installed in a permanent hospital to see what could be done for me.

'You'll have to lie on your back,' he told me, 'for a goodly length of time.'

'What if I don't bother with any of this?' I asked.

'You may die,' he said.

It seems strange to me now that up to then I had not really noticed my illness. Certainly, I was thin, and had been coughing for the last few months in Malaya, but that was nothing out of the ordinary. And here I was suddenly confronted with the fact that if I did not agree to spend an unspecified time in the hospital lying down the world would end for me and I would not need to think about any kind of future. All my thoughts on what I would do were no longer valid. With tuberculosis eating away at me what sort of job would I be able to get? The future was a whiter sheet than ever. It was like being told today that you had cancer, because at that time there was no specific cure for TB.

It was the biggest shock of my life. My body was something I had never thought of. It was indestructible, I had thought. There was no amount of walking or swimming or labouring it could not do. But obviously there was. Sooner or later you have to pay for having lived in oblivion.

For weeks I was in a state of shock, not feeling at all ill, however, imagining that some kind of grim mistake had been made, and that any day now one of the medical officers would come up waving an X-ray and wearing an embarrassed smile to tell me so. But science cannot lie, I found. Or it did not with me at twenty.

I went on leave, and remember trying to tell my father I was ill and would have to spend some time in hospital. I was full of rage and shame and despair (and self-pity, I suppose) at the thought that I had caught tuberculosis, and could not manage to get that bloody word out while talking to him. All kinds of euphemisms came to me, so that he ended up by thinking I was too embarrassed to tell him I had syphilis from my sojourn in Malaya.

When I went by train to Swindon, to get to the RAF hospital at Wroughton, I walked out of the station to be confronted by a coffin with a flag over it being unloaded from an RAF lorry to be put on a train. I asked the driver what the person inside had died of, and was told he had been a patient at Wroughton hospital who had coughed his last. I was in uniform, and he asked me if I wanted a lift back to Wroughton, not realising that I was going into the hospital there. But I turned down his kind offer, preferring to walk around the town for an hour or two on what would be my last freedom for nearly eighteen months.

One of my lungs was collapsed. In order to stop myself going mad (there is no other way I can put it) I read every book I could get my hands on. I began with translations from the Greek and Latin classics, and as much English poetry as I could find. This led me to study prosody, and also to write dozens of poems of my own in empty wireless log books brought from Malaya. I wrote sketches and stories, and a book-length manuscript which contained glimmerings of my future novel *Key to the Door*.

Another education was beginning, for I was reading scores of books. I had read hardly any adult books before, and now a great and prolonged feast began. A bad illness seemed to have many advantages, though it was difficult to think so at the time. With the arrears of pay that accumulated in hospital I bought a reconditioned Remington typewriter, a machine on which I typed my early unpublished novels, and then *Saturday Night and Sunday Morning* ten years later.

National Service ended for me when I was finally discharged from the hospital and the RAF at the end of 1949. As far as I was concerned it had started in 1942 as an ATC cadet. My total time lasted seven years, that period of fatal length that makes or unmakes many lives.

I was by no means cured of tuberculosis, but the rot had been stopped, as it were. There was no need to think about getting a job anymore because I had had the first intimations that I was going to be a writer. No one knew of this at first, because there was no one to tell, and in any case who would believe it? I was helped at least from the material side because I was awarded a total disability pension of a few pounds a week, which would keep me in food and a sort of shelter till I was able to get something published. Naturally, I did not know how long this was going to take.

I was pensioned off at twenty-one, so what else could I do but start a new life? It had already begun, anyway, born I suppose out of the old one.

JOHN ARDEN

I never thought that there was anything particularly odd about it. I was eighteen and a half, I had been at school for as long as seemed natural, I had passed the requisite examinations for future entry to university, National Service came in between as everybody knew: and it lasted eighteen months. The Second World War had been over for four years but conscription had been in force ever since I was eight. After ten years – formative years at that – one easily took for granted a state of affairs which would have produced constitutional apoplexy among an earlier generation of British democrats. I was aware, from my history lessons at school, that a Standing Army had at one time been regarded as a shame and a disgrace to any civilized country: but when one read that, one did not form in one's mind an image of the archetypal British Squaddy with his shapeless khaki battle-dress, furtively puffing at a fag-end in the corner of a railway-train corridor. Not at all: Standing Armies were either great blocks of shaven-headed Prussian ploughboys being screamed at by Feld-webels and huge Obersts; or else, maybe in a more academic mood, one thought of farouche seventeenth-century mercenaries, with their boots on the furniture, roaring drinking songs, puffing long clay pipes, and interfering with the servant girls in some terrorised Cotswold inn. When present-day Englishmen were conscripted, we did not become 'conscripts': 'servicemen' was the word, and our modest needs, as enlisted voters, (or sons of voters at any rate), were supplied by the NAAFI organisation. There were also request record programmes on the BBC. We wore uniform for purposes of 'defence'. Throughout the two World Wars we had been defending ourselves against the Germans: now, it appeared probable, the Russians would be the enemy. But it made little difference. Having been born almost exactly in the middle of the interval between the two wars, I had my father's experience of the first and my own schoolboy knowledge of the second to form my notions on the subject: world conflict, with Great Britain playing a chivalrous defensive role, and necessarily winning each rubber, was the twentieth-century norm. It was always the other side who massacred civilians, tortured prisoners, laid waste cities, and operated a secret police. I do not think my education can have been as good as the size of my school-bills (public school-bills) suggested. But then everyone else had much the same attitude – at least everyone else whom I knew (I had lived a very sheltered life, so this generalisation is much more limited than may at first appear).

At school I had been in the cadet corps, which was compulsory. No one ever thought of attempting to opt out of it except a boy called Haskin who had diabetes and was therefore excused all sorts of other school activities. When old boys returned after a year or so to revisit the school they usually came in uniform, and the uniform was usually that of an officer. I expected, therefore, that unless things went seriously wrong I too would become an officer. I did have certain doubts about this, however, because my record in the cadet corps was something of a joke. But I knew enough of the world to realise that by the standards of the real Army the cadet corps itself was something of a joke, and I did hope for a commission. I also half-hoped I would not obtain one, because I could foresee myself getting into all sorts of dreadful messes in the Army and I fancied it would be safer to get into a mess as a private responsible to nobody rather than as a subaltern in charge of twenty men. I was also very nervous lest I should be granted an Officers' Selection Board interview, and ignominiously failed.

In the event, however, they discovered at my medical that I was second-rate all over. Physically, that is. My educational qualifications seemed extraordinarily high in comparison with everyone else's, but then I was examined in a municipal office somewhere in the darker parts of Sheffield and nearly all the other examinees were rough lads from the steel foundries whom nobody would have dreamed of suggesting for Officers' Selection Boards except in a revolutionary Peoples' Army – and, despite the then current

Attlee Government, that was not quite where we were at. I was informed that I was unfit for a commission, and indeed unfit for service except 'on lines of communication only'. This made my mother very sad: but I later discovered it meant nothing at all. Three-quarters of the Army seemed to have such a health classification: and they posted them wherever they chose. In a modern mobile war all lines may be said to be lines of communication, if only because every fighting unit carries its own radio. But it did prevent anyone putting me into the Paras or the Commandos. I had never wanted to join either.

When I was called-up I was sent to the Royal Artillery at Oswestry; and shortly after that I was posted, on probation, to the Intelligence Corps at Maresfield in Sussex. My first two weeks as a Gunner were not at all bad. We were kept very busy learning to do all the things which I had already learned in the school-cadets and, although I did not do them very well, I never got into trouble. The competition was not high. I then had to wait for another two weeks to be posted to Maresfield. I spent the time in a sort of deadly military limbo known as the Holding Troop. This was presided over by Sgt Ramsbottom, a very bad-tempered elderly man, who had under his charge about thirty youths who were about to be moved on elsewhere; some (like me) to other units, but the majority were due for permanent discharge. I had not realised that despite the preliminary medical so many conscripts would later be discovered to be unfit for service for either physical or psychological reasons. The psychological reasons were often alarming. Half the barrack-room, in fact, were quite barmy. They ran up and down in the nude on moonlit nights, urinating out of the windows, screaming obscenities, and putting boot-polish on the face of anyone who was asleep. They sometimes fought with knives. The ones who were not quite barmy, but were being sent home because it seemed that they might one day become barmy, occupied the days of waiting by stealing as much of everyone's kit as they could for the purpose of selling it when they got clear of Oswestry. Most of them had a cousin in the Black Market. One of them lifted Sgt Ramsbottom's best pair of trousers from his bunk one evening. But the Army insisted that they must wait a fortnight beford being sent home even if they prepared to take half the camp with them in that time. Documents, it appeared, had first to be processed.

There was no normal disciplinary activity in the Holding Troop. Sgt Ramsbottom – except for the vain but appalling explosion of fury he brought in with him into the hut the night his trousers disappeared – used to leave us absolutely to our own devices, once he had allotted us our work for the day. This was always some class of tedious fatigue. I seemed to spend most of that fortnight cleaning obscene writing from the walls of the latrines in company with a lad called Burke who was also destined for the Intelligence Corps. In the evenings we would go to Oswestry and see a film (it was invariably a B-class musical or western) and then we would quietly slip into bed and hope to get at least a little sleep before the moon came up and the lunatics stripped off. I spent the whole fortnight (except for the evenings at the cinema) in denim overalls which got very wet and smelly because of the work in the latrines. At the time we did not know – nobody had thought it their business to tell us, and we were altogether too intimidated to ask – that we were to stay in the Holding Troop for only two weeks. Burke and I made ourselves very miserable by speculating that we might be there for ever. It was as though the regular flow of military life, along with which we had been for a while so cheerfully travelling, had suddenly let us be sucked into this terrible backwater and we could discover no way by which we could get out of it at our own volition. The only time we saw an officer was on payday: and he could not be spoken to. There was a drill for receiving pay (one pace forward, two-three, salute, two-three, take-pay-and-paybook-in-right-hand: open-left-top-pocket-with-left-hand, say 'Pay and Paybook Correct, SIR!', place-pay-and-paybook-in-left-top-pocket, two-three, salute, two-three, about turn, left right left right left right LEFT – something like that, I think it went): you did not interrupt a drill to ask if you were going to be posted soon, please. Sgt Ramsbottom knew nothing and if he did he would not say.

'It's my fucking job to keep you fucking at it while you're here and that's all my fucking job is. Fuck off.'

And then suddenly, one day, out of the blue. We were in the latrines: Burke was applying Ajax to an inscription which read: 'My sister has a hole like a horsecollar,' and I was scratching with an unbristled WD brush at a picture of what I suppose (allegorically-speaking) could be described as an enormous horse's neck. The wet concrete floor was darkened by the shadow of Sgt Ramsbottom.

'Yo' two – Burke, Arden: posted in t'morning. Intelligent Corpse, Maresfield. Going to mek yo' into fucking spies, they are. Get to t'troop office and get yo' fucking documents.'

We couldn't believe it. And then, all of a sudden, Sgt Ramsbottom became human.

'Eh – yo' two. Yo' mek sure and check yo' fucking kits afore you go. Yo' don't want that Shower of fucking nut-cases in t'barrack-room whipping owt of what yo've been issued with. Let alone your Possessions Personal. By God, but I'll bet yo' be glad to get out of this! . . .'

And with a sour but almost paternal chuckle that disappointed old man turned and slouched away.

Life in the Holding Troop at Oswestry had been awful. The Holding Troop, by anybody's standards, had indeed been a Shower. It was the one really low spot of my service career. It was, of course, exceptional. I never at any other time felt quite so forgotten, quite so useless, quite so cut-off from all normal human intercourse. Gunner Burke had been a nice fellow, but very very gloomy to talk to. Yet, looking back after twenty-three years, I am inclined to think that the Holding Troop was really typical of the entire Conscript Army in which I had to serve. Everyone in it was either daft or crooked or pissed-off. As an institution it served no useful purpose except to get the walls of the latrines clean for once in a while, and to keep the documents at HQ in a reasonably ordered condition. The Holding Troop was an enlargement to a thirty-man-sized-scale of the contents of somebody's pending-tray on a War Office desk. Yet it did contain people. The lunatics, no doubt, when at home, were merely 'Poor Charlie's lad, you know he's never been quite right – but he's a good lad, all considered,' or 'So unfortunate for Angela, my dear – her boy was born *handi-capped:* but in a way it was a blessing – he didn't have to go through the Army: she was so afraid they would insist on it, and he would not have been at all suited to the life . . .' The not-so-lunatic element, with their fly commercial relatives, are no doubt nowadays company directors, property speculators, great-train-robbers, and other pillars of the EEC. The rest of us kept quiet and endured it. On the whole I had forgotten it until I came to write this essay. But I wonder about Sgt Ramsbottom. How long had he been in charge of the Holding Troop before I was put in it? How long did he remain in charge of it after my release? What had he done to be there in the first place? And what on earth did he think of the work that he had to do? If the man who stole his trousers was no more than a 'fucking nut-case', Sgt Ramsbottom, by comparison, must surely be called sane. But is a sane man in a lunatic situation really an expression of human sanity at all? The fact is, the entire Army, as a conscript organisation, was an insane institution.

I do not think it had been so, a few years earlier, when there was actually a war on, and any oddity such as the Holding Troop was an unfortunate but unavoidable flaw in the whole system of Hun-and-Jap-destruction which was going on at the time. It was, during the war, generally recognised that wartime was a time of madness on an international scale: and the only thing to do with it was to get it over as briskly as possible and to try to keep one's wits still with one for however long it took. It was also possible, during the war, to actually be good at soldiering: people gained promotion, won medals, carried out successful operations against the enemy. One can even imagine an NCO boasting (at least to himself) that he ran the smartest Holding Troop in the entire Army; and that, if we won the war, his own genius for organisation would have provided small but measurable part of the sum of that victory. But in 1949 there was no war at all. At any rate there was none that was very present before our imaginations. I fancy that repressive operations were taking place in various colonies such as Malaya. There was perennial trouble with the Egyptians along the canal. Korea began before I was demobbed. But the Berlin airlift crisis was over and BAOR was as cushy a posting as could be looked for. So we had a defence force which was trained to attack (as all good defence forces must be), which was very large in numbers, filled with a genuine cross-section of the nation's youth: and was in the end nothing more than a gigantic compulsory Holding Troop. The whole Army, that is to say, was a Shower: and quite barmy.

I will illustrate this by one or two anecdotes. They are not very unusual anecdotes; indeed everyone who did National Service can come up with a whole string of very similar ones (and only too often does). But they do all tend to the same conclusions.

First. During the war, as I have said, it was possible to be good at soldiering because there was some end in view. But in peacetime? At Maresfield Camp, the depot of the Intelligence Corps, there was a conscript called Brown. He was determined to be good at soldiering. He was good at it. He grew a moustache that would have been a credit to a guards major. He practised all and every evening laying out his kit, 'as per photo' on the barrack-room wall. His shirts were stuffed with cardboard so that they lay square on his bed; his blankets, when folded, had plywood templates in them to preserve their square outline. He blacked the soles of his boots and polished with Duraglit the heads of the nails therein. In the bottom folds of his trousers, when turned down over the tops of his gaiters, he placed a string of lead weights (as used by fishermen) so that the outline of the tucked-in trousers remained

235

stiff and vertical (the weights rattled rhythmically as he walked – he might have been an oriental dancer). He occupied whole hours with an electric iron pressing extraordinary pleats in his outer garments. He even pressed fan-pleats in the back of his denim overalls – the only man I ever knew to do so, for the texture of denim is such that any pleats must inevitably disappear after ten minutes' wear. Then he looked one day at his kitbox (known officially as his Box Soldier) at the foot of his bed, on which was placed (as per photo) a pile of haversacks and pouches, all stiffened with cardboard and thick with pea-green blanco. On top of the pile was his Helmet Steel. The box was a dull grey-green colour, the helmet was matt-green. Brown got himself down town one Saturday to an ironmongers' in Uckfield and returned with brushes and paint. Everyone was out at the pictures, watching a B-western. When we came back to camp we found that Brown had painted his Box Soldier a beautiful gloss veridian with white lining-out round the edges. He had painted his Helmet Steel a beautiful gloss black with a white rim and the little screw on top was picked out in two circlets of colour, red outside and white inside. We gazed appalled. The sergeant came in.

'Ho yus. Very tasteful. Shows initiative, dunnit? Yer-ss. But it does like disrupt the symmetry of the room. So what are we gointer do then? You've got all Sunday, an't you? So get weaving. Get all them boxes painted. All of you – jump to it!'

So we did. We did not like Brown. His nickname was Bullshit Brown and the oaf was *proud* of it. But we did use his paint and his brushes (we had to: it was Sunday, the shops were shut) and we did not offer to pay him for the privilege. I do not think any of us ever spoke to him again. In the end he received exactly the same sort of posting as we did. We had not, by the by, been made into 'fucking spies' – the Intelligence Corps units overseas were at that time being run down and trained personnel were drafted into ordinary clerical jobs in all sorts of offices, where promotion went by seniority and by the class of desk to which one had the fortune to be originally assigned. Brown may have made lance-corporal before he got demobbed. So did I: and no-one ever accused me of initiative in the bullshit line. He discovered too late that Nobody Cared.

Secondly. I was eventually posted to Edinburgh Castle, a Command HQ, where the office staff worked normal nine to five-thirty civilian-type hours. We worked with an admixture of genuine civilian civil servants, all elderly gentlemen who might have done exactly the same sort of work in the town hall or the post office. We had their sort of tea-breaks, and we wore civilian shoes in the office. On Saturday mornings we were allowed to wear civilian clothes. We never did any guard-mounting duties or anything of that: there were real soldiers, from the Highland or Lowland Regiments, to do that kind of thing, in kilts or trews, white gaiters, with bagpipes. They got photographed by tourists at the castle gates while we strolled out in the evenings to go to the cinema. One day a new clerk arrived to take up his duties. He was a Regular, a corporal in the Service Corps, who had been a clerk for a while, in the adjutant's office at a regimental depot somewhere in Scotland. But for most of his career he had been a drill-instructor at the RASC training-camp. He would not wear shoes, and he had no civilian clothes. They would have had to be paid for out of his own savings, and he was a married man with a thrifty disposition. He therefore wore boots and stamped everywhere through the Command offices. When he had to deliver a document on to an officer's desk he would enter the room like an elephant, come to a crashing attention, salute, bang the paper on the desk, stamp, salute, stamp, about-turn, and march out of the room like a rhinoceros. The colonel or brigadier behind the desk, dapper in his neat charcoal suit, would press a white-cuffed gentlemanly hand to a brandy-throbbing temple, saying:

'Oh, God . . ,' in an agonized whisper, 'please, Corporal Turnbull, do you not think you could possibly wear shoes . . . ?'

The chief clerk (a Sgt-major) got on to him.

'Godsake, lad, have a bit of common – the staff-officers don't want all that bloody bull all over their lino – shoes, lad, shoes – for Gawd Sakes!'

Turnbull was adamant. No King's Regulation in existence could force a serving soldier to wear his own Possessions Personal on duty. The Army paid for his boots: he would have to pay for his shoes. It was his right to decline the privilege. His argument was unanswerable. After a month they shifted him off – a medical board had passed him as 'psychologically-unfit for clerical service'. I do not know what they did with him. He was probably sent back to Aldershot to instruct recruits at drill.

Thirdly. The chief clerk in that office was an enthusiastic little cockney called Mr Bones. He was not enthusiastic about bull: but he regarded his office and its filing-system and all its various bureaucratic procedures as a kind of model of the Ptolemaic Universe. Like the Ptolemaic Universe it was a perfectly satisfying system as long as you absolutely believed in it: a dash of Galileo would be enough to upset the entire structure. But Mr Bones was as rigid as any seventeenth-century Cardinal Inquisitor. Because he was a sgt-major and we were privates and corporals our vulgar scepticism never reached his insensate mind. But he was now and then troubled by the heretical remarks of his friend Sgt-Major 'Chalky' White from the next office, who used to inflict real hurt on him by saying:

'It's all a lot o' balls, really, old man, isn't it?' – or:

'All right, all right, old man, you've lost a file – so you've lost a fucking file. It's not Top Secret, no court-martials, so no one's going to miss it . . .'

Mr Bones would retire into his own little cubby-hole, crouch behind his desk and mutter to himself for hours after one of these random shafts.

Mr Bones played hockey, with great enthusiasm, every Saturday afternoon. One Saturday he broke his leg. He was carried off to the military hospital, a dreary clutch of corrugated ironware in the outer suburbs of the city. He was given a private room, in deference to his rank. He demanded, and obtained, a private telephone by his private bed. The following Monday we all rejoiced in the office, officers and men alike, and prepared to take things very easy for a week or so. But no such luck. The phone rang at nine-thirty sharp. I answered it. It was Mr Bones, ringing from his private ward.

'Right, then, who's that? Corporal Arden? Right. So what's come in the mail this morning? What d'yer mean, lad, you haven't had time to look at it yet! Get them letters to the phone at once and stop bloody idling!'

I then had to read out to him every letter that had come in. He passed comments on it as I read it:

'Oh, no, not that bloody ammunition inventory again! I thought that was settled last month – I wrote to them on file number GW/39678, get it out of the cabinet . . . now, find me my letter date 13 ult. signed if I remember by Colonel Purvis, yerss . . . didn't I make it clear that the Command HQ was held responsible, only if and providing that the returns had not been filed at Lowland District HQ within the past six months? Yerss, I thought so – of course I made it clear – write to them a snorter and tell 'em to look their bloody files up and sort out their backlog. When you've written it, ring me up and read it over to me . . . Right, so what's next?' And so on.

One day there was a real difficulty we could not clear up on the phone. I had to bring out the relevant files on a tramcar to the hospital. I found Mr Bones sitting up in bed, with a glass of hospital lemonade on a table beside him. He was fretting.

'I can't get about at all – stuck with me foot in bloody plaster – Gawd knows when I can be back at the castle and in the meantime the whole bloody lot is going to rack and ruin . . .'

I sat with him for an hour or two going through his wretched files. Then I had to leave them all with him and come back the next day. I left him surrounded by files and sheaves of paper; he was exhilarated and quite prepared to sit up in bed all night and work at the documents. The next day when I turned up he had finished it all. He was depressed. He felt deprived. I am sure he would have wished me to bring even more files out to him that day too: but as some of them were classified, it was all strictly against security regulations and he did not want to push it too far. Supposing someone robbed me while I was on the tram? There were known foreigners in Edinburgh, and not a few suspected native reds.

'Trouble is,' he said plaintively, 'they give me this private room so I can get on with the work: but I would like to get about into the other wards don't y'see – and have a bit of a chat with the lads . . .'

But none the less, he was a happy man. Corporal Turnbull too had been happy in his elephantine way. They were neither of them National Servicemen. Even though there was no war, they were keeping their own professional Army alive until there was one. Bullshit Brown had had no such incentive. I honestly do not know what Bullshit Brown thought that he was doing. 'Serving his King and Country'? Yes, well: but to what end?

The purpose of Armies is to kill people. Our Army in those days was not killing people. So it went mad inside of itself. This insanity was quite different from the present lethal madness which infects the Army in Ulster. The Army in Ulster has got people to kill: it is a professional Army, its drill-squares no doubt manned by Turnbulls, its office-labyrinths threaded with the Ariadne-clues of countless busy Boneses, even the ageing Ramsbottoms presumably find some degree of fulfilment. The madness inherent in this set-up is therefore expressed outwardly and takes its fearsome effect upon those people who do not share it: the thirteen dead men of Derry's Bloody Sunday were not 'terrorists', but no one has attempted to claim they were not inimical to the Army, as an Army. Therefore they died: and, although it would not be true to say that no questions were asked, the questions were not the right questions and the answers were suppressed. The very discipline of the Army itself was seen to be deliberately bent to permit the lunacy of the individual soldier to go undenounced in public.

Remember the case of the anonymous paratrooper who fired no less than nineteen shots at a non-existent IRA sniper who was supposed to have been spotted behind a frosted-glass bathroom window? Every time the soldier shot at him, he bobbed down, every time he bobbed up again the soldier fired at him once more? You can put that one to the test yourself: go outside into your back garden, look up at your own bathroom window, ask your wife or someone to get inside the bathroom and take aim at you with the lavatory-brush, reconstruct the situation which the soldier claims obtained in the Rossville Flats that day. Lord Widgery did not believe the story: but he forebore to press it further. If he had, of course, he would have had to discover where the nineteen shots had in fact gone (only one of them went through the window). It was better to let it be assumed that the soldier was simply barmy: his barminess was accepted as normal, for no proceedings were taken against him. Had the Army consisted of conscripts as well as professionals, the public at large would have become rather more disturbed. The American Army in Vietnam, the French Army in Algeria have been all but destroyed in the past few years by having made use of conscripts to deal with persistent guerilla movements. I do not think the condition of those two forces would have deteriorated nearly so much (from the point of view of their generals) had they been entirely professional; that is, made up of none but committed madmen.

The British Army today is not unlikely to be used in Britain for purposes of strike-breaking and the like. After what has happened in Ulster, the conclusions to be drawn are ominous. I travelled recently on the Irish Mail train from Euston to Liverpool. In the long open carriage was a group of very young 'skinhead' soldiers, in full battle-gear, on their way to the Belfast ferry. Nearly every passenger in that carriage was obviously Irish, from their speech. The soldiers sat in a mute savage huddle, their eyes twitching to follow the movements of each man who passed them on the way to the toilet or the buffet-car. For them, it was clear, the Falls Road began in Euston Square. I have said these boys were 'skinheads': their haircuts were civilian and cultic, even though they wore uniform. What is a 'skinhead' but the most alienated and rancorous product of our present state of industrial opportunism compounded by induced unemployment? The rejects join the Army; already disturbed, they are inducted into an already lunatic system.

And the National Holding Troop is no longer simply holding them: it is letting them loose at the rising of the moon.

One potent source of recruiting for our contemporary professional Army is the orphanage. It is no doubt the large number of young soldiers with literally no next-of-kin that has given rise to the many (and frequently well-attested) stories prevalent in Ulster that there are more soldiers killed by the IRA than is ever admitted in the War Office statistics. Imagine what use an unscrupulous government could make of an entire Army of orphans with no relatives to worry about them: it would, I suppose, be the military maniac's dream.

Perhaps I am exaggerating? So many people will be able to quote soldiers of their acquaintance who do not feel the need to kill as an essential of their life, and certainly retired members of the British Army are often noted for their humanity and gentleness of demeanour. But who can say what has gone on beneath their normal exteriors at some point in their past careers? I remember Colonel McDonald, a staff-officer from a Highland Regiment, a courteous and sympathetic gentleman, who always said, 'Good morning, Corporal, beautiful day, isn't it?' or, 'Abominable this weather, I really don't know why the boffins don't do something about it . . . far better than wasting their time with all these nuclear bombs, what?' as I brought in his mail to his in-tray in the morning. One day he was at his window, looking out over the castle battlements at the wide expanse of Princes Street Gardens and the mathematically-ordered New Town of Edinburgh, from that height a kind of dream-memory of all the noblest aspirations of the Age of Enlightenment. One felt that Haydn was suspended somewhere above in the light fog of chimney-smoke, playing softly on his harpsichord . . .

'Good morning, Corporal,' said Colonel McDonald, a mystical look in his kind gray eyes. 'Extraordinarily fine view today . . . you know, if I had a battery of large calibre mortars mounted on the battlements, *there*: I could sweep the whole thing quite clean – from *there* to over *there* – not a house left standing . . . extraordinary, *devastate* it – what . . . ?'

241

His own gracious Georgian flat was immediately below us: he was not thinking of that. But when I read in the Widgery Tribunal reports of how the officers in command of the Bloody Sunday operation in Derry were standing high up on a rooftop surveying the expanse of the Bogside, I thought of him . . .

DAVID HOCKNEY

At first I just went and registered, and did not actually think much about it. I was eighteen, and that was 1955. I had been at the Art School in Bradford until then, and qualified for two years' deferment. And then in 1956 they had the Suez invasion, and it was the first thing that made me politically aware. At the same time the war in Cyprus was also quite active, and I began to think about it and realised it was a kind of colonial war which I disapproved of, really. And all in all, I suppose, what happened was that without any particularly clear thinking I decided I would not do military service. I felt I couldn't. So I re-registered as a conscientious objector.

When I left the Art School in July 1957 I had to go to a Tribunal in Leeds; I think it was September. Before I went I was asked to write a statement giving my reasons. Most of those going as conscientious objectors did so for religious reasons, but I wrote a statement saying that I was not really a Christian. I simply said I could not take part in anything military.

The Tribunal was held in the County Court at Leeds, and there was a County Court Judge as Chairman. I am not sure how many others there were: three or four, perhaps, one of them a woman. I had never been in a court before in my life, and I was very nervous. I must have given my answers in a very nervous way, but it did not take very long: I was in there only about five minutes.

Looking back on the questions they asked me, there was no

243

really wise question and there was no really stupid question. The questions just seemed irrelevant to me, and I think my answers might have sounded evasive to them. For instance, they asked me what I would do if my mother were attacked, and I just could not see this as a real question, the question showed they did not understand how I was trying to think, that I was trying to suggest to them that cowardice in that situation certainly would be worse than violence.

Anyway, they accepted my case and directed me to work on the land or in a hospital for two years.

There had been about six cases in front of me, all Christians, Quakers or Jehovah's Witnesses, and they knew all about it: they said they were not going to do any service, not on the land or in hospitals either. The truth is, I knew too little about it beforehand. I just did not want the military or any part of it; I had not really given too much thought to any consequences.

I went to the Labour Exchange in Bradford, and there were, of course, no jobs on the land for me there (if there had been, I would have preferred one) but there were jobs in hospitals, and that is how I came to start work at St Luke's Hospital about the end of September 1957.

I had never been in a hospital before in my life, and at first I absolutely hated it: I could not stand the smell of Dettol, I could not stand the smell of Lysol, which seemed to me to permeate the food, and I thought it was in the bread, and I thought it was in everything. I could not bear it. And then they put me to work on a skin disease ward. Most of the people had skin diseases, which meant they were not in a way too ill, they were not confined to bed, for example, they could actually get up and walk about and a lot of them looked after themselves quite well; it was just that they had psoriasis or eczema or some form of dermatitis. And after about a month I suppose I adapted to the situation fairly easily, and in many ways I quite enjoyed it. It was quite a pleasant job in that you met people all the time and chatted with them and they were nice, little ordinary people from Bradford, and it was a change from the Art School in a way, it was more like a real world, I suppose. I used to have to do things like be the caller for Housey-Housey, or Bingo, it is called Bingo now. Things like that. One porter used to collect all the bets and take them to a bookie nearby and I used to have to collect them from the ward for him and things like that. But otherwise it was just a ward orderly's job.

Then, after a year, I thought it would be useful to do another job somewhere else, and with a friend of mine who was also doing the same thing (he was supposed to work on the land or in a hospital), I moved to Hastings, and rented a cottage at St Leonards-on-Sea, in Sussex, overlooking the sea. I worked in a hospital at Hastings, St Helen's Hospital. This friend of mine worked on a farm, and we lived there for about five months. I did not earn as much money there, as you were paid on a different scale: I used to collect about £5-15-0 there for a forty-eight-hour week, whereas in Bradford I had collected about £8-10-0. And so in the end it was very difficult living with very little money so I went back to Bradford for the last six months.

Now I worked in a medical ward mostly; I mean a male medical ward where people were much more ill, people who had had strokes and heart attacks and thrombosis and things like that. It also happened to be in the winter, almost, and a lot of people in Bradford, especially in those days, suffered with bronchitis: old people who had got bronchitis just came in and died, there were always lots of people dying in that way. And so I came into contact with corpses and that side of hospital, and somehow again I realised it is amazing how one gets kind of used to it. But partly I think we got used to it easier because of course they were mostly old men, and I was young, and so one did not identify with them really: they were mostly near seventy-five or eighty, it seemed, not a bad life-span, so I don't know, that's how you cope with it really; or me, at any rate.

Then finally I gave up before I should. I think they sent me one notice saying if I did not get back to work I was liable to six months' imprisonment. But I just painted for a bit because I had not done any painting while I was in the hospital. I actually had to work a forty-eight-hour week, which is six days of eight hours, and it's quite exhausting work, really. I found I did very few drawings in the two years, but I read quite a lot. In the other time I had I simply sat down and read. I read Proust, as a matter of fact, forced myself to read him: I had never been to France then but somebody had said he was one of the greatest novelists of the twentieth century, so I thought maybe I should acquaint myself with him. It was very difficult, but I did force myself to read him. I think it took about fourteen or fifteen months.

Then I went back to the Royal College of Art in September 1959 and I think, looking back on it now, at the time when I was in the hospital I was always conscious that somehow two years were being robbed from me. A friend of mine who had been at the Bradford

School of Art went on to the Royal College of Art straightaway because he was crippled with polio, and so did not have to do National Service, and I felt, compared with him, I was wasting two years, and I was always conscious of it, really. When I went to the College of course the effect of it was that I felt that somehow I had to make up for it, so in my first year (well, I suppose in all the years I was there) I did work really very diligently and hard. I just spent all my time drawing or painting there, and, anyway, I had gone back to being a student with a little less money again, so I could not really afford to do anything else, and anyway that is what I wanted to do.

I think I did sense at the end of my first year at the Royal College of Art that perhaps the two years in the hospital were not wasted, because of course I had enjoyed an experience that I began to use later: first of all it made me much more conscious of time, then the reading I had done had had an effect. I had thought more about painting: when I could not do any I had thought about it. And the training I had had at the Bradford School of Art, for example, was the old Arts School training which was really quite academic. I think it is probably terribly good, I think it is probably the only kind of training you should have, actually, but the point was it had ignored modern art and what I knew to be modern art and what I knew to be good painting; and so in the two years I had also read more books about art, I think, and I had got a better knowledge of it simply from reading, so that when I went back to art school I was more serious about it and thought of it in a much deeper way than I had when I was a younger student. I suppose that's really just being twenty-two instead of twenty, as well. But later on, by the time I left the Royal College of Art, I had realised that somehow it was better that I had gone there as a student older than twenty. I realised it was better that I had gone there when I was twenty-two because I was more serious about it, therefore I benefited from all that free time just to paint and draw. Yet I think probably five years at the RCA would have had the same effect after the fifth year anyway, perhaps. But, I do not know, I suppose that is the thing I am not that sure of, whether the fact that in between going from one art school to another I saw a bit of a more realistic world and that had an effect. The point was I could not have considered the Army a real world in the way I considered that job in the hospital. I would always have thought of the Army as an unnatural world. I think I would have had a bit of difficulty adapting to it: I mean I do not know, but I might have possibly walked around with a Manual of Military Law under my arm, or I would have certainly kept checking it to make sure that I was not somehow just being pushed around. Whereas I would never have dreamt of letting them down while working in a hospital, I mean, although you were supposed to leave work at five if a little emergency cropped up or something, one would stay; I would never dream of just saying, 'Well, at five I go.' One became a part of it in that sense, even though I was paid by the hour, whereas the nurses and doctors are on salary of course and are expected to do things like that. But workers who are paid by the hour are simply expected to be there at the appointed hour and leave at it, and are really not supposed to have any kind of responsibility.

Looking back at it now from, what, twelve years (I don't think about it too much, I suppose; I had not thought about it lately until I was asked to now), I think it certainly did not do any harm to me in any way. I am not sure how much good it did; I think somehow I would have eventually finished up with the same attitudes and conclusions; or, rather the same attitudes and questions as I do now. But maybe that is just because one is looking back now over twelve years, you tend to forget things, forget how boring things were, sometimes. You forget how down you were at times, I think, people never remember the pain, really.

NICHOLAS HARMAN

On the whole I'm bad at anniversaries. My wife's or my children's birthdays creep up on me unawares. But I remember Armistice Day. I commemorate it privately, to myself, by refusing to buy an Earl Haig poppy. Beribboned commissionaires and self-appointed lady patriots approach me with confident smiles. Dear Sergeant or Madam, I say to myself, kindly remove your eyes from my empty buttonhole: today isn't for me to help you, it's for you to help me. Because I too, in my day, was fodder for cannon.

I remember as though it was yesterday the taste of the bread and golden syrup – the impossible treat of a war-time childhood – that I swallowed when I woke on 11th November 1952. The sharp evening chill was coming down as I ate it. Later that night I brought it up again over an Indian doctor who was wearing a red paratrooper's beret. I was nineteen, and after my bread and syrup I had shaved carefully around the traces of a moustache that were the feeble result of ten days' growth. One of the other times when I woke up in hospital during the next few days there was a black man's face in front of mine, a few inches away and upside down. As I opened my eyes he asked, in a concerned Southern manner: 'I hope that wasn't a moustache on your lip there, sir, because if it was I just shaved it.' And he straightened himself up over the bed-head and walked away round the transfusion unit, the crane for my arm, the leg-brace and the tray of pain-killers.

The night before, John Larrett's legs had been smashed on night patrol. A prisoner blew himself, and John, up on a grenade. The shooting, and the cold night wind from Manchuria, had kept me awake until after the dawn stand-to. Then, as the sun began to suck up the mist, I got back to bed. But almost at once the company sergeant-major was shaking my leg through the tent-flap. The CSM had won a medal for gallantry, in Italy – and he showed fear as an old soldier shows it – with joy that the casualty was not himself, this time. He wanted to talk about Mr Larrett. He knew it was my turn on patrol that night, and so did I. No doubt he quite enjoyed looking at the young officers to see if they were scared.

On the whole we were not scared. Nor, in so far as we knew what we were doing in Korea, did we have doubts about doing it. The job, that night, was straightforward. I was to move just after dusk to a position between our own battalion front and the Chinese front, and there I was to wait, listening, until just before dawn. If I heard enemy movement I was to record it. If I detected enemy in the open I was to call by radio for artillery fire on them. But I was not to engage the enemy myself, except in self-defence.

I took two men with me. The lance-corporal had lately, in a panic, fired a shot into the heel of my boot while I was wearing it. I had neither shot back nor reported him, so we were friends. The fusilier was my new wireless operator, replacing Fusilier Garner-Jones who snored on night-patrol. Both men died that night. I suppose they would not have died if I had not ordered them on patrol. I am sorrier about the wireless operator. He took a long time to die, and by then I was too weak from my wounds to get at the morphine to stop him screaming.

It is worth recording just what it was that these two soldiers died doing. Roughly half-way along a mountainous promontory of eastern Asia two armies faced each other, each composed largely of men quite unconnected with the land where they were fighting. The lines of trenches had for over a year lain opposite one another, along swift rivers or steep mountains which made advance by either side impossible. At a few points there was a break in the natural frontier: a valley ran from one side deep into the other's territory, or a hill overlooked the other side's front line. We were at one of these points, and at these points gunfire and skirmishing continued. But it was not intended by either side's generals that their troops should in fact advance. It was not that sort of war.

A few miles to the west, clearly visible from my own company's position, and cutting vertically into the night sky, searchlights had shone through the summer nights to show where the generals from both sides were talking about peace. By November, in some complicated manoeuvre or bluff by one side or the other, the talks were suspended, and the lights went out. (Now, twenty years later, those talks are still going on in that same place, called Panmunjom.)

The job of the soldiers then was to ensure that the other side did not gain a bargaining advantage, however brief, at the truce talks, by winning a few yards of ground. To resist a swift attack with a limited purpose soldiers must be ready to fight hard at a moment's notice. Soldiers fight best and fastest when they hate their enemy. They will hate their enemy if the enemy is shooting at them. So, most nights, some of us went out into the gap between the armies to be shot at by them, while some of them similarly came out to be shot at by us.

Officially, of course, the purpose of these night patrols was to gather information about the other side, and if possible to take prisoners from whom such information could be extracted. I do not remember that we English soldiers ever brought a prisoner safely in. They used to tie grenades to their bodies and blow themselves up if in danger of capture. For linguistic and other reasons we did not process prisoners ourselves. We handed them over for interrogation to our allies of the South Korean military police. In the officers' mess we agreed that our enemies were very sensible to avoid that fate, at any cost.

So, as dark fell, I passed with my two soldiers through the front trench of the front platoon, out of the last machine-gun post, and down through the gap in the wire to the track across the minefield that led to no-man's-land. From the front platoon three men were detailed off to show us the way through the wire and the mines. We were half-way through the minefield, down the slope where our own people could no longer see, when the Chinese caught us.

They must have moved in the night before, detecting and removing the mines one by one, and lain there all day waiting for dusk and an unwary English patrol. In close-quarter fighting in the dark it is best to start by throwing hand-grenades, since you can't fire a gun without a flash that betrays your own position. As I led my patrol into the ambush their first flight of grenades cracked my right shin and slashed my scalp. Then they fired, the short groaning bursts of what we knew as burp guns, from ten yards off. My own first grenade went off between two of them, and they went over. The next part happens to me now, in my mind, with the clear, gliding slowness of an action replay. I am sure it happened like this.

I was on my knees, holding a second grenade in my right hand ready for throwing. My left hand was reaching to remove the safety-pin from this grenade. In the darkness, where the only light came from the pearl dusk above the trees and the flash of gunfire, I saw a man in a British steel helmet – one of my escorting party – aim and fire his Sten gun point blank at my chest. My left arm seemed caught in a hurricane of wind, a gust fluttered the arm away from my body, the man firing fell back, another man in a strange cap fell forward by me. My escort had shot a Chinese soldier who was standing behind me about to fire at my head. In doing so he had also shot me across the chest, from which the bullets were deflected by my flak jacket into my arm. Then somebody in turn shot him. I was still on my knees, unable to walk because of my broken leg, with the grenade in my right hand, the safety-pin still in place, and enemy soldiers still moving where they had been before.

I moved the grenade towards my left hand, which was to remove the pin. The hand would not take the pin. Instead the arm bent, backwards, above the elbow, with a gritty sound like a rotten board smashing. I put the grenade to my mouth, pulled the pin with my teeth in a gesture that I was at the time aware of imitating from a child's comic, and threw the grenade towards where the Chinese soldiers had been. Then I lay forward. My mistake was to fold my right arm across my chest, where the weight of my body in the hard flak jacket pinned it to the ground. From then on I could move my left boot, but nothing else.

I think the Chinese survivors touched me. But either they thought me not worth taking, or they had enough of their own people to carry home, and they left me. In the quiet I heard the earphones round my wireless operator's neck, near me on the ground: the 'mush' of a signal, my own call-sign over and over. 'Indian Mound Four Able report my signals over.' Perhaps it was that which started the wireless operator talking. He told me what had happened to his stomach. He wanted to get it back inside himself. He told me about this, louder and louder, crying in small screams. On my thigh I could feel the bulge of the first-aid kit. In it was the morphine on the needle. I think I could have moved my arm if my weight in my flak jacket had not been on it. When I tried, I began to scream like the wireless operator. I felt weaker after that. I could only tell him this was the sort of wound that would get us home ahead of time. After half an hour or so he got quieter and died. Everybody else was dead too.

They came to pick me up quite soon after that, an artillery screen whistling over, the sky lit up with flares, and the rescue patrol creeping out in danger that the ambush would still be in place. They put me on a stretcher and carried me back up the track and along the trenches. Once the other side sent some shells in at us, and the stretcher-bearers dumped me on the edge of a trench while they got down into it. Next to me they dumped another stretcher, with a dead man on it. He was the first Chinese soldier I had seen close up.

Then the bandages took over, and the morphine floated me off, putting a little man in my head to give orders to my limbs to see if they were still alive, telling an arm or a toe to move, calling back the order – always too late – when a bit of rough bone grated on another, or a part just failed to work at all. In the main surgical hospital I heard a kindly American colonel say he would try to save my arm. In a transit tent there were several Puerto Ricans with identical wounds in the foot, caused by applying a rifle to the instep on receipt of the order to advance. An old American signals sergeant was kind and talked to me in a gap when the morphine stopped working. He said he had survived going across the Yalu river into China with his telephone cables, at the moment when the Americans thought the war was won, and before the new Red Army had appeared and driven them back; now the war was dead-locked, and he had slipped in mud and broken his leg. In a long post-surgical tent everyone was kind and clean and food came in a sort of tray with aluminium compartments so that the jam got into the frankfurters. The bed opposite mine was flanked by two large black military policemen. The stump of the patient's leg lay on top of the covers, bandaged white and still. In the night he cried out, 'Kim, Kim, Kim': he ripped the bandages off the stump, started the bleeding and managed to die before they could get the plasma to him. He was a North Korean prisoner.

Before I went on the plane back to base hospital in Japan, the regimental padre came down to visit me. He was a kindly man, incarnating all the innocent absurdity of the Church of England. My friend Kit Hoare sent down a bottle of mess champagne with him, as a present to cheer me up. When my gear arrived in Japan the bottle had been stolen from it. Kit was killed that night, on patrol.

Ten months later I was released from the Army with a disability pension of £168 a year. I went to university, to Cambridge, and at the age of twenty I started my real life.

One peculiarity of the Korean war was that you got not one but two campaign medals for having been in or near it. The heavy, shiny one had the new Queen's head on, like any decent British medal. The other, a lightweight, anodised job suitable for armies that do not believe in Brasso, bears the message: 'For service in defence of the principles of the charter of the United Nations.' The wording skilfully indicates drafting by a committee not all of whose members can command the rhythms of English prose. And it was an especially odd citation for a young person such as me. I don't remember ever having heard of the UN at Eton: if I had it would have been only as a pinko joke, and that was a view of the organisation certainly shared by my brother officers in the regiment. I remember loud laughter in the mess at a rumour that there were *Belgian* soldiers engaged with us in the fight against whatever it was.

Nowadays it is fashionable to pretend that soldiers, to fight bravely, need to be animated by a clear structure of loyalties and antagonisms (although how that notion fits with the fact of the men who dismantle bombs in Ireland beats me). Anyway, I think we did sometimes fight rather bravely: but I know we felt no particular loyalties except to ourselves, and no antagonisms except towards the Americans. I speak, of course, for the officers. I had, and still have, no idea at all of how the ordinary conscript soldiers got through the whole business, or what they thought it was all about. It was said that two Jewish fusiliers, at the final kit inspection before we went on embarcation leave, left out on display their newly-acquired Communist Party cards – and were promptly returned as security risks to civilian life and their barrows in Petticoat Lane. Whether or not they really existed they were heroes and legends in my platoon, but nobody had the nerve to follow their example. Our only talented escaper made himself vomit blood by drinking native liquor before a dangerous night march, and had to be sent away to guard ammunition dumps out of the front line – but I never knew if this was an intelligent evasion of peril or simple drunken foolishness.

I suppose what kept the English soldiers going was best explained by my platoon sergeant one night, when I cautiously praised the apparent informality and first-name-calling of some Australian officers and men with whom we had been sharing a position:

'It may be all right for them, Sir,' said Sergeant Taylor, 'but in the British Army you can tell an officer even in the dark.'

It was the class structure that did the trick. A conscript army, on a mission it did not understand, was resting on a social system devised to build an empire.

If I was a quite efficient officer (which, within the demands of the job, I was), it was the result of a deliberate training which had seen my father through one war and which saw me through another. It almost went wrong with me. On leaving Eton I had naturally been intended for a National Service commission in the Foot Guards. But the brutality I saw among recruits at the Guards Depot in Caterham had led me to choose a line regiment (and Korea) rather than two years' membership of that sort of nastiness. Only afterwards did I see that my little rebellion was absurd. ('But, Harman,' said the guards major at the Officer Training School, 'you have been offered a Commission in the Coldstream Guards. It is *an honour*.') I now see that if you want to turn ordinary men rapidly into good soldiers, you must first strip them of their ordinary manhood – and regular bullying and humiliation does this faster and more efficiently than other means. Our fusiliers were worse soldiers than guardsmen largely because they had not been so roughly handled as recruits.

For soldiers, and most particularly for soldiers conscripted in times of apparent peace for warlike tasks, what matters is the unquestioning acceptance of the role chosen by the authorities. For upper-class lads like me the role was absolutely plain: to give clear orders even when nobody quite knew what the point of them was, and to seem in control even when most confused or afraid. At nineteen the upbringing and education of my class had made these things easy. Afterwards, with the easy self-discipline of sport removed by my injury, and with the beginnings of an intellectual life forced on me by months of involuntary physical idleness, I was disqualified from these simplicities.

Maybe some other accident would have done it in the end. But in the event National Service treated me like my son treats a toy train, switching the points to run it on to some quite different piece of track. Those who suggest that, as a general principle, universal military service was a good thing and turned out a better sort of young person seem to me grossly mistaken, usually motivated either by malice towards or envy of the young. But I do know for myself that the person I should have been without National Service would be even more foolish, more ignorant, more arrogant and more unpleasant than I now take myself to be. And heaven knows what, straight from Eton, I could have made of the etiolated subtleties of the English tripos at Cambridge in the 1950s.

The war I was in as a conscript put in place a regime whose achievements for the Korean people are highly questionable. It utterly failed in its main objective, which was to limit at birth the wider ambitions of the new Chinese Communist state. It effectively discredited for many years – perhaps for ever – the idea of a United Nations force as an impartial power for peace. It killed a fair number of young people, a few of whom were friends of mine. It did not even teach the Americans not to try it on again. And, as I write, the treaty to end it is still not signed. I had an expensive education.

KARL MILLER

I paid virtually no attention to the Army till the Army paid attention to me, sending a writ and summoning me to Aldershot. I joined like a lamb.

At school I'd been in my element as a hard-working scholarship boy, a dux, a valedictory orator, a prefect and a poet. I'd been brought up by a kind grandmother and aunts, and there wasn't much money: but I'd never felt deprived or lower-class. My experiences at school may have been partly responsible for that, and they may have made me complacent. I thought of National Service, when I thought of it at all, as a pause between school and university, as a kind of seventh form. The two years would be spent in the posture of a pastoral poet, mooning by a Nissen hut with a book in my hand. This is what the verse of Alun Lewis and Sidney Keyes and many a *Penguin New Writing* had led me to expect of the Forces. It would be Woodbines, Woodbines all the way, and short stories, and yielding girls. Soldiers were sensitive and solitary. They were like Denton Welch. Privates enjoyed private lives of rare quality.

At about the same time, I wrote a short story called 'The Nether Fields' which expressed without restraint this notion of the soldier as poet and loiterer (in the Army itself, loitering was impugned as skiving). The story was a visionary effort in Dylan Thomas prose which described how a wounded soldier – loitering even unto death – studied the indifferent behaviour of a fair-haired boy. The situation was reminiscent of the last pages of *Death in Venice*, a work which, when I later read it, I rashly supposed I'd mystically foreseen. When I got to Cambridge, the story was published, and there were worries that it might be held to have a homosexual content. If so, this could only have helped it, for homosexuality was then in high fashion, as I was to discover in the Army. But the truth is that it was charged with adolescent narcissism: I was admiring my own youth in a military mirror which had precious little to do with the realities of military life. My own hair, I fear, was fair, and I played the part of the soldier as well.

Well, of course, the Royal Engineers of Farnborough proved a very different element from the Royal High School of Edinburgh, and my experiences in basic training were a great come-down for the scholarship boy. After that delusive pastoral prelude, my National Service became burlesque – a comedy in two acts, inter-larded with scenes of horror and desolation. In one way, what happened was that the respective social systems collided, and the earlier was effaced. School was meritocratic: scholars and athletes were promoted and awarded badges. This was an authoritarian system, just as the Army was: but it was apparent that the Army was something other than meritocratic, or at any rate that authority rested, in the Sappers, on a highly specialised conception of merit. You were likely to be made a second lieutenant if you had been to a public school (each with its unit of the Junior Training Corps) and could stand up to the rigours of an Officers' Training School, for which public schools were a fitting preparation. You were not likely to be made a second lieutenant if you had not been to a public school, and if you spoke with a regional accent.

As soon as I entered my first Hampshire hut, it was plain that there were two types of inmate: the public schoolboys and the working-class. And it didn't need exhaustive research to establish which of the two was earmarked for abrupt and exalted promotion. Given the country's various complementary and competing hier-archies, it is possible for an individual to be high and low, in and out, at the same time: as a working-class scholarship boy, I felt torn and uncertain when confronted with these two castes. I made friends for a while with a cadet whom I'll call David, a quiet, stylish boy, a rich man's son who referred to yachts, who'd been to a Scottish public school but who was no Jock and didn't sound like one. When he left to win his spurs, I thought I wouldn't see him again. But I did.

On arriving at Farnborough, we discovered we had fallen

through a hole and landed in the eighteenth century. Even in an unglamorous regiment like the Engineers, an Army unit behaved like an appendage of the landed interest and its suburban simulations: the game we were playing was gentry-and-mob, with touches of knights-and-serfs. The class arrangements of modern Britain had been collapsed into a simple dualism. There were two of everything: officers and other ranks, mess and cookhouse, cheesecutter and beret. The Army had yet to develop a middle class, and the sergeants' mess was no approximation to one. During the war, I gather, this dualism was to some extent dismantled, in order that we might win; and merit, together with a measure of solidarity, was given a chance. But the two tiers had returned. The subaltern from Oundle and his soldier-servant – Robin and Batman – loomed large over Hampshire. It looked like a damned good way of restricting the supply of competent leaders: most of the really impressive soldiers I came across were warrant officers who reckoned they'd never go any higher.

I'd thought the Army would be sweet and secluded. Before long Robin was sneering at me as I stood to attention in front of him, having made a mistake: 'You know what thought did.' Again, during the war, the military code of bullying and threats and sneers was suspended for efficiency's sake and out of respect for what was going on. In peacetime, as a rule, the Army hadn't much to do, so that this code – certainly in training and in the more 'regimental' units – became its sole concern.

The initial humiliations appeared to be contrived to break you and toughen you simultaneously. The result was that the more impressionable members of each intake, sitting in their 'spiders' or huts, began to feel like displaced persons, refugees, subject to unbeatable sanctions and controls, miserable and desperate. In the troopships at Harwich the tannoy used to request the officers to stay on shore while the other ranks were 'being loaded', like a netful of gorillas or a deck of refrigerated whalemeat. Making a man of you turned you into cargo. I remember one corporal who used to work himself into cleverly paced and modulated fits of raving Hitlerian rage every time he took charge of a squad. He turned us into his Jews. One inept, depressed and probably backward boy whom I knew was made to double round the square, I was told, until he dropped. They can only have made a mess of *him*. A death was rumoured: I'd like to see the suicide figures for the National Service intakes. It must have been difficult for the Regular Army to cope with the conscript swarms of the Fifties, even with the machinery left over from the war, but it didn't make sense to specialise in having them hate, despise or deride you. And these were the only responses I encountered among my friends.

Night fell once as I arrived in a new camp. I'd been to the Q Stores to draw my kit, and had stumbled out into the dusk carrying my possessions in my arms. Presently they toppled over on to the wet road: blankets, denims, beret, cap-badge, shoulder flashes, belt, blanco. My 'housewife' exploded and its needle, thread and buttons flew off into the dark and took a long time to retrieve. I fully understand that this was not like being shot in the groin, or being tarred and feathered, but for a moment there I seemed to lose all hope.

I made my way to the spider where my mates were lying on their beds, reading comics, listening to 'Truly, truly fair' on the radio and displaying and discussing their erections. Privates, it turned out, led very public lives.

They were a rough lot, my mates, but I got on with them well enough. I wasn't disgracefully poor at marching and drilling, and I grew to be obsessed, as you had to, with the business of tending your boots and uniform and rifle and housewife. The battledress we wore was ugly, uncomfortable and inconvenient, but you had to generate a fetishist's awareness of its textures and tortures. Those gaiters! The Army's idea of cleaning things was to make them dirty – if possible, to smear them with black lead. I became a connoisseur of salutes, and I'll never forget one corporal's performance in that area. His salute started as a foppish grovel and flowered into a soaring semaphoric orchid or flamingo: a show of exotic servility which sent up the officer and was clearly prejudicial to good order and military discipline, but which was quite unchargeable as such: a masterpiece of false ceremony richly deserved by the very many of our superiors whose only role was to be saluted.

I learnt some of the tricks of the trade, but I wasn't a success even as a skiver, and there were a number of catastrophes. I entered a mill where octogenarian millers were hefting bags of flour: when one old man placed a bag on my narrow shoulders, I melted – illnamed – to the floor. I scored nothing out of twenty in an intelligence test in which you assembled the parts of a bicycle pump and other objects: for this I was placed among the clerks for what was left of my basic training. A psychiatrist talked to me with distaste, and on the train to Germany I pried into my personal documents to find that I wasn't considered to be leadership material. This was not such a bad blow as it might seem, since I had joined up believing that you couldn't be an officer unless you signed on as a Regular: I'd simply never heard of Robin. Later, I passed the exam for the Administrative branch of the Civil Service: neither the military nor the civil assessment of my abilities now strikes me as realistic, and, in particular, I have decided to ignore that nil rating for intelligence.

And so to Act Two – in which I escape to Germany and spend the remainder of my National Service there. The British Forces Network radio station in Hamburg was a bizarre posting, and a huge deliverance. I now think that it would have been better if I'd been posted to a conventional sort of unit, and suffered out the insulted existence of the average squaddy, but I was panting for the microphones, and I had an interesting time in Hamburg.

William Drummond of Hawthornden was my deliverer. I had written a feature programme on the life and times of this seventeenth-century pastoral poet – 'A hyacinth I wisht me in her hand' – for the Scottish BBC: it was entitled *Damon in Albany*. And I'd also done some broadcasting after being called up. Officers who'd been sneering and jeering the day before would tiptoe up on parade and pass on in whispers telephone messages from producers: Robin respected the BBC. Anyway, this was why I was posted to Army Radio.

BFN was a quaint place, but it did a pretty good job. It was a kind of local radio station really, in advance of what there is now in that line, and it served the British Army of the Rhine in a fashion that would nowadays be called participatory: soldiers, wives, Church Army canteen manageresses, often came to the microphone. It took many of its programmes from the BBC, but put out many of its own as well, and of every variety. On Sunday mornings *Two-Way Family Favourites,* the blue-riband record-request programme, was broadcast jointly with London. BFN's military broadcasters were divided into regulars, who lived both in barracks and in 'married families' housing in the city, and conscripts; there were civilian broadcasters on secondment; there was an admin group of earthy soldiers who were contemptuous of all broadcasters; and there was a German staff as well. The broadcasting was done in the Hamburg Musikhalle, where we occasionally slept on guard duty. A tirade of nineteenth-century orchestral music flowed continually at our elbow: Furtwängler and Hindemith would conduct, and Gieseking play.

I worked as an assistant to a padre from Ulster, Major Robert Crossett, a striking man, gruff and bitter, who talked to persuasive perfection on the air. This meant that I travelled round BAOR seeing to the transmission of church services. I also wrote reams of book and film reviews in an office whose windows gave on to an ancient red-light street. My grandmother had defined a brothel for me (one had been mentioned in Walter Scott) as 'a place where bad people go, and dance.' I asked: 'Is there a brothelle in Gilmerton?' I was never able to believe in Scotch brothels, but here were authentic German ones. Spent from my church services, I would sit and watch the whores as they displayed themselves in shop windows of a sort, like so many second lieutenants, served with refreshments by maids in caps and frilly aprons.

The head of the station was a civilian, Leslie Perowne, bright as a bird, a lover of opera and of bygone regimental uniforms, who was sent out from the Gramophone Department of the BBC to spread the Spoken Word, and the values of the Corporation, in outlandish spots. I used to like talking to his second-in-command, Dennis Scuse: my first ordinary engrossing conversation with a superior felt like an illicit pleasure. A neat captain, with a sharp look and a moustache you could shave with, warmed the hearts of Rhine Army with peripatetic human-interest shows of the Wilfred Pickles stamp. There was a cadre of disc-jockeys, two of whom – Chris Howland and Derek Jones – were probably better at it than anyone in the BBC at that period, if you except Jean Metcalfe. These were the station's silver tongues.

So my military service had taken a literary turn, after all. I was back in my element, reading Proust in the evenings. I listened a lot to Haydn's *Clock* Symphony, which seemed to chime me towards Cambridge. Hardly anyone read comics. There was no more public hoisting of penises, no more virtuoso masturbation. On the other hand, there was some consenting of adults in private. I was rapidly alerted to this when the soldiers in the unit staggered shambolically onto parade early one morning in uniforms that might have been slept in. There we all were, in brilliant disarray, a platoon of cissies and loitering, prejudicial Damons, a bunch of hyacinths in the Army's incredulous hand. A weary RSM caused a convulsive movement by doing up a hip button, and roared out the arresting words: 'It's all right – my name's not So-and-so!' Naming one of his comrades-in-arms.

We were more like Dad's Army than Proust's. We had no one who resembled his beauties from the barracks at Doncières: we were never strong on spruce, delicious lieutenants. But there was a very definite poovishness in the air and on it, as you'd expect of a unit composed of entertainers, sensitives and regimental rejects, at a time when homosexuality was regarded as exciting and subversive. I was no mad, marauding bugger myself, but I wished them well – if only because Robin would have been so sickened.

We may have been a bit of a comic-opera outfit, but, in a rather malicious, greenroom sort of way, we were reasonably happy and reasonably busy. We did our duty – perhaps because there was more of it to do – more efficiently, I imagine, than quite a few conventional units. We refrained from grinding the face of the Germans, and dispensed with the apparatus of servility and invective which we'd fled from in the training camps: no doubt the majority of postings provided some relief from that.

But it wasn't the case that features and drama and family favourites were the closest we came to soldierliness. They also served who only drove through the Eastern Zone to Berlin in order to broadcast groaning hymns and not very godly homilies. Why, I was even captured by the Russians. Our equipment was impounded at Helmstedt, on the border of the Eastern Zone, and, standing between a portrait of Lenin and a portrait of Stalin, I was interrogated by an officer, who was civil enough: he did not ask if I knew what thought did, but, consulting my documents, he did inquire why I had four names, including two middle ones. It was some while after the Berlin Airlift, but the Russians were still behaving in a regimental manner, so there had to be this charade that I might be smuggling in some second sapper, or Third Man, by means of an excess of names. The Germans with me were thrown into a camp for a week or two, and then released. These were my only hostilities.

My two years passed, and I moved from Cissy Street to Civvy Street via a demob centre in Hampshire where punishment drills and shouting matches and filthy huts were the Army's idea of a worthy send-off, and where some soldiers were getting ready to go to Korea to fight in a war: I don't claim that my version of National Service had much in common with theirs.

What *do* I claim for those two years? They seemed momentous at the time, but that was largely because I was young and green. I felt I had discovered that, at this stage in its history, the Army in

Germany, as perhaps in other theatres, was a dud organisation. Loaded down with bewildered adolescents, it did nothing that a small, wholly professional army, fully abreast of the new weapons that became available, could not have done far more effectively. Sir Arthur Young, who was head of the Royal Ulster Constabulary for a while during the current troubles in Northern Ireland, is reported to have said: 'You can't just leave an army standing around. They always have to be *doing* something.' In Germany, the Army was left standing around. Its deterrent operations within the Nato context could as well have been conducted from bases in Britain, and the decision to maintain a presence in Germany was, I'm sure, a mistake, which may in part have issued from some obscure desire for the sensations of conquest. The Army's occupation of that country left its soldiers singularly unoccupied. Its presence there was like a piece of the expiring British Empire, complete with memsahibs and married families, awkwardly attached to the resurgences that were to become the German Miracle. It stood around like some great shambling animal put out to grass and chewing the cud of its traditions – which were mostly to do with Officers' Mess silverware.

In general, or so I'd claim, the Army had slid back several decades to its pre-war condition of institutionalised snobbery, humming with eighteenth-century overtones. Each training camp suggested a country house awash with a nightmare accession of unemployable underlings: no wonder these public schoolboys had to be summarily promoted to deal with the problem of insubordination. But in fact there wasn't any insubordination to speak of. Even more than the ferocity of the authoritarianism, what seems astonishing now – after a decade of protest, and of preaching about democracy and partici- pation – is the depth of the abasement. There were few rebels: only the Kray brothers come to mind, who are said to have made nuisances of themselves when called to the colours. (I was once accused of mutiny, for riding the German Underground instead of going by Army truck, but the charge was 'camped' out of court by everyone involved.) It looks as if there is less snobbery in Britain now: if so, National Service may well have been considered a nadir in the lives of the generation that experienced it, and, as such, it may have assisted the change. There are matters on which prac- tically no one of my age would want to quarrel with the protesting young.

The story is that it is good for young men to be kept down and bullied and made to despair. But since all lives are laid end to end with restrictions and humiliations, it isn't clear why we should extol the military varieties when they were so often the product of little more than egotism and mismanagement. I realise, incidentally, that the public schoolboys had themselves been bullied – at school: hence the tears shed in memoirs, and hence – in retaliation, as it were – certain of the traditions of the British Army. Despite the silliness of that story, however, I think it was good for young men to know, to suffer the certainty, that the post-war Army was corrupt, unjust and oppressive, if only because it enabled them to doubt the familiar view that merit will out, and will thrive, and will invariably deserve to thrive. In some cases, it enabled them to conclude that promotion is shameful.

National Service made me turn to the working-class as to a beautiful woman. After Cambridge, I ceased to be sensitive and started playing football, partly because I reckoned that there must be virtue in something rated so low. Just as, in certain moods, I loved to drink-in the awfulness of the Army, so I love to hear football condemned as morally inferior. These are experiences that help you to know what you respect. In reality, football is an education, and the nurse of some important virtues.

Several of my friends, who included public schoolboys, felt the same, perhaps more strongly, after being demobbed and after graduating from the university. In its more objectionable features, the university struck them as rather like the Army: there was Robin, none other, sitting among the college silverware, being waited on. So they joined or re-joined the working-class, dressing in rough textures and dark, dangerous shades, and looking more like displaced persons than spruce mechanics. Social mobility was seen as a new name for snobbery. I presume that it's also a new name for talent, but these people have a point, and I am on their side. Many of their compatriots are not: Britain still remains a country – there are others – where you are treated better, wherever you go, if you wear a suit.

The attitudes of these dissenters can't be made to match any of the usual kinds of progressive politics. It would not be true to say that these people had been radicalised by their taste of the Army. But their attitudes are quite widely diffused, and they are present in a number of books, plays and films which appeared in the fifties and early sixties. I'm thinking especially of the only decent film that has been made about National Service, *The Bofors Gun,* and of its bleak account of the anxieties of the boy who quits the unit in Germany to be an officer cadet. Such anxieties are a counterpart of my own eagerness to abscond to the microphones, and I now believe they are something to be ashamed of.

These recollections of mine may be accounted vengeful and resentful – poisoned by my failure to flourish in the Army. In fact, I enjoyed myself on the whole; I'd accept that, in my own time, many of the public-school élite who'd been trained to command were likely to be able to do so well and without offence; and I take a more benign view of the profession than most of those I meet. I would be willing to fight in any war I judged was necessary, such as the Second World War. And I am convinced that there *is* such a thing as a good soldier. (I don't mean the kind that is charged with assault or rape and is then defended by an officer who goes on about what a good soldier he is.) A good soldier is likely to have the decency and calm of a good soccer professional, and one reason for this is that both men have lived in a state of subjection to unearned authority in the shape of officers and directors. Subjection to merit can be equally painful: particularly since, in certain respects, merit has been consistently overrated. Merit, of whatever kind, does not always deliver when institutionalised or placed in authority, and it isn't absurd to suppose that the Army has traditionally recognised and responded to this. All the same, there are ways of bearing with institutionalised paltriness which can make people virtuous.

The British Army is now a small, wholly professional organisation, no doubt happy to be so, and to be rid of its conscripts. Perhaps I should explain why I am on the side of the Army in Ulster, even though many of the officers interviewed on television have proved patently upper-class. There has been plenty of evidence to indicate that the troops who've been trying to do the impossible and keep the peace in Northern Ireland have included a large number of good soldiers, as well as some bad ones. What I like about the British Army is that, during my lifetime, it has almost always fought for good reasons, and almost always in a disciplined fashion. It has done no tarring and feathering that I know of, beaten up no pregnant women that I know of, blown the faces off no shopgirls that I know of. And it has not chosen to kill any fathers that I know of in front of their wives and children. This may seem like a rather simple test to apply – like assembling the parts of a bicycle pump. But if these things are true, they can scarcely be unimportant. I write this with a fairly extensive knowledge of the charges of brutality that have been levelled at the troops in Ulster. And I do so without retracting any of the criticisms I've made of the Army as I knew it in its pointlessness twenty-five years ago, at a bad time in its history, exhausted by a world war.

I went camping with the Territorials once or twice after I left the Army, and there was nothing very awful about that. For most of the men it was a holiday. 'What are the pleasures of Paris,' I heard one of them cry in a pulpit voice, 'compared with the humdrum fuckeries of Findhorn?' On another occasion we were marching along George Street in Edinburgh when we found ourselves approaching a tall stone column: at the top, a figure appeared to be gazing down at us in a posture of qualified displeasure. 'Look,' said a soldier: 'There's the OC!' In a way, he was right. For this was a statue of Henry Dundas, Lord Melville, one of the most astute of the eighteenth-century grandees. There on his pillar, never to detumesce, stood the favourite führer of the Northern gentry. That gaze, I felt, had rested on the whole of my military career.

It was when I went to Lancashire with the Territorials that I met my friend David again. I was standing in a long queue outside a cookhouse tent, all of us keen to reach the food, despite the fact that it was covered with a hundred thousand wasps. David came round with his cane. With difficulty we recognised each other, and with difficulty we spoke. Then he walked away, having inspected the wasps. I wondered if he would get in touch with me during that fortnight: I couldn't very well get in touch with him. Well, he didn't. I don't want to break anybody's heart: we hadn't been Damon and Pythias, as in some pastoral poem by William Drummond of Hawthornden. And I don't much blame my ex-friend for what happened. It was mostly the Army's fault.

TREV LEGGETT

I am glad to get this off my chest. Time has not sufficiently erased the memory of National Service: perhaps writing it down will finally purge my system.

I did not find the two years enjoyable. I would like to suggest this to be the reaction of a sensitive, cultured, teenager; but in fact I was (and remain) an insensitive clod, much given to Old Boys' Soccer and swilling bitter. Rather, it is the utter mindlessness of military life; particularly, I suspect, in time of peace. I was (and remain) an intellectual snob, however. Particularly depressing was the bombardier, filling in a form at my arrival in one unit, in response to learning of a degree in mathematics, saying: 'Yers, but 'ave you got School Certificate?'

Of course it was not all bad. And at least it was interesting, even amidst the mind-shattering boredom of it all, watching the effect of it all on one's own character. Military training is designed so that movements become so drilled in that they can be carried out in the heat of battle, come shellshock or high water. To that extent, therefore, individual thought becomes an embarrassment. The training is far more effective than is immediately apparent. Certainly individuality, but most of all the power of individual decision, is eradicated with terrifying speed. Entering the Army on a Thursday, my first sight of the outside world was nine days later, on a Saturday afternoon: by which time the best manner of apportioning the modest twenty-four shillings (one week's pay) between pictures, meal, or other refreshment became a decision of such major importance as to be almost impossible to take unsupported.

The brain dies. It came as a surprise to find that after a spell on guard duty my mind had been a complete blank for two hours. I had thought of nothing at all. Even better was Gus Johnstone's story of waking up lying on his face on the ground, having fallen asleep standing on guard.

I have suggested that there was some interest in an objective view of one's own reaction to events; but this must be true of any human experience. It can hardly be put down as an item to the credit of Army life. What, then, was there in National Service?

On the debit side, undoubtedly the waste of it all. My permanent posting was Lyemum barracks, on the island of Hong Kong. The British keep (or kept) a total strength of twelve thousand men there. Estimates varied, but the understanding was that if the Chinese attacked in force, this would be sufficient to hold the island for between 36 and 72 hours, provided that the troops fought to the last man. This would just have sufficed to evacuate the married families by way of boats kept standing off Stanley peninsula. I believe the idea was that if the Chinese had to kill twelve thousand men to take Hong Kong it would prove (to the rest of the world?) that they were committing an act of aggression. Considering that the smuggling going through Hong Kong was China's only trade contact with the outside world, and her only source of hard currency, it seemed to me patently obvious that it was in China's interest to maintain the status quo. I do not know the figure in the Army estimates for the entire Hong Kong garrison, nor its official purpose in being there: neither figure nor reason was vouchsafed to a mere lance bombardier. And this absence did nothing for the utter sense of the futility of it all.

An easier example was that of a friend who was a member of a small British unit attached to an American air station in Mildenhall, Norfolk. Analysis showed that every one of the unit's thirty people was there only to service the other twenty-nine. One was a cook, one a pay clerk, one a driver, and so on. There was no outside reason for the existence of the unit at all. If liaison with the Americans were required, one man would have sufficed.

Don't misunderstand me. I am no pacifist. Albeit reluctantly, I am driven to the conclusion that any nation needs to be able to defend itself. But there must be some way accurately to assess the real military needs of that nation. I do not, nor did I seventeen years ago, say that National Service was a complete waste of time in the sense that it may be desirable, or necessary, to give every able-bodied man some military training. My training spread over a period of eight months, during roughly half of which I was actually being instructed. Parenthetically quite a heated discussion ensued one evening as to whether the Army's Surveyors' Course, lasting fourteen weeks, could be compressed into four days, or whether five days were desirable for full benefit. This being mentioned to our sergeant the following day, we were assured that for pre-war Regulars the fourteen weeks had been a six months' course! Of the remaining sixteen months of my twenty-four, two-and-a-half months were passed on troopships, twelve-and-a-half in Hong Kong, and one in Malaya – then an active service zone.

Of the sixteen months, perhaps sixteen hours were fruitfully spent.

Even accepting the desirability of some military training, there seems no military justification for a period longer than, say, six months. Politically, as a means of masking unemployment – possibly. Socially, to control rebellious youth between eighteen and twenty years of age – probably. But to hide it behind military necessity – no.

Before descending into the futility of it all, let me remember the sixteen profitable hours. Even part of that was doubtful. Four hours I spent, from eleven p.m. to three a.m., in barracks in a transit camp in Singapore, talking to a sixteen-year-old. He was the son of a regular warrant officer, and was en route somewhere to enlist for twenty-two years, yet not, at that time, having actually signed anything. Four hours of my beauty sleep I gave him – at my persuasive best, I thought, albeit rather desperately towards the end – trying to talk him out of such a drastic step. I believe I weakened his resolve somewhat; but I shall never know now whether I was successful. It is probably a fair measure of my hatred of Army life that, although time has blunted some of the feeling, I can still recall, vividly, from February 1956, four hours of passionate denunciation of all things military.

The other twelve hours of fruitful occupation were spent terracing out a hillside for the good Miss Mildred Dibden at Shah Tin Orphanage. In order to do some building extension flat ground was required, and such as existed was entirely taken up by clothes lines. It was necessary that some more flat ground had to be hewn out of the hillside, as a new site for the clothes lines. Several times during the day buckets of home-made lemonade appeared for us: and at the end of the day we learned that every drop of drinking water had to be carried up from the valley below. The men's answer to that was to put every last Hong Kong cent we had between us into a collection and donate it to the Orphanage. The trouble with the Army is the system: the blokes in it are quite decent, really.

To return to the theme of development of character, or lack of it. It was striking to observe my first real example of people behaving like sheep. The same had no doubt been true of school and college; but I had not had the same awareness of it. I realised some of the reasons for the behaviour of troops abroad. I was just old enough to have some appreciation of what happened to foreign servicemen in London during the war; but they were, of course, decadent foreigners, with lower moral standards than the fine British. But the latter becomes a drunken lecher; in part, because one is expected so to do. Four of us spent a weekend in Macao (five hours by the midnight ferry from Hong Kong) where we clearly were not the first servicemen to visit. In our hotel room by seven-forty a.m., it was at seven-fifty a.m. that we were first offered by the floor waiter 'four Portuguese girls.' Parenthetically we spent the day sightseeing and soaking up gin. Eventually, suffering from brewers' droop, we turned down the last offer of 'four Portuguese girls' at midnight; by which time the tune almost changed to 'four Portuguese boys.' Clearly by that time the floor waiter was having grave doubts.

One behaves badly because it is expected, although there are probably two subsidiary reasons. There is the removal from parental influence of young men in their late teens – a time when they would anyway be turning towards alcohol and the sweet sin of lechery. More than that, however, is probably the cloak of anonymity given by the Army. Khaki, or in this case olive green, hides a multitude of sins. When this is allied to the control system which still makes 'two-three-zero-six-three-eight-two-five' more easy to remember than one's own name, there is a good base for ill behaviour. 'Oh, hello, 3825, I'd like you to meet 4716.' Could it ever really have been like that?

Perhaps the lack of encouragement to moral discipline explains the ludicrously harsh approach by the services. In what other walk of life could one get anything up to, say, three days in jail for an officer not being satisfied with the shine on a pair of boots? For any small misdemeanour in the services, the punishment is always completely out of proportion to the crime. This must be the source of the saying in the Army that the one cardinal sin is to be found out.

So the net effect of the Army, an observable general effect, on virtually everyone's character is that one becomes less able to think, one's morals sank considerably in relation to behaviour towards females outside the Army, in relation to increasing use of bad language (used extensively to make up for paucity of vocabulary) and in relation to petty theft (whosoever kit is deficient it will not be mine), and one became an accomplished liar.

Allied to all this in my own case was the development of a passionate, and so far lasting, hatred of all Army officers. In 1970, in Edinburgh for the Commonwealth Games, I saw an officer I had not seen for fourteen years. It came as quite a shock afterwards to find that my instant reaction was to go up and literally spit in his eye. In the end I allowed myself to be led away by my wife; both of us sadly shaking our heads, though perhaps for slightly different reasons.

Within my experience the only remaining place where class-consciousness plays any part in British life is in the services. The rubric 'Officers and their ladies, NCOs and their wives, other ranks and their women' was still in use a few years ago at least. On one troop camp in Hong Kong a small group of us erected, in the rain, first a tent for each officer's sleeping quarters, then a large tent for the officers' mess, then a large adjoining tent complete with wicker armchairs for the officers' bar. Finally, in the dark, we were allowed time to erect a small tent to house six of us plus all our (by this time soaking) equipment. I found this bred considerable resentment on my part, hardly helped by the fact, learned subsequently, that the officers received additional pay for the time spent in camp, as a hardship allowance.

I do not think that I resent discipline, properly founded. But this was my first and only experience of discipline imposed entirely by the system, regardless of one's respect for the individual responsible. At home, school, university, or subsequently in commerce, discipline can be acceptable, since one respects parents, teachers, lecturers or managers for their knowledge and ability. But it appeared to me that all officers were fools, and pompous fools to boot: and, Lord, how I felt like booting them! Chosen, apparently, on the basis of a loud public school accent, they were entirely and brashly self-confident. As a side effect, the experience left me with a healthy contempt for all public schoolboys. This has since evaporated somewhat: I now number a few among my friends, although I still do not think I would allow my daughter to marry one of them.

Before leaving the subject, it is fair to point out that my attitude does not spring entirely from intellectual snobbery. I conceived great respect for NCOs. The British Army is held together by the calibre of warrant officers and sergeants particularly. It was said that an Army comprising German officers and British soldiers could take on the world. So long as the British included the Ghurkas, I would agree. Conversely, an Army of British officers and men from anywhere I would not back to outmanoeuvre a Brownie pack at full strength.

What was the use of National Service? Even, is that a question which is now worth asking? That is to say, did the individual gain anything? Obviously, yes. Undoubtedly most individuals matured in personality. A measure of human experience must be its memorableness. Of the last twenty years of my life, only two were spent in the Army; but it certainly contributes more than ten per cent of the memories of that period. Most of all one remembers characters. That, and tiny anecdotes, 'in' jokes. Memorable trivia. Probably because service life was so different from other experience, for the majority it had the effect of broadening all experience.

Characters? The first engraved himself on my memory after an harangue by the sergeant-major following too many fainting on parade. The importance of a good night's sleep was stressed, followed by a good breakfast. It was Geordie Minto who politely enquired of the sergeant-major if the latter knew where a good breakfast might be available. During a discussion on Army numbers, it was Chico Simpson who turned to the sergeant-major and said, 'I presume you don't have a number. When you first joined you both knew one another.' Out of context, neither sounds much. To suggest, obliquely, to a sergeant-major that he is so old that he was one of the first two men in the British Army is hardly the greatest wit imaginable. But within the bounds of Army discipline, one needs real character to say anything but 'Sir' to a warrant officer. Great men, both. And Davidson, who took a three-tonner up a track forbidden to anything but jeeps or land-rovers. At the top he was charged by an officer for 'conduct prejudicial to good order and discipline.' He very reasonably pointed out the impossibility of taking the truck down again and thereby incurring another charge. He was finally allowed to take the truck down again, with all charges dropped.

My favourite anecdote stems from the troop camp we attended, ostensibly as relaxation after a GOC's inspection of the battery. Whilst there, the other troop planned a mock attack on us, and came through our camp in the dead of night, scattering thunder-flashes, loosening guy-ropes, and creating a fair amount of havoc. Fortunately my own tent was not disturbed; but the comparison of stories the following morning was interesting. Of six men, three did not even wake. Of the three who did wake, one believed the noise to be thunder, and went back to sleep. One believed it to be a Chinese festival (always accompanied by a number of crackers) and went back to sleep. One seriously believed it was the promised invasion by Chinese communist troops; but someone else must already be aware of it, so, whilst awaiting further orders, he, too, went back to sleep.

Memories drift back. They say that you are in more danger from your own side than from the enemy. Whilst travelling through Malaya a party of a dozen or so of us were formally acting as an escort to a truckload of ammunition being moved through the jungle, then hiding an unknown number of communist guerillas. Unfortunately the ammunition truck scraped the side of a civilian truck coming the other way, and ripped the side from its petrol tank. With the temperature in the nineties, the sight of about two tons of various explosive devices standing in a large pool of petrol is reasonably unpleasant, particularly to a devout coward. Neither did the calming influence of nicotine seem a good idea, smoking not being encouraged under the circumstances. I was one of the six detailed to stand guard while the ammunition was transferred to another truck, three on each side of the road. With fixed bayonet all but touching a solid wall of green foliage, my guard value seemed low. My dominating thought was the question of whether an explosion six feet to my rear would prove a painless death.

My surveying unit's responsibility on active service was to set up a row of four observation posts on reasonably high forward ground and observe either the flash or the smoke from enemy guns, and, by cross-observations, fix their positions. Three shots from the same gun should enable its position to be fixed to the nearest yard. The fact that armies the world over were by now using flashless powder by night and smokeless by day should not be allowed to detract from our effectiveness. It is the thought that counts. Practice was achieved by setting up the posts, then having an officer drifting around the countryside in front throwing out an occasional thunder-flash. On one such occasion the posts were on predetermined positions, one of which by a freak of weather was on the top of a hill which for a week remained obstinately shrouded in low-lying cloud. Mechanically, the posts' visibility reports came up as A, C and D posts visibility fifteen thousand feet; B post three feet.

Twenty yards down B's hill visibility was perfect. Yet in a solid week of the scheme there was never a suggestion that B post should be moved down the hill. An officer had reconnoitred beforehand, assigned the posts' positions, and that, as they say, was that.

Skiving is an army tradition. Any soldier spends most of his time working: but what he is working on is evolving means of avoiding work. A good skive always excites admiration. A man in my unit once avoided the chore of pay parade, which seems to take an interminable time, by walking up, looking at an empty balcony immediately above the head of the paying officer, and saying, 'Yes, sir, I'll be with you in just a monent, sir, I'm just getting paid now.' His name was called out of turn, and he was paid without delay. Another excellent effort was by Rampton, a lad who was frightfully willing, but always dead slow. If called by an officer, his approach speed was slow, with short strides. On being told to double he would do so enthusiastically, lifting his knees high and quickly, but his forward speed would remain unchanged. It probably took two months, without anyone actually being able to reprimand him, before it was accepted, and thereafter he was left to himself: Rampton was never chosen for any extraneous jobs.

The nub of it all is the inflexibility of the military system, and the ingenuity demonstrated to avoid certain aspects of it. There is a code for all emergencies. Army orders: 'if you observe a fire, shout loudly, "Fire, fire, fire." Send the next person on the scene to alert the fire picquet, etc.' Presumably only to shout 'Fire, fire' would be put down as a practical joke. Also (peculiar to Hong Kong), if you are bitten by a snake, you are ordered to catch it and take it with you to the MI room. Incidentally, the orders covering sick parade are more meticulous than most. Great perseverance is needed; or, as they say, it takes a fit man to go sick in the Army.

The ingenuity was well demonstrated in a neat practical joke. Even on a long weekend, there were some half-a-dozen from outlying parts who could not satisfactorily reach home and back to Salisbury Plain. Those who did leave found, on return to the barrack hut, the beds piled on top of one another. This is possible, the beds being of tubular steel frames: when the feet, and circular foot and head pieces, have been removed, the tubular steel uprights fit into one another. The first person back in after all remaining beds had been filled climbed to the top of the stack only to find that the top one was touching the roof and was impossible to remove.

After ten or so people had slept a precarious night sleeping somewhere in the stack the trick was explained. The stack had to be
moved to the end of the hut where, utilising one knot-hole and
three further holes drilled in position, the bottom bed could be
lowered into the floor. The top bed and each subsequent then
became removable.

Such, of course, form the brighter side of military life. Curiously
enough it is on such incidents that the Army's esprit de corps is
built up. On these, and on a carefully fostered competitive spirit.
Competition between different platoons, different companies,
different regiments. The camaraderie engendered in the Army is a
real one. Probably the saving grace of Army life is that the Army
is composed of human beings – at least in the main, one had
occasional doubts. Also one appreciates the difficulties of running
a National Service system. I think it was Rousseau who said that
a problem every state or nation faces is what to do with its young
men in times of peace. A system of National Service has to grasp
the nettle of this particular problem in its most acute form. By its
very nature, soldiering in peacetime is a fiendishly dull business.

Nevertheless, perception of the problems of National Service
did not necessarily render it the more attractive or endearing. The
fact is that National Service was bloody awful. Its only consolation
was that everyone else was stuck with it as well as oneself; two
years of every life wasted. On looking back through this piece, I
am amazed at the bitterness. The anecdotes with which I have
bored friends related more to time spent in Hong Kong than to
time spent in the Army. What is left has become, sad to realise, a
panegyric of hate against the system. Yet the wish expressed in my
opening paragraph has to an extent been realised. I feel that writing
it down has purged my system. But the final absolution must come
from publicly quoting, verbatim, from the testimonial written in
my discharge papers by some unknown yet perceptive hero: '... was
rather more mature than the average National Serviceman and as
such at times tended to resent discipline. He will make a better
civilian than a soldier.'

Mark that well – 'He will make a better civilian than a soldier.'
It was the kindest thing that anybody said to me in two years.

NOTES ON CONTRIBUTORS

JOHN ARDEN

Born in Barnsley, Yorkshire, in 1930. Studied architecture at Cambridge and Edinburgh Universities. He is married to Margaretta D'Arcy, the actress, with whom he has collaborated on a number of plays. He has written for stage, television and radio, and his plays include *Live Like Pigs, Serjeant Musgrave's Dance, The Workhouse Donkey, Armstrong's Last Goodnight, The Bagman,* and *The Bally Gombeen Bequest.*

MICHAEL BAKEWELL

Born 1931, went to King's College, Cambridge, joined the BBC in 1954 and worked in radio and television as director, producer and Head of Plays. Productions included plays by Beckett, Pinter, Ionesco and Kops. Left to work as freelance director in television and theatre. Activities have ranged from filming 1,200 military bandsmen at Wembley Stadium to directing a stage version of Frank Dickens' *Bristow* at the ICA. Stage productions include *Miss Julie, Juno and the Paycock* and *Twelfth Night.* Has worked extensively in France and Germany on television co-productions, including *Songs of the Celts* and *La Vie de Chateau.* Currently working as director and literary agent.

ALAN BURNS

Born in the Great Depression in Cricklewood, London. When war broke out he got under the dining room table and stayed there until he was evacuated to Great Missenden. He went to Merchant Taylors' School, where he learned Latin. Called up for National Service, he volunteered for Hong Kong and was posted to Aldershot, Bulford, and Bodmin. He practised as a barrister for a time, spent a year at the LSE, then worked in Fleet Street as a libel lawyer. Leaving London to live in a cottage in a field near Whitchurch Canonicorum, Dorset, he wrote five novels: *Buster, Europe After the Rain, Celebrations, Babel* and *Dreamerika!*, all published by Calder. His play *Palach* was produced by Charles Marovitz at the Open Space Theatre. He has been generously assisted by the Arts Council, and was Henfield Writing Fellow at the University of East Anglia, and subsequently C. Day Lewis Writing Fellow at Woodberry Down School. Recently he edited *To Deprave and Corrupt* for Davis-Poynter Ltd., and is now working on a documentary novel for Allison & Busby.

PETER BURNS

Born in 1931 and educated at Merchant Taylors' School. After National Service in 1952 he sold films for British Lion in Cardiff, Birmingham and Glasgow. He then worked for Central African Airways in Rhodesia, and for Shell Chemicals in South Africa. He tried copywriting in London from 1956 to 1960, went to Paris to write a novel, returned home as, successively, a Persian carpet salesman, mini-cab driver, petrol pump attendant. In 1962 he got a job with Oxfam's publicity department, later becoming assistant to the Director. He left Oxfam to spend twelve weeks promoting a new socialist newspaper, *The Morning News,* which folded, then twelve months with Amnesty International. Five years ago he joined the National Council for Civil Liberties as promotion secretary, a post he held until 1973 when he was appointed General Secretary of War on Want.

MEL CALMAN

Born in London in 1931. Educated at the Perse School, Cambridge, St Martins School of Art and Goldsmith's College, London.

He has worked as a cartoonist for the *Daily Express, Observer, Sunday Telegraph,* television, publishing and advertising. He now draws regularly for the *Sunday Times,* freelances and runs a small London gallery, The Workshop, specialising in drawings, illustrations and cartoons. He is very interested in animated film and has made one, *The Arrow,* for the British Film Institute.

He has recently done more writing, though he thinks of his cartoons as ninety per cent writing anyway.

IAN CARR

Jazz musician. Born in Scotland, lived in Northumberland until 1956 when he left King's College, Newcastle, to do his National Service. After leaving the Army he spent two years wandering around the Mediterranean, returning to England in 1960 to devote his energies to music. Joined the Harold McNair Quintet in 1962 and later became co-leader with Don Rendell of the Rendell-Carr Quintet, one of the most successful British jazz groups of the mid-sixties. His current band, Nucleus, has a widespread international reputation and won the first prize at the Montreux International Festival in 1970. He has made many LPs, writes music and is involved in journalism and broadcasting. His book on the British music scene is to be published by Latimer Press in 1973.

STUART CRAMPIN

Born in Tiptree in 1935. Educated at King's College, London, gaining BSc in Mathematics, Jelf Memorial Medal; active in mountaineering club, drama society and as Art Editor of literary magazine. Then to Pembroke College, Cambridge, gaining PhD in Geophysics. Eighteen months' enforced vacation recovering from climbing accident attempting Pilier SW on Aiguille du Dru.

Employment: dogsbody to Roma, Liss-Carin, Amelia Catharine.

Gainful employment: sometime Research Fellow, Seismological Institute, Uppsala University; Research Fellow, Seismology Unit, Edinburgh University; Gassiot Fellow in Seismology, NERC. At present, PSO, IGS Geophysics Laboratories in Edinburgh.

He has written more then twenty papers in *Geophys. J., Mon. Not. R. Astr. Soc., J. Geophys. Res., Bull. Seism. Soc. Am.,* etc.

JOHN FURNIVAL

Born in South London in 1933. His first major memory is seeing Crystal Palace burn down from his back garden, and of flying kites in a park called Hilly Fields. He wreaked considerable damage as an evacuee. Educated at Haberdasher Aske's and later at Wimbledon School of Art and the Royal College of Art with National Service sandwiched in between. After leaving the Royal College he returned to teach there. At present he is at the Bath Academy of Art, where he has been teaching in the Fine Art and Graphic Design departments for the last five years.

NICHOLAS HARMAN

Nicholas Harman is the son of a distinguished lawyer, Lord Justice Harman (who was himself wounded and imprisoned in the First World War). After schooling at Eton he was conscripted into the Army, and then went on to Cambridge and later became a journalist. He worked in Paris for three years, returning to London to join the staff of *The Economist* magazine. He left after nine years, the last of which were spent as assistant editor in charge of domestic affairs. After a brief spell as a foreign affairs writer on the *Sunday Times* he joined the *Panorama* programme on BBC television, where he now works as reporter and front man on *Midweek*. He is married, has three children and lives in South London.

DAVID HOCKNEY

Born Bradford, 1937. Studied at Bradford College of Art, spent the next two years as a conscientious objector, working in hospitals. Studied at the Royal College of Art 1959-62, winning the Royal College of Art Gold Medal. Since then he has taught in England and USA and continues to travel and exhibit throughout the States and Europe. His first one-man exhibition was at the Kasmin Gallery in London in 1963. In 1967 he received first prize in the 6th John Moores Exhibition, Liverpool. In 1970 the Whitechapel Gallery, London, held a retrospective exhibition which then toured Hanover, Rotterdam and Belgrade.

BILL HOLDSWORTH

A Kentish Town boy, born 1929. After an elementary school education a wartime examination gave him a chance to study Building at the Northern Polytechnic.

Six years ago (having been an apprentice fitter, draughtsman, salesman, builder's labourer, contracts engineer, and designer) he formed his own firm of building services and environmental engineers under the design consortium name of Atelier St. Albans.

He lives with his wife and three children in Hemel Hempstead, and keeps alive an active interest in art and politics. This has included being a Borough Councillor, Trades Union activist, member of CND and Committee of 100; he was co-founder of Arts Movement that established Centre 42 and the Roundhouse. He likes to write poetry and short stories; and runs a small avant-garde art gallery.

MICHAEL HOLROYD

Born in London in 1935. Mother Swedish, father Anglo-Irish, and various step-parents Hungarian, French and occasionally English. Educated at Eton, where he studied science, and at the Maidenhead Public Library, where he read literature.

Since National Service he has published two literary biographies, *Hugh Kingsmill* and *Lytton Strachey,* one novel, *A Dog's Life,* and a collection of essays, *Unreceived Opinions.* Edited *The Best of Hugh Kingsmill* and *Lytton Strachey by Himself.* Is currently at work on a life of Augustus John, and has been appointed official biographer of Bernard Shaw. Lives in London, carefully.

B. S. JOHNSON

Born 1933, brought up in Hammersmith and other parts of west London. He worked as a bank clerk and accounts clerk before going to King's College, London, at the late age of twenty-three to read English. His first novel *Travelling People* and a volume of *Poems* won a Gregory Award in 1962. Other books include *Statement Against Corpses* (short stories with the Pakistani poet Zulfikar Ghose), *Street Children* (text for photographs by Julia Trevelyan Oman) and five more novels: *Albert Angelo, Trawl* (which won the 1967 Somerset Maugham Award), *The Unfortunates, House Mother Normal* and *Christie Malry's Own Double-Entry.* He has also worked in films and television: his first film, *You're Human Like the Rest of Them,* won the Grands Prix at the 1968 International Short Film Festivals at Tours and Melbourne. He is married with two children.

RICHARD KEY

Born 1938 at Bath. Educated Clifton College School, Bristol, and went to work at Fry's chocolate factory as trainee salesman at age seventeen. Drifted back to Fry's from National Service, but after two and a half years left and came to London to fulfil ambitions as editor and director in film industry. Entered BBC as trainee assistant film editor in June 1963, but left, after fifteen months, disenchanted with the size of the operation. Joined small documentary film company, and for three and a half years worked on a large variety of documentaries in a number of technical capacities. Became freelance editor in 1968, and has since worked successfully for nearly all the English television companies and several others. Has just completed editing his first full-length feature film, and hopes to fulfil second half of ambition by directing documentaries soon. Married, with two children.

JOHN LAWSON

Born in Dundee, Scotland, in 1939. He left school at fifteen and went to work in a hat factory where he rose to the position of progress chaser before National Service. Returning to Dundee after service in the RAF, he worked as a labourer in a jute mill before emigrating to London. Since then he has had a variety of jobs (hospital cook, building trades, street trader, general labourer), mainly around the Angel district.

TREV LEGGETT

Educated at Shene Grammar School and then read for a mathematics degree at London University. Completed a Fellowship of the Chartered Insurance Institute and has been with a reinsurance company for sixteen years. Writes occasional technical articles for the insurance press and lectures on the same topics. Speaks Spanish, French and German, and is widely travelled. He is married and lives in Chessington, Surrey.

EDWARD LUCIE-SMITH

Born in Jamaica, 1933. Came to live in England in 1946. Educated at King's School, Canterbury, and Merton College, Oxford. Is well known as a poet, anthologist and writer on art. His books include *The Penguin Book of Elizabethan Verse, Eroticism in Western Art,* and *A Tropical Childhood.*

WES MAGEE

Born in 1939 in Greenock, Scotland. He left school at fifteen and worked as a bank clerk until being called up for National Service in 1960. After a basic training course with an infantry regiment he was transferred to the Intelligence Corps and worked in West Germany for eighteen months. While in the Army he began writing and has since contributed poems to many magazines and anthologies. He was awarded the New Poets Award for 1972 and his first volume of poems *Urban Gorilla* was published in autumn 1972.

He is now a teacher at a junior school in Swindon and is married with two children.

ALAN MARSHFIELD

Born 1933. He was educated at the Portsmouth Technical School, Portsmouth College of Technology and King's College, London, where he graduated in 1958 in English. He has travelled widely in Europe and worked in the Ordnance Survey and in various teaching posts. Currently he is Head of English in a comprehensive school. He has broadcast his poetry and published poems regularly in periodicals. Two collections of his verse have appeared: *Mistress* (Anvil Press) and *Dragonfly* (Oasis Press). He has also translated Asklepiades and Rufinus for the Penguin *Greek Anthology,* and a selection of the work of the Finnish poet Eeva-Liisa Manner for BBC Radio 3. Recently he completed a novel, *Heliodora,* set in first century BC Tyre. He has a Finnish wife, two children, and lives in Edgware.

KARL MILLER

Born 1931, and educated at the Royal High School, Edinburgh, and Downing College, Cambridge. From 1956-57 he was an assistant principal at HM Treasury. He then joined the BBC as a television producer before becoming literary editor of the *Spectator* in 1958. Since 1961 he has also been literary editor of the *New Statesman* and is now editor of *The Listener*. He has compiled a Penguin anthology, *Writing in England Today: The Last Fifteen Years* (1968), and edited *Memoirs of a Modern Scotland*. He is married with three children.

JEFF NUTTALL

Born in 1933. Trained at grammar school and art school and finally qualified as a teacher. He taught in secondary modern schools for approximately fifteen years and now teaches Fine Art at Leeds Polytechnic which has assimilated the old and justly distinguished Leeds College of Art. He is remarkable for the breadth of his activities. Whilst the commercially-sponsored *Bomb Culture* has drawn disproportionate attention to his work in popular sociology, he continues to pursue careers as a poet, sculptor, novelist and director of experimental theatre, all with equal success.

Collections of his poems are available from Penguin and Fulcrum. Novels are available from Turret Press, Kensington Church Walk; and from Fulcrum. More advanced literary work is published by Writers' Forum. Sculpture may be seen at the Angela Flowers Gallery. Performance scripts and ideas are carried out from time to time by the People Show, the John Bull Puncture Repair Kit, Jack, and the Oval House Theatre Group. Books are forthcoming from McGibbon and Kee, Routledge and Kegan Paul and Trigram.

BERNARD PALMER

Lifelong Londoner: almost certainly oldest living inhabitant of Notting Hill Gate. Product of its Elementary and Grammar schools. Only child. Evacuated to Lacock Abbey and Cornwall. Back in London, occasional schoolboy broadcasts prompted the idea of the BBC as a career which National Service delayed. Afterwards to King's College, London, for a diet of Proust and Dr Joad. Crossed zebra into Bush House to become BBC studio manager and producer on *London Calling Europe*. Seconded to Botswana for year's broadcasting at time of Independence, 1966, and travelled widely in central and southern Africa. Private interests include choral conducting, playing viol consorts, natural history and drinking. Unmarried as yet. Club: Portobello Road on Saturdays.

ALAN SILLITOE

Born 1928. He was brought up in Nottingham and went to school there. In 1942 he started work in a bicycle factory and later worked at various other jobs (labourer, capstan lathe operator, airfield control assistant) until going into the RAF. Discharged with a pension due to tuberculosis caught in Malaya, he spent the next eight years in France and Spain and came back to England in 1958 for the publication of his first novel, *Saturday Night and Sunday Morning*. Since then he has travelled a great deal, mainly in France, Morocco and Spain. His last three novels have been *A Start in Life* (1970), *Travels in Nihilon* (1971) and *Raw Material* (1972), while earlier collections of stories have been *The Loneliness of the Long-distance Runner* and *The Ragman's Daughter*. He is married with one son.

PATRICK SNAITH

Born 1937. Now warden of a residential hostel for students and young people in Camden. Educated at Wolverton Grammar School and King's College, London, where he took an honours English degree. Since then he has spent his time teaching, lecturing, writing, and organising farm camps and language courses for foreign students in the Fens. As a teacher of English as a second language, he was a State school teacher in Ostfold in Norway for two years; and after that in four West Jutland towns in Denmark for a year. These experiences have made him very critical of the educational system of this country. His leisure interests are the theatre (and writing for it), sport and music.

BILL TYLER

Born in London 1934. Thoroughly enjoyed the war in different parts of England and has had a secret love affair with the countryside ever since. Returned to suburban London with family in 1945. He found private prep. school hard going; with extra coaching he achieved entry to public school (Mill Hill) in 1947 but disliked the discipline and Latin. Eventually he accepted the former. He found arts subjects more rewarding and hoped to become a photographer, but preferred sports to chemistry and physics. Architecture seemed the ideal combination of art and technology and he entered Architectural Association School in 1952. He travelled widely in France and Italy in summer vacations and completed diploma course in 1957 without fully appreciating the freedom of a very liberal academic training. After National Service, and an extensive tour of Scandinavia, he joined an architectural practice on a temporary basis, became an associate partner in 1966 and finally left in 1969. He formed Tyler Design Unit in 1970 to undertake all types of design work and was Art and Architecture co-ordinator at the 1971 Bedford Square Book Bang. He is married.

LES WILES

Born in Woolwich 1936. Privately evacuated to Northamptonshire during the war. After twenty-five years as Senior Mixer at Shepherds Bush Film Studios, his father was unemployed for two years from 1948 when Lord Rank closed the studios. This caused the family to uproot itself from Welling in Kent and emigrate to Islington. An unsettled education led to two 'O' levels and deadend jobs as a labourer and in a brewery before National Service. Afterwards he sold office machinery for five years before realising it was a waste of time and talent. He therefore decided to do something 'worthwhile', and after eighteen months landed himself a job as a trade union organiser with the Association of Cinematograph and Television Technicians which he still has.

BIBLIOGRAPHY

National Service has attracted very little documentary writing since it finished, and most of the following therefore date from 1946-1962. The fiction published on the subject is too numerous to list here.

BARCLAY, Brig. C. N. National Service: a Survey. (Extract from *Brassey's Annual*) 1956.

BAXTER, D. Two Years To Do. (Elek) 1959. *Lively, readable autobiography*.

BURCHER, Maj. J. A. C. Clowes Memorial Prize Essay 1955, commenting on the training of National Servicemen. (Extract from *Army Quarterly*) 1955.

CENTRAL OFFICE OF INFORMATION. National Service in Britain's Armed Forces. 1956. *Handout for those about to register*.

CHAMBERS, P. and LANDRETH, A. Called Up; the personal experiences of sixteen National Servicemen. (Allan Wingate) 1955. *Claims it takes no attitude towards National Service, but seems at this remove to be definitely in favour*.

CRAWFORD, Maj. W. K. B. Training the National Service Officer at Eaton Hall. (Extract from *Journal of the Royal United Service Institution*) 1951. *Useful detail and explanations*.

ELLACOTT, S. E. Conscripts on the March – Story of the Soldier from Napoleon to the Nuclear Age. (Abelard-Schumann) 1970.

FERGUSON, T. and CUNNISON, J. In their Early Twenties; a study of Glasgow youth. (OUP) 1956. *Heavy statistics, but valuable.*

HOUSE OF COMMONS SELECT COMMITTEE ON ESTIMATES. Third Report, Session 1952-53. The Call-up, Posting and Movement of National Servicemen. (HC 132) 1953. Departmental Replies (HC 295) 1953.

HUDSON, Major E. R. B. New-Style National Service. (Extract from *Army Quarterly*) 1951. *Presumptuous proposals never (fortunately) implemented; new meant more.*

KING GEORGE'S JUBILEE TRUST. Citizens of Tomorrow; a study of influences affecting the upbringing of young people. 1955. *Important; very much the 'correct' attitude of its time.*

LANNING, Flt.-Lt. G. E. National Service–the Education Officer's part. (Extract from *Journal of the Royal United Service Institution*) 1950.

LEE, Maj. F. L. Compulsory Service in the Armed Forces. (Extract from *Brassey's Annual*) 1954. *Useful notes on conscription from King Alfred onwards.*

LLOYD, Maj.-Gen. C. Integration of National Service with the Country's Economic Future. (Extract from *Journal of the Royal United Service Institution*) 1955.

LOW, Brig. A. R. W. Army Manpower; the case against wishful thinkers. (Extract from *Army Quarterly*) 1949. *An answer to the next item which has a certain period charm.*

MARTEL, Lt.-Gen. Sir G. The Case against Conscription. (Extract from *Army Quarterly*) 1949. *Something of a hardliner, but he underestimates Russian strength.*

MARTEL, Lt.-Gen. Sir G. National Service. (Extract from *Army Quarterly*) 1950. *A rejoinder to the answer to the above in which much the same is said, but more shortly.*

MINISTRY OF DEFENCE. National Service (Cmd. 9608) 1955. *Announced cut in strength of forces.*

MINISTRY OF LABOUR & NATIONAL SERVICE. Call-up of Men to the Forces 1957-1960 (Cmnd. 175) 1957. *Announced the end of National Service.*

MINISTRY OF LABOUR & NATIONAL SERVICE. Report on the Enquiry into the Effects of National Service on the Education and Employment of Young Men. 1955. *80% of all those demobbed in September 1953 took part in a simple interview/questionnaire. The purpose was to discover whether National Service caused problems in employment, vocational guidance and resettlement. It concluded that 90% of young men settled down satisfactorily, only a small minority would benefit from vocational guidance if it were to be provided at the end of National Service; so all was right with the world.*

PRASAD & SMYTHE. Conscription: a World Survey of Compulsory Military Service and Resistance to it. (War Resistance International) 1968.

RADCLIFFE, Lt.-Col. R. A. C. The National Serviceman and Industry. (Extract from *Army Quarterly*) 1952.

RAITT, Capt. R. I. Clowes Memorial Prize Essay 1961, on National Service 1945-1961. (Extract from *Army Quarterly*) 1961. *Very useful and informative.*

SCOTT, Brig. F. C. National Service and the Territorial Army. Extract from *Journal of the Royal United Service Institution*) 1953.

TINKER, Lt.-Col. E. H. National Service without tears. (Extract from *Army Quarterly*) 1950. *Start the indoctrination earlier seems to be the message.*

WAR OFFICE. Report of the Committee on the Employment of National Servicemen in the United Kingdom. (Cmnd. 35) 1956. *The decision to end National Service must have been very much influenced by this report.*

APPENDIX A

Table Showing Allocation of all those
Registering for National Service 1951-1955

	1951	1952	1953	1954	1955
Drafted into the Services, or entered as volunteers	201,900	199,700	160,000	142,700	101,000
Medically unfit	48,600	44,700	41,500	40,900	33,300
Available or awaiting medical	1,400	3,200	10,600	2,800	23,000
Awaiting decision on deferment	500	600	900	900	2,400
Call-up deferred:					
apprentices	500	3,700	31,700	62,400	73,200
post-apprenticeship	700	800	400	—	—
articled pupils and others training for professional qualifications	3,000	4,700	6,400	7,700	8,800
agricultural workers	4,100	4,900	5,800	6,200	8,200
coalmining workers	9,100	10,300	11,000	12,000	12,300
seamen	5,800	6,500	5,200	4,800	4,200
scientific research workers on high priority work	300	200	—	—	—
schoolboys taking GCE, etc.	—	—	—	1,200	10,800
university students and student teachers	4,600	7,300	10,400	11,400	7,800
Emigrants and others gone abroad	1,600	1,300	800	600	300
All others (including hardship postponements, approved school cases, conscientious objectors, etc.	900	1,100	1,300	1,400	3,700
TOTALS of men registering	283,000	289,000	286,000	295,000	289,000

APPENDIX B

Table of BRITISH ARMED FORCES' STRENGTHS 1939-1964

Male and Female Officers and Other Ranks

Date		NAVY		ARMY		RAF		TOTAL	
		Regulars	NS men	Regulars	NS men	Regulars	NS men	Regulars	NS men
December 1939	TOTAL	214,000		1,128,000		215,000		1,557,000	
December 1940	,,	333,000		2,075,000		491,000		2,899,000	
December 1941	,,	449,000		2,340,000		813,000		3,602,000	
December 1942	,,	566,000		2,516,000		936,000		4,068,000	
December 1943	,,	756,000		2,680,000		999,000		4,435,000	
December 1944	,,	780,000		2,760,000		985,000		4,525,000	
April 1945	,,	852,600		3,007,300		1,124,400		4,984,300	
June 1945	,,	783,000		2,920,000		950,000		4,653,000	
April 1946	,,	475,800		1,592,700		616,000		2,685,000	
June 1946	,,	410,000		1,436,000		602,000		2,448,000	
April 1947	*	112.3	81.2	168.4	705.3	98.1	227.2	378.8	1013.7
	TOTAL	193,500		873,700		325,300		1,392,500	
April 1948	*	121.9	22.6	183.2	347.6	121.2	134.8	426.3	505.0
	TOTAL	144,500		530,800		256,000		931,300	
April 1949	*	127.4	17.1	194.3	221.4	128.3	96.6	450.0	335.1
	TOTAL	144,500		415,700		224,900		785,100	

*in thousands

continued over

Date		NAVY		ARMY		RAF		TOTAL	
		Regulars	NS men	Regulars	NS men	Regulars	NS men	Regulars	NS men
April 1950	*	129.0	11.0	195.0	182.6	126.0	76.0	450.0	269.6
	TOTAL	149,000		377,600		202,000		719,600	
April 1951	*	131.0	7.2	209.7	223.5	148.9	88.9	489.6	319.6
	TOTAL	138,200		433,200		237,800		809,200	
April 1952	*	140.6	4.6	222.7	224.0	181.7	89.1	545.0	317.7
	TOTAL	145,200		446,700		270,800		862,700	
April 1953	*	138.9	6.7	220.4	228.0	199.0	78.1	558.3	312.8
	TOTAL	145,600		448,400		277,100		871,100	
April 1954	*	126.0	7.8	225.7	221.2	195.8	69.3	547.5	298.3
	TOTAL	133,800		446,900		265,100		845,800	
April 1955	*	118.9	9.5	231.8	205.2	188.0	70.2	538.7	284.9
	TOTAL	128,400		437,000		258,200		823,600	
April 1956	*	110.5	11.6	205.4	202.6	167.8	74.8	483.7	289.0
	TOTAL	122,100		408,000		242,600		772,700	

*in thousands

continued over

Date		NAVY Regulars	NAVY NS men	ARMY Regulars	ARMY NS men	RAF Regulars	RAF NS men	TOTAL Regulars	TOTAL NS men
April 1957	*	106.4	9.6	200.9	174.3	159.2	68.7	466.5	252.6
	TOTAL	116,000		375,200		227,900		719,100	
April 1958	*	101.3	5.3	183.7	144.7	145.4	45.6	430.4	195.6
	TOTAL	106,600		328,400		191,000		626,000	
April 1959	*	99.4	2.2	178.9	125.0	147.2	26.0	425.5	153.2
	TOTAL	101,600		303,900		173,200		578,700	
April 1960	*	97.2	0.6	166.2	98.1	145.1	18.4	408.5	117.1
	TOTAL	97,800		264,300		163,500		525,600	
April 1961	*	95.2	0.1	166.5	64.8	144.8	13.4	406.5	78.3
	TOTAL	95,300		231,300		158,200		484,800	
April 1962	*	94.3	—	176.9	25.8	143.5	5.4	414.7	31.2
	TOTAL	94,300		202,700		148,900		445,900	
April 1963	*	95.8	—	188.0	2.6	143.8	—	427.6	2.6
	TOTAL	95,800		190,600		143,800		430,200	
1 April 1964	TOTAL	97,600		189,400		136,100		423,100	

*in thousands

APPENDIX C
Table showing Selected BASIC Pay Rates*
Army

From:	† Private	Corporal	Sergeant	W.O. I	2nd Lieut.	Lieut.	Ref.
	WEEKLY RATE				DAILY RATE		
July 1946							Cmd.
Regular	35/–	52/6	73/6	105/–	11/–	13/–	6750
NS man	28/–	52/6	73/6	105/–	11/–	13/–	*et al.*
Nov. 1948							Cmd.
Regular	35/–	52/6	84/–	115/6	13/6	15/6	7588
NS man	28/–	52/6	73/6	105/–	11/–	13/–	*et al.*
Sept. 1950							Cmd.
Regular	56/–	73/6	115/6	157/6	17/6	19/6	8027
NS man	35/–	52/6	73/6	105/–	13/–	16/–	*et al.*
Sept. 1951							Pay
Regular	56/–	77/–	115/6	157/6	17/6	19/6	Warrant
NS man	35/–	52/6	73/6	105/–	13/–	16/–	
April 1954							Cmd.
Regular	56/–	91/–	136/6	185/6	17/6	19/6	9088
NS man	35/–	52/6	73/6	105/–	13/–	16/–	*et al.*
April 1956							Cmd.
Regular	70/–	98/–	164/6	217/–	21/–	26/–	9692
NS man	38/6	56/–	77/–	108/6	13/–	16/–	*et al.*
April 1958							Cmd.
Regular	84/–	112/–	171/6	224/–	25/–	30/–	365 *et al.*
NS man	38/6	59/6	80/6	112/–	13/–	16/–	
April 1960							Cmd.
Regular	91/–	119/–	182/–	231/–	29/–	34/–	945
NS man	38/6	63/–	84/–	115/6	13/–	16/–	

NB – Rates for Navy and RAF were similar.

NBB – These are basic rates; allowances were also made for wives and dependents where appropriate, and for classes, grades, and trades.

*Old currency.

†Rate given for Regular Serviceman is 1-Star, i.e. 6/12 months service (normally). Rate given for National Serviceman is that after 6 months service.

THE PERFECT STRANGER
P. J. Kavanagh

This celebrated autobiography, winner of the Richard Hillary Memorial Prize for 1966, is as readable and funny as it is hauntingly tender. It is P. J. Kavanagh's tribute to the memory of his first wife, Sally, the perfect stranger – and it is also the absorbing, amusing tale of his early years, from schooldays and undergraduate life to the time he spent in Korea as a soldier and his happy, but short-lived, marriage to Sally.

'A real book; human, tender, gentle, loving, intelligent' – *Sheffield Morning Telegraph*

'A love story beautifully told' – *Sunday Telegraph*

Autobiography 40p

This book is obtainable from booksellers and newsagents or can be ordered direct from the publishers. Send a cheque or postal order for the purchase price plus 6p postage and packing to Quartet Books Limited, P.O. Box 11, Falmouth, Cornwall TR10 9EN